# Black Muslim Religion in the Nation of Islam, 1960 – 1975

# Black Muslim Religion in the Nation of Islam, 1960–1975

Edward E. Curtis IV

The University of North Carolina Press

Chapel Hill

Designed by April Leidig-Higgins
Set in Ehrhardt by Copperline Book Services, Inc.
Manufactured in the United States of America

This book was published with the assistance of the
Anniversary Endowment Fund of the University
of North Carolina Press.

The paper in this book meets the guidelines for
permanence and durability of the Committee on
Production Guidelines for Book Longevity of the
Council on Library Resources.

Library of Congress Cataloging-in-Publication Data
Curtis, Edward E., 1970–
Black Muslim religion in the Nation of Islam, 1960–
1975 / Edward E. Curtis IV.
p. cm.   Includes bibliographical references and index.
ISBN-13: 978-0-8078-3054-3 (cloth: alk. paper)
ISBN-10: 0-8078-3054-2 (cloth: alk. paper)
ISBN-13: 978-0-8078-5771-7 (pbk.: alk. paper)
ISBN-10: 0-8078-5771-8 (pbk.: alk. paper)
1. Black Muslims—History—20th century.   2. African
American Muslims—History—20th century.   3. Black
nationalism—United States—History—20th century.
4. Nation of Islam (Chicago, Ill.)—History.   I. Title.
BP221.B864   2006
297.8'7—dc22                          2006013094

cloth   10 09 08 07 06   5 4 3 2 1
paper   10 09 08 07 06   5 4 3 2 1

To Regan Lee Zwald,
with love and thanks
for our life together

# Contents

# Illustrations

# Acknowledgments

This book took a long time to percolate, and then, during one glorious year at the National Humanities Center (NHC) in Research Triangle Park, North Carolina, it poured onto the page.

Some of the book's ideas can be dated back to my initial encounters with African American Muslim life in 1993 and 1994, when I conducted fieldwork at Masjid al-Mu'minun, an African American Muslim mosque in St. Louis, Missouri. There, I regularly observed Friday prayers, visited the Clara Muhammad parochial school, and attended banquets hosted by the local community. I also ate a lot of fried fish and talked with the brothers and sisters about their experiences as former members of Elijah Muhammad's Nation of Islam (NOI), the African American Islamic movement that attracted national and international attention during the 1960s. Since that time, much of my academic work has focused on gaining a deeper historical understanding of the NOI and its importance both for U.S. history and Islamic studies. This book represents the culmination of my thinking; the reader will have to decide whether my claims deserve to be called insights.

So many folks have helped me along the way, and it is a pleasure to thank them. Since most of the manuscript was written at the NHC, let me first thank the entire staff there. I am especially indebted to librarians extraordinaire Betsy Dain, Jean Houston, and Eliza Robertson; copyeditor Karen Carroll; IT gurus Phillip Barron and Joel Elliott; ringleader Kent Mullikin; and Marie Brubaker, whose friendship and conviviality buoyed me throughout my year there. So many faculty fellows at the NHC became essential conversation partners. Special thanks go to Tim Tyson, Tom Kaiser, Lisa Lindsay, Joel Marcus, Julia Clancy-Smith, Israel Gershoni, Peter Sigal, Margaret Humphreys, Lynda Coon, Gregg Mitman, Maura Nolan, and Richard Jaffe for their collegiality.

At Indiana University-Purdue University Indianapolis (IUPUI), where I revised the manuscript, Carrie Foote-Ardah, Philip Goff, Tom Davis, Kelly Hayes, David Craig, Peter Thuesen, Rachel Wheeler, Robert White, Sherrée Wilson, and Bill Jackson made me feel incredibly welcome. Debbie Dale helped me with manuscript preparation. The Millennium Seminar on Black Studies, including participants Monroe Little, Marianne Wokeck, Jennifer Thorington-Springer, Obi Nnaemeka, Natasha Flowers, Najja Modibo, and Missy Kubitschek, reminded me how much fun this business can be.

Before sitting down to write the book, I tested some of its ideas in academic journals, conference presentations, and student seminars. Thomas Tweed and Ebrahim Moosa offered advice on an article about African American Islamic history narratives, which was published by the *Journal of the American Academy of Religion* 73, no. 2 (June 2005): 659–84. Some of my arguments in chapters 4 and 5 first appeared in *Religion and American Culture* 12, no. 2 (Summer 2002): 167–96. That journal's fine anonymous readers pushed me to see the larger implications of my claims, as did Robert Orsi and Ahmet Karamustafa in other venues. Members of the American Academy of Religion's Afro-American Religious History Group, Study of Islam Section, and North American Religions Section have all offered apt criticisms and encouragement over the years. Peter Wright, Micah Gilmer, Bruce Burnside, and other students in my seminars on African American Islam at the University of North Carolina took my work seriously and challenged me, and I especially want to thank my undergraduate honors student, Katherine Currin, who gave me permission to quote from her oral history interviews with former female members of the NOI.

I am deeply grateful to my friend and colleague Kathryn Lofton for reading and commenting on the entire manuscript. Elaine Maisner of UNC Press expressed interest in this work before I wrote it, and I have been lucky to have her guidance. At the Walter Royal Davis Library of the University of North Carolina-Chapel Hill, John Rutledge, Tommy Nixon, and Robert Dalton helped me identify and acquire the sources necessary for the research of this book. Financial support for this work was generously provided by the National Endowment for the Humanities, the National Humanities Center, IUPUI, and UNC.

I thank colleagues from far and wide for helping me think through various issues related to the book and for answering pesky, but important research questions, especially Jamillah Karim, Amir Hussain, Juan Campo, Bart Ehrman, Bruce Lawrence, Robert Coolidge, Yaakov Ariel, Ashraf Dockrat, Gordon Newby, Laurie Maffly-Kipp, and Kris Baclawski of the Michigan State University Libraries Special Collections. Colleagues who offered support in different but equally important ways have included Carl Ernst, Sarah Shields, Jeremy Rehwaldt-Alexander, Genna Rae McNeil, Melani McAlister, James O. Horton, Karen Leonard, Marcia Hermansen, Randall Styers, Sarah Pinnock, Michael Feener, Niklaus Steiner, Debra Majeed, Judith Weisenfeld, and G. J. A. Lubbe.

Thanks to you all.

# Black Muslim Religion in the Nation of Islam, 1960 – 1975

# Introduction

I give my life to this great man,
The Most Honorable Elijah Muhammad;
For in the principles by which he stands,
I envision a code of honor.
He gave me a God whose name is Allah;
One Who really answers prayer —
In place of a spook, who, in times of great need,
Was never, ever there.
I revere this man who filled me with pride
Such as I've never known before;
A road to success and true happiness,
Elijah has opened the door.
Each time I pray, some five times a day,
I beseech that Allah keep him strong;
For I know down life's way there'll be many like me
For Muhammad to teach right from wrong.
— Edward 6X Ricketts, "A Muslim's Allegiance,"
    *Muhammad Speaks*, 29 December 1967

This book shows what it meant, during the 1960s and 1970s, for thousands of Americans like Brother Edward 6X Ricketts to practice a religion that they understood to be Islam. These Muslims, like Brother Edward, were members of an African American Islamic group called the Nation of Islam (NOI). They pledged their allegiance to Elijah Muhammad, the Messenger of Allah, a prophet who taught them "right from wrong" and a "code of honor." They believed that, in following Elijah Muhammad's prophetic pronouncements, they would achieve "success and true happiness." This volume offers a systematic and comprehensive analysis of their rituals, ethics, doctrines, and religious narratives, revealing the unambiguously religious nature of a movement that was founded, according to NOI members, by God Himself.

It all began in 1930, when W. D. Fard, or Farad Muhammad, a mysterious peddler and purported ex-convict, established the Lost-Found Nation of Islam in the Wilderness of North America. Working from house to house in Detroit, Michigan, Fard reportedly told others that he was from the Holy City of Mecca, although scholars still dispute whether he was indeed a foreigner and whether he was Arab, Turkish, or African American.[1] No matter who he was, he delivered an important message to African Americans in the midst of the Great Depression. He told his black customers and associates that their true religion was Islam and that their original language was Arabic, stolen from them when they came over in slave ships from the Old World. Fard stayed in Detroit only a little while, and he had few followers, but his movement would have an impact on the entire country.[2]

According to the traditions of the NOI, Elijah Poole (1897–1975), a smallish man from Sandersville, Georgia, became Fard's chief assistant and eventually recognized Fard as God in the flesh. By 1934, Fard disappeared from Detroit, and Poole emerged as leader of the nascent movement. Poole, who became known as Elijah Muhammad, used several aliases throughout the 1930s and 1940s in order to confuse the state and federal authorities who thought him to be a black troublemaker and a dangerous sympathizer with anti-American forces, perhaps the Japanese Empire. In fact, he was apprehended by federal authorities in 1942 and convicted of draft evasion.[3]

Once released from jail in 1946, Elijah Muhammad began building an Islamic movement that would cement itself in American historical memory as a black nationalist organization committed to racial separatism and ethnic pride.[4]

It started as a small group of people at two temples in Chicago and Detroit but spread across the United States and even to Jamaica and Bermuda. By 1973, the NOI claimed to have over seventy temples or mosques—they used both words by that point—and thousands of members from coast to coast.[5] The growth of the movement during the period after the Second World War can be attributed to a number of factors, although none was more important, at least for a time, than the emergence of the fiery, articulate, and charismatic Malcolm X (1925–1965).

Malcolm X, whose life story was famously enshrined in the *Autobiography of Malcolm X*, became Elijah Muhammad's chief missionary and a national symbol of black resistance and black anger.[6] Giving voice to Elijah Muhammad's teachings during the 1950s and early 1960s, Malcolm X emphasized the need for self-determination and openly advocated separation from whites. He spread Elijah Muhammad's message to the rest of America and the black world. In the midst of the campaign for civil rights, this black Muslim portrayed Martin Luther King Jr. and other leaders of the black freedom struggle as a bunch of self-hating Uncle Tom Negroes fooled by the chimera of integration.[7] Rather than grovel for scraps from the white man's table, he said, black people should "do for self." He advocated the establishment of a separate territory in the United States where blacks could have land of their own. He also repeated the calls of Elijah Muhammad for black-owned businesses, black schools, and other exclusively black institutions.[8] During a period in which African Americans were still the victims of legal discrimination, his lambasting of white people as "blue-eyed devils" rang true in the ears of many black Americans. Perhaps more than anything, Malcolm X stood as a defiant voice against internalized racism. Echoing calls by African intellectuals for a black consciousness freed from the scars of colonialism, he urged African Americans to reject feelings of inferiority. Blackness, especially black manhood, was to be embraced and treasured, he said.[9]

By 1963, Malcolm X grew tired of what he identified as Elijah Muhammad's moral failings and lack of political activism. He left the NOI, famously traveling to Mecca to declare his allegiance to what he called orthodox Islam.[10] But even after his defection in 1964, the NOI continued to grow. Its mosques multiplied, and new members came in to replace those who, like Malcolm, left in disappointment. The organizational infrastructure of the NOI also grew during the 1960s and 1970s. In many of the NOI's temples, members participated in chapters of an all-male organization, the Fruit of Islam, and an all-female organization, Muslim Girls Training and General Civilization Class. By this time, believers also oversaw the operation of several primary and secondary schools called Universities of Islam. Wherever Muslims lived, they established small businesses associated with the local temple, including barbershops, bakeries, clothing stores, and restaurants. Many non–Muslims patronized these establishments. Still more businesses were owned personally by Elijah Muhammad, who presided over a multimillion-dollar business empire which consisted of a printing press, farms, restaurants, a meat packing plant, homes, apartments, trucks, a clothing factory, and a small bank.[11]

It is difficult to calculate exactly how many persons called themselves followers of the NOI during the 1960s and 1970s. Estimates have ranged from below 10,000 to over 100,000, with no reliable census to confirm these numbers.[12] Some members stayed in the NOI throughout this period, but many converts also left the movement, sometimes returning later.[13] No matter what its exact size, it is safe to conclude that the NOI was a relatively small group when compared to other African American religious communities and organizations.[14] But this was a small group that, like other marginal groups and new religious movements in American religious history, made a big splash.[15]

For two decades since its founding in the 1930s, the NOI had remained a rather obscure movement, noticed mainly by African American urban dwellers, scholars of black sociology and religions, and the Federal Bureau of Investigation.[16] Most Americans had no knowledge of the NOI until the late 1950s, when New York's WNTA-TV aired a five-part series about the movement hosted by Mike Wallace entitled "The Hate that Hate Produced."[17] Following this program, stories about the NOI appeared in national magazines such as *Time* and *U.S. News and World Report*. This coverage was generally negative, criticizing the movement as an anti-American or black supremacist organization. African American civil rights leaders, including Roy Wilkins of the National Association for the Advancement of Colored People (NAACP), denounced the NOI as a hate group.[18] Wilkins, like noted sociologist of religion C. Eric Lincoln, argued that the failure of the United States to provide equal opportunity for African Americans had fueled movements like the NOI.[19] Inside the FBI, investigators ignored the social contexts in which the NOI found success, instead citing it as an example of black racism: "The Muslim Cult of Islam is a fanatic Negro organization purporting to be motivated by the religious principles of Islam, but actually dedicated to the propagation of hatred against the white race. The services conducted throughout the temples are bereft of any semblance to religious exercises."[20]

As negative portrayals in the mainstream press and criticism from black leaders increased, more and more Muslims in the United States joined to condemn, dispute, and reject the teachings of Elijah Muhammad and the NOI. Many of them were immigrants or foreign students who did not want the "hatred" of the

NOI to become associated with the religion of Islam. The Islamic Center of Washington, D.C., for example, actively disassociated itself from Elijah Muhammad, denying any claim of Islamic legitimacy for the group.[21] One Algerian Muslim wrote to the *Pittsburgh Courier*, a historically black newspaper, asking readers not to "confuse the sect of Muhammad with that of true Islam. Islam does not preach hate," the writer said, "it does not preach racism, it only calls for love, peace, and understanding." Another letter to the *Courier*, a newspaper for which Elijah Muhammad had written numerous religious articles, asserted that the leader "twists the Koran around to fit his hate teachings."[22] Similarly, African American Muslim leaders opposed Elijah Muhammad as an illegitimate Muslim leader. For instance, Talib Ahmad Dawud, who agreed with Muhammad's anti-integrationist and anti-Christian views, criticized Muhammad's belief in the divinity of W. D. Fard. Dawud also claimed that Muhammad had violated the fundamental tenets of Islam in his "denial of a future, bodily resurrection, and his follower's failure to adhere to the proper Muslim prayer rituals."[23]

These attacks from both immigrant and African American Muslims continued until Elijah Muhammad's death in 1975.[24] In 1972, the Islamic Party of North America published an article in its in-house periodical, *Al-Islam*, accusing NOI members of being "heretics" since they "are not Muslims according to the Qur'an and Sunnah [traditions of the Prophet Muhammad]." The NOI, they said, was a "polytheistic racial cult" that does not follow the five pillars of Islamic practice.[25] During the same period, Hammas Abdul Khaalis, a former jazz musician and African American Sunni Muslim leader in Washington, D.C., appeared on television to criticize the Messenger Elijah Muhammad, leading to several responses in *Muhammad Speaks*.[26]

The mainstream press, rather than presenting "both sides" of the story, often reported these criticisms of the NOI's Islamic legitimacy as facts. In 1972, for example, Merv Block of the Associated Press published an exposé of the movement that simply assumed that the "Black Muslims" were not real "Moslems."[27] Also in 1972, John Day of WBEE's "Opinion" program invited Shukar Ilahi Husain onto his program to criticize the NOI as a fraud and did not allow the NOI to respond. Interestingly, Husain was a member of the Ahmadiyya movement, itself considered heretical by a growing number of Muslims in the post–World War II period.[28] But that fact was apparently less important than the role Husain could play in discrediting the NOI.

In other words, the mainstream American view of the NOI in the 1960s and early 1970s was that the movement was neither legitimately religious nor authentically Islamic.

## Reconsidering the NOI as a Religious Group

This book takes a different view. NOI members may have held political positions about integration, Vietnam, and white supremacy, and they may have been looking for solutions to their political and social problems. But what made them cohere, what made them a movement, was their devotion to a comprehensive religious system. These Muslims created a rich religious culture defined by the development of religious narratives and treatises, the performance of religious rituals, and the practice of ethical commandments.[29] They practiced their religion not only by reciting their prayers and their creeds but also by paying attention to what they ate, how they dressed, and what music they listened to. For NOI practitioners, Islam was not only a theology but also a system of ritualized practices that brought them what they described as dignity, hope, civilization, self-determination, pride, peace, security, and salvation.

In sum, this volume charts how members of the NOI imagined, performed, and practiced Islamic religion during the 1960s and 1970s.[30] Of course, not every activity of NOI members was religious in nature, and it is important to emphasize that their religious activities, like those of all other human beings, were tied inextricably to their politics, social location, and their cultural orientations. Often times, the religion of the NOI was powerful precisely because it was simultaneously a form of political activism and religious expression. But this book examines the political and social aspects of the NOI through the lens of its believers' religious activities. When I use the word "religion" to describe the activities of NOI members, I am referring to "a system of beliefs and practices that are relative to superhuman beings."[31] While this definition of religion, like all definitions, is problematic, it has one enormous advantage in this case. It captures the spirit of NOI discourses that focused on the nature of God, ethical commandments from God concerning human behavior, mythical views about God's authority over the beginning and end of the world, beliefs about God's role in human history, and ritualized behaviors meant to signify and enact God's and Elijah Muhammad's authority over the believers. For the most part, this is a definition of religion that the subjects of this study would recognize.

In foregrounding how persons in the NOI understood their religious activities, this book analyzes religious expression not "as abstracted windows into belief or as essential statements of religious truth," but as "specific events of speaking, commenting, and reflecting" that help to illuminate what it meant, for the believers, to be members of a religious community, to perform religious acts, and to abide by religious rules.[32] The activities of African American Muslims were a form of identity-making, and their identities, like all human identities, were "dynamic, not stable; negotiated, not given."[33] African American Muslim contests over the meaning of their symbols, texts, rituals, doctrines, and narratives are the discursive arenas in which this study traces the historical development of religious culture in the NOI. Religious activities are thus examined as the "cultural processes whereby individuals and groups map, construct, and inhabit worlds of meaning."[34] And religious discourses are analyzed with an awareness that meaning-making is always shaped by several different interests and within multiple historical contexts.

This book therefore provides a profile of the rich religious landscape of African American Muslim members of the NOI. It begins with how Muslims defined and described what being religious and being Muslim meant for them. Literally hundreds of their personal stories appeared from 1961 to 1975 in the *Muhammad Speaks* newspaper. Members often described their commitment to Islam not only as the conversion of their souls but also as a demystifying of their minds and the liberation of their bodies. In analyzing their stories of Muslim life, I demonstrate how the movement combined certain elements of Afro-Eurasian Islamic traditions, especially Sunni traditions, with African American religious traditions in creating a form of Islamic practice.

The following chapters then focus on the ways in which African American Muslims in the NOI constructed their Islamic identities through intellectual and creative activity, including the writing of treatises, the drawing of cartoons, and the creation of religious poetry. These chapters emphasize the more cognitive aspects of religious practice in the NOI. Chapter 2 explores the intellectual defenses of Elijah Muhammad mounted by a professional class of intellectuals, often in the employ of the Messenger, who defended their leader as a genuine Islamic prophet. I analyze cartoons and line drawings that depict Elijah Muhammad as an Islamic prophet, the exegeses of the Qur'an used to bolster Elijah Muhammad's Islamic bona fides, and various theological arguments about his prophetic status. Chapter 3 broadens the scope of inquiry to explore the discourse of both intellectuals and rank-and-file members that linked the history of black people to the history of Islamic places, figures, names, texts, events, and themes. These historical imaginings represent another form of religious narrative in the NOI that helps us understand what it meant to be a Muslim for some members of the movement.

Later chapters consider an even wider range of sources and experiences in analyzing aspects of religious practice in the NOI, focusing on the NOI's ethical discourse on the body and the ritualized nature of religious activity in the movement. Chapter 4 scrutinizes how members attempted to discipline, strengthen, purify, and cleanse their bodies by altering their dress, diet, labor habits, and more. Chapter 5 examines the ritualized activities of members in other venues, including men's and women's organizations, NOI schools, temple meetings, conventions, and rallies. Closing with a summary of changes in the movement after the death of Elijah Muhammad in 1975, I emphasize important continuities in religious culture and suggest that the "mainstreaming" of the NOI indeed built upon traditions established during the 1960s and early 1970s.

Although this story provides the first comprehensive examination of NOI religious culture, I also seek to place this movement in larger historiographic contexts. A study of the NOI not only reveals the complex religious context of particular believers, but also illuminates the importance of Islam and Muslims to American debates over the politics of identity and the structure of American religions. First, the growing influence of Muslim immigrants on African American culture from the late 1950s through the 1970s is revealed. The 1965 immigration bill was a watershed moment for religious diversity in the United States. In its wake, the numbers of non-Christian religionists from Africa and Asia increased dramatically.[35] But well before 1965, immigrant Muslims had been making their presence felt in black America. Their criticisms of the NOI prompted an elaborate defense of Elijah Muhammad's Islamic legitimacy and, in an ironic turn, led to an increased awareness of the Qur'an and other classical Islamic texts and traditions among members of the NOI.

Second, the shift in African American Muslim consciousness had important consequences for black culture and identity politics more generally. It is often argued that, during the 1960s, many ordinary African Americans turned their gaze toward Africa, took an interest in pan-Africanism and, eventually, in African history, culture, and such languages as Swahili and Yoruba.[36] In the late 1960s, Ron Karenga established the festival of Kwanzaa and urged a reorientation of black consciousness that focused on what was seen as the unique cultural heritage of all black African peoples.[37] This movement and others like it would establish a foundation for what today is often called Afrocentrism.[38] While some African American Muslims shared this renewed interest in Africa—Malcolm X is the best-known example—many members of the NOI came to disagree explicitly with advocates of the black consciousness movement.

These African Americans began to map their identities with a view not only toward Africa but also toward the Islamic world, toward any place where Muslims had been, including Asia, the Middle East, and even Latin America. They looked beyond the transatlantic world to form their communal identities and created black history narratives that linked the history of black people to this history of Islam. Their cognitive map went well beyond the boundaries of what has been called the black Atlantic. African American Muslims were not simply creating nationalist identities in the 1960s and 1970s; they were also creating transnational identities. They felt allegiance not only to the black nation but also to a community of Muslims who might be members of several different nations. If one wants to understand why some African Americans are attracted today to various transnational Islamic movements, including conservative Islamic movements like the Salafiyya and various Sufi or mystical orders, one has to understand this pivotal moment, this reorientation of black Americans toward the Islamic world and Muslim religionists.

Third, this study's focus on the religious culture of the NOI illuminates the debates over that movement's impact on the relationship between religion and politics in the United States during the 1960s and 1970s. Scholars of religion in the United States often see these decades as a time when the political clout and cultural authority of Protestant Christian institutions, especially mainline churches, declined.[39] Not only did the 1965 immigration bill lead to an increase in the number of non-Christians in the United States, but alternative religions and nonaligned evangelical churches also challenged the Protestant establishment for members and for influence in the public sphere.[40] The civil rights movement and the Vietnam War also widened the divide between conservative and liberal Christians.[41] The NOI was yet another challenge to the institutional hegemony of Protestants in the United States and the link between Protestant Christianity and the state. At the height of the Cold War and the Vietnam conflict, the NOI rejected civil rights, Christianity, and American identity.

This rejection was complicated, however, since the NOI did not reject what are generally accepted as middle-class American Protestant ideals, including clean living, modest and neat dress, thrift, punctuality, dietary restraint, economic self-sufficiency, heterosexuality, and monogamy. All of these norms were embraced as Islamic values, and the African American Muslims who chose to practice them were viewed by the press, the academy, and the FBI as potentially radical. That is also how the believers viewed themselves. They were both politically conservative and radical. NOI members certainly perpetuated American Protestant middle-class ideals and thus may have avoided a direct attack on American political economy, but through their "Islamization" of these norms, they challenged the cultural and ideological foundations of the American nation-state, its social structures, and its dominant religious institutions. One might say of the NOI what historian Darlene Clark Hine said of Afrocentricity: it "blurs easy distinctions between conservative and radical because it fosters liberation *and* fuels essentialism, empowers people *and* polices boundaries."[42]

## But Was the Nation of Islam Really Islamic?

In arguing for the Islamic character of the movement, my account begins with a rather simple view of Muslim identity — that of self-identification.[43] If someone calls himself or herself a Muslim, I want to know what that means to them, and, as a fair-minded observer, I accept, for the purposes of both scholarly understanding and dialogue, that he or she is indeed Muslim. But this stipulation of Islamic legitimacy does not restrain me from pointing out the particular contours of an individual's or a group's Muslim identity and how that identity may differ from other Muslim orientations.

To be sure, the religious thought of Elijah Muhammad was decidedly heretical from the point of view of traditional Sunni Islamic orthodoxy. Elijah Muhammad taught that W. D. Fard, the founder of the NOI, was God in person, Allah Incarnate. God was "no spook in space," said Muhammad; He was a real man.[44] In the minds of many Muslims outside of the NOI, this idea violated a fundamental principle of Islamic faith — the declaration that there is no god but God. For his Muslim critics, Elijah Muhammad had committed the grave theological sin of *shirk*, the association of God with any other entity.[45] And this was not Elijah Muhammad's only doctrinal mistake, according to his opponents. He also declared that he was the Messenger of Allah, divinely chosen to lead black people to salvation. This notion contradicted a time-honored and authoritative Muslim interpretation of the Qur'an that Prophet Muhammad *of Arabia* was the seal of the prophets and, so, the last prophet of God to appear on earth.[46] When most Muslims witness that Muhammad is the Messenger of God, they are inevitably referring to Muhammad of Arabia. Elijah Muhammad, however, created his own version of what students of Islam would recognize as the first pillar of Islam, the *shahada*, or the declaration of faith. According to Elijah Muhammad, believers should declare the following: There is no god but God (that is, W. D. Fard) and Elijah Muhammad is His Messenger. For most Muslims, anyone who declared such a thing was not a true Muslim but a heretic.

It is important to note, however, that despite its distance from so-called Islamic orthodoxy, Elijah Muhammad's teaching did refer to a legitimate Islamic tradition. Elijah Muhammad's doctrine of God and His Messenger was a variation on an older Islamic formula; or at the least, it appropriated traditionally Islamic theological vocabulary into a new religious framework. It took the traditional declaration that "there is no god but God and Muhammad is the Messenger of God" and interpreted it to mean that God was W. D. Fard and that Elijah Muhammad was the Messenger. For believers inside the NOI, this interpretation became the fulfillment of prophecy, an expression of Allah's original intentions.

Elijah Muhammad's religious thought also included a myth of black origins and a story about the fall of man, both of which bore little resemblance to other traditions of Islamic thought. Elijah Muhammad taught that blacks were the original human beings on the earth and that blacks were self-made—that is, they were both the creators and the created. After a series of cataclysmic galactic events that occurred trillions of years ago, which included the separation of the moon from the earth, blacks came to inhabit the holy city of Mecca in Arabia. According to Elijah Muhammad, they were called the tribe of Shabazz. They spoke Arabic, practiced the religion of Islam, and lived in an Edenic civilization that continued for epochs—until around 4600 B.C. At that time, one of their own, a mad and evil scientist named Yacub, began a series of genetic experiments that produced the white man, a genetically inferior, brutish, and evil creature. The white man existed on raw meat and lived in the caves of Europe from 4000 to 2000 B.C.E., at which time he began a campaign to usurp black hegemony on the earth. Eventually, the naturally violent white man enslaved the black man, bringing him to the New World on a slave ship called John Hawkins in the 1500s. In the New World, the tribe of Shabazz forgot its language, its religion, and its traditions of civilization. It adopted the evil lifestyles and especially the horrible religion of its oppressors, Christianity.[47]

Muhammad thus offered followers a black theodicy: a story grounded in a mythological view of history that explained the fall of black civilization, the Middle Passage from Africa to the Americas, and the practice of Christian religion among slaves and their descendants.[48] This narrative assured African Americans that they were good by nature and had been the victims of an evil plot. While blacks may have been powerless to prevent the unfolding of this history, Elijah Muhammad said that God had not abandoned them. It was their destiny as the chosen race, the original man, to be offered salvation, to regain their former status as rulers of the earth. In 1930, God, in the person of W. D. Fard, appeared on the earth and commissioned Elijah Muhammad his Messenger to "mentally resurrect the so-called Negro." Messenger Elijah Muhammad called on African Americans to reject the slavemaster's religion and to reclaim Islam. He told them to separate from the white devils and unite with their own kind. Elijah Muhammad explained that black people had been fooled by the "tricknology" of the white man's religion; he told them that there was no heaven in the sky and argued that such pie-in-the-sky religion was meant to make them docile, to trick them into waiting for true equality and freedom, which could be theirs now. Like other practitioners of an American religious tradition called New Thought, he proclaimed that heaven and hell were states of mind and that it was high time to leave hell.[49]

In order to enter heaven, however, African Americans would have to follow his moral teachings, said the Messenger. He taught them to observe a strict code of ethics that theoretically governed every aspect of their lives. For many Americans, Elijah Muhammad's prescriptions for moral renewal were the least shocking aspects of his doctrines. Advocating Victorian notions of gender segregation and control of the body, he incorporated many American middle-class norms into his system of Islamic ethics. Some of these ethical directives paralleled elements of the *shari'a*, or Islamic law and ethics, while others did not. Believers were to practice clean living: to regulate their diets, eschew alcohol and tobacco, avoid gambling, dress modestly, control their sexual desires, practice thrift, work hard, be punctual, use proper English grammar, pray often, and treat others with respect. In addition, said the Messenger, they should use violence only to defend themselves and should observe all laws of the United States, so long as they do not contradict the laws of Islam. Believers were also encouraged to "do for self," that is, to practice economic self-sufficiency and avoid as much as possible the white-dominated economy. Instead, Elijah Muhammad told them to buy from black-owned business and especially from the many businesses that came to be created in the 1960s and 1970s under his leadership.[50]

If followers practiced these principles, the Messenger said, they could enjoy salvation in the here and now and await their restoration as the rulers of the earth. He rejected calls for blacks to return to Africa, since it was North American blacks that would lead other persons of color toward the restoration of black greatness. Instead, he demanded a separate black nation-state or territory within the United States—though he did little to advance this political agenda. Believers were often told to refrain from participating in U.S. elections, and they were discouraged from joining the armed forces. But there is no evidence to suggest that Muhammad planned or even desired the violent overthrow of the U.S. government. Rather, Muhammad assured his believers that God would redeem them at the end of times through a violent destruction of white civilization (although, in 1972, he said that white people could be saved if they, too, would convert to Islam).[51] Combining apocalyptic views with certain themes from science fiction, the Messenger said that, at the end of days, a mothership—a huge UFO—would appear in the sky and dispense bombs that would destroy whites and leave blacks unharmed. Only he and his believers would be able to see this horrible object, a deus ex machina that would bring justice down from the heavens upon the evil and immoral society of white persons.[52] In declaring that, at the end of the world, God would target whites, rather than evil human beings in general, Muhammad once again offered a teaching unacceptable in the eyes of most Muslims.

In sum, Elijah Muhammad's thought violated many fundamental precepts of what has come to be known as Sunni Islam, or the Islam that follows the traditions of the Prophet Muhammad of Arabia. But that does not mean there was no connection between Sunni Islam and the religious culture of the NOI. By exploring the ways in which members of the NOI interpreted and adapted historically Islamic traditions as part of their religious culture, this book makes the case that these believers increasingly identified, in one way or another, with the Islamic beliefs, rituals, ethics, and symbols of "mainstream" Islam. From a normative point of view, they became increasingly "Islamized" during the period under examination.

In charting their "Islamization," my approach is informed by recent scholarly developments in the anthropology and history of Islam that offer new directions for understanding the various religious, cultural, social, political, and economic processes by which human beings, in various places, have become Muslims. Rather than assuming that Islam is a fixed entity that over time spread from the Arab and Persian Middle East to the rest of the Afro-Eurasian landmass, scholars have remapped Islamization and stressed indigenous processes of identity formation and local appropriations of Islamic traditions.[53] Historian Richard Eaton explained this re-siting of Islamization thus: "Instead of adopting the perspective of one standing in Mecca, looking out upon an ever-widening, ever-expanding religious tide that is uniform and monolithic, one adopts the perspective of someone standing in a remote and dusty village, incorporating into his religious system elements considered useful or meaningful that drift in from beyond the ocean, from over the mountains, or simply from the neighboring village."[54] In addition to questioning the mapping of the Islamic world as "heartland and periphery," Islamic studies scholars have challenged assumptions about the nature of religious conversion itself.[55] Many have criticized the Protestant biases embedded in the assumption that religious conversion must be "understood as a fundamental change in *beliefs*, an act of replacement perfect and complete when all pre-Islamic beliefs disappear in favor of Islamic tenets." As one scholar of Indonesian Islam puts it, such understandings of conversion create a false dichotomy between "true" Muslims and "those who emptily perform Islamic rituals while retaining behind this façade their original beliefs."[56]

All of these charges against marginal Muslims have a familiar ring—they have also been made about members of the NOI.[57] Rather than dismissing NOI members as fake or unorthodox Muslims, I argue that religious life in the NOI can be understood and analyzed as a subtle process of Islamization in which members of the NOI debated the meaning of their religion, accepting and rejecting various elements of *other* Islamic traditions as they struggled to practice a form of Islam that was relevant to their historical circumstances. This new approach, furthermore, looks at religious identity not only as a matter of one's theological beliefs but also of one's ritual activities, ethical imperatives, and communal affiliations. Even those readers who continue to make a stark distinction between the religion of the NOI and the religion of Islam might be surprised by the extent to which some members of the NOI incorporated various traditions from Sunni and other historically Islamic symbols, texts, and practices into their religious activities.

In the end, the quest to understand Islam in the NOI is not only a quest to complicate our understanding of a single, small religious group. It is also an attempt to take religion, and religious believers, seriously. The theological convictions, ethical impulses, and rituals of religious persons are not merely cultural accessories or veiled politics. They constitute categories of human activity worthy of our attention and respect.

## CHAPTER 1

# What Islam Has Done For Me
## Finding Religion in the Nation of Islam

I believe in Allah, God of the Muslims, creator of all the worlds, and in Elijah Muhammad, his last Apostle, who was conceived by a black man, born of a black woman, suffered under the white man, was economically cruci-fied, mentally dead and racially buried. He is still in hell (America) but has risen from the dead the so-called Negroes, and is raising his people from their graves of ignorance, to inherit heaven on this earth. . . . Thence Allah shall judge the living (devils) and the dead (so-called Negroes). I believe in no "Holy Ghost" tales; no murderous Spanish Inquisition Catholic Church; no com-munion of saints, angels, spirits or spooks; no forgive-ness of your [white] people's sins against mine; no dry bones and decayed flesh resurrecting; and no life after physical death.

— Sylane X, *Muhammad Speaks*, April 1962

iven the ways in which powerful interpreters of culture framed the NOI during the 1960s and 1970s, it is no wonder that many Americans came to regard the movement primarily as a political and social movement rather than a religious one. NOI leaders also contributed to this image of the group; their sometimes heavy-handed use of the word "religion" was partly a political strategy used to claim social legitimacy and legal protections. NOI leaders frequently cited the American tradition of religious liberty as a powerful symbol in their fight to protect NOI males from the military draft, to repel the interference of local police forces and the FBI, and to defend Elijah Muhammad's status as a religious leader.

At the same time, if one takes seriously the words of NOI members, it is clear that many of Elijah Muhammad's followers understood themselves to be practitioners of a genuine religion. In fact, members of the NOI used the word "religion" over and over again to describe their belief in Islam.[1] Their eloquent and enthusiastic writings show that, while these narratives may have sometimes performed political functions, they were also expressions of religious feelings, ideas, and experiences.

Hundreds of Muslim followers contributed letters to the editor of *Muhammad Speaks* and especially testimonials about the impact of Islam on their lives. The testimonials appeared in a running feature of *Muhammad Speaks* called "What Islam Has Done For Me." Many of these stories were classic American religious conversion narratives whose form will be familiar to many readers, and they evidence how the styles of religious practice and patterns of conversion in the NOI echo those of other American religious groups. These testimonials often described how a convert faced a crisis or lingering problem before they found Elijah Muhammad and the NOI. Converting to Islam provided a way out and a solution to their problems. Some of these narratives, like those of born-again African American Christians, discussed conversion as a sudden and powerful moment in which the believer experienced God's presence.[2] Others framed their conversions in less numinous terms, instead explaining their conversions as a gradual transition to Islam that nevertheless yielded equally important results. In this chapter, I offer a reading of those narratives, foregrounding the words of the believers themselves. In so doing, I highlight first-person narratives of Islamization, stories that explain what it meant to members of the NOI to become Muslims. For these persons, Islam was certainly a religion, but it was also a path to self-improvement and a source of physical and psychological safety or protection. For some, it was a complete way of life.

## Islam as a Religious Alternative

Many believers in the NOI embraced Islam as a religious alternative to Christianity.[3] As shown by the epigraph at the beginning of this chapter, Sylane X from New York City even crafted a creed of Muslim belief—one that was not part of regular NOI literature—that transformed a well-known Christian formula into a statement of theological and doctrinal protest. His creed is a rejection of Christian religion, which was associated in the minds of many believers in the NOI with black suffering and white racism. It also denied the existence of any "spooky" God or afterlife. Over and over again in the pages of *Muhammad Speaks*, believers contrasted what they saw as the superstitious and spooky religion of Christianity with the rational and practical religion of Islam. For instance, Dr. Leo X McCallum, the semi-official dentist of the NOI, praised the scientific and rational elements of Islam. "There is nothing more scientifically, biologically, physiologically or mathematically correct than Islam," he claimed. Unlike Christianity, he argued, Islam is compatible with logic. The "basic dogmas of Christianity," including the teachings about the divine nature of Jesus and his resurrection, are not believable to the rational man, especially those black professionals with higher education in the scientific fields, Dr. McCallum said. (He made no comment about the mythological teachings of the NOI.) Thus, Islam can better serve as the scientific man's religion, he asserted.[4] Likewise, Marie Atterbury of Macon, Georgia, emphasized the extent to which Islam appealed to her thirst for rational answers to life's persistent questions. A former Methodist, Atterbury wrote, "Islam teaches more than Christianity. One learns more basic facts of life, because the ministers are trained to give more detailed explanations. . . . The Honorable Elijah Muhammad inspires me with his sincerity. I am also impressed by his logical answers to the problems that plague the black man."[5]

For some believers, Elijah Muhammad and the NOI also offered interpretations of the Bible that were simply more convincing than the readings offered by the Christian church. John X Lawler, for example, said that when he converted years before, Elijah Muhammad helped him understand the confusing aspects of the Bible. "Only when I discovered Islam," he wrote in 1963, "were the most puzzling aspects of the scripture made clear. And not only I, but others have found that the Messenger of Allah's teachings to be the key that unlocked not only the mystery of the Bible, but of life itself." According to Lawler, Elijah

Muhammad taught him both the "reality of the Supreme Being [read W. D. Fard]" and his "duties to my fellow man."[6] Sister Beatrice X of Washington, D.C., also praised Elijah Muhammad's teaching about the Bible, arguing that her former Baptist minister, a thirty-three-degree Mason, had used only part of the teachings of Islam to illuminate the difficult sections of the Bible. Elijah Muhammad, on the other hand, "pointed out some things in the Bible with which I had to agree."[7] Another, Sister Georgia X Thompson of Monroe, Louisiana, simply said, "This religion gave me a better and clearer understanding of the Bible."[8] Though some believers never explained why they were convinced by Elijah Muhammad's Biblical exegeses, others said that it was Muhammad's "unlocking" of certain Biblical passages, especially in the book of Revelation, that convinced them. These interpretations of the Bible were used to support the Messenger's theories on the origins of the black man, on the role of the white devil in God's divine plan, and on the coming apocalypse.[9]

In fact, many believers thought that Elijah Muhammad had access to esoteric science, a kind of gnosis that paved the way for a perfect understanding of the universe. Theodore F. X Peyton of Detroit said that before he became a Muslim, "I professed to be everything except a Christian. I went from an atheist to a skeptic to an agnostic. . . . I never could understand Christianity, nor could I bring myself to pretend I did." For him, the fundamentalist Christian teaching claiming that human beings were only 6,000 years old was unscientific: "I could not understand how the Christian preachers could stand up and claim that the earth and man were only 6,000 years old when untold numbers of fossils dating 750,000 and 800,000 and more years old of man's bones are found nearly every day. I could not see how they (the preachers) could ignore these facts."[10] Islam, as interpreted by Elijah Muhammad, offered an alternative view — that the earth and human beings were millions of years old, as outlined in the introduction to this book.

Of course, one might argue that Elijah Muhammad's pseudoscientific myth of the black man's origins were just as scientifically implausible as any Christian myth. But for this believer, Elijah Muhammad's myth made sense. As Warner X Berry, another believer who saw Islam as a scientific faith, put it, Allah "knows the natural laws that govern the universe. He knows the chemical and mathematical secrets of life."[11] And Elijah Muhammad made that knowledge available to believers. George X Tucker said, "In history and science Elijah stands by himself as unbeatable. He has taught us the history of the earth and its inhabitants and of the moon which is a part of this planet earth, separated by an explosion by a black scientist 66 trillion years ago."[12] These "facts," which had clear numerological significance in their use of the evil number "six," were featured in the NOI's catechisms, called the *Actual Facts* and *Student Enrollment*.[13]

In addition to being more rational and scientific than Christianity, Islam was also cast as a religion of resistance and action. Former Christian minister Marvin Omar of Maywood, Illinois, who identified himself as a graduate of Howard Law School, contrasted the this-worldly nature of Elijah Muhammad's Islam with the other-worldly and deceptive character of the white man's Christianity. Christianity, he said, was a white man's religion meant to turn black people into docile and powerless beings:

> Thank God for sending the Honorable Elijah Muhammad to open my eyes. It seems incredible that I once believed the white man's Christian dogma. Through black preachers, the white man told me that Jesus was white; that God is white; that angels are white women with wings; that black men, after they die, would fly around with Jesus in 'heaven'; that Jesus flew away and someday after I die I would be like him and fly away to some never-land in the sky; that after I die everything would be all right; that I should be good on earth and turn the other cheek so that after I die and shed this body some blue-eyed stringy-haired white God was going to give all little black boys bodies like his; that I would lay up in the sky where all God's children have shoes and eat and drink milk and honey forever.[14]

After his conversion to Islam, Omar said, he rejected such "pie-in-the-sky stories," and decided to work in this life for "justice, freedom and equality." Similarly, for Brother Hiram X, a former Black Student Union volunteer who converted during his student years at one of the California State University branches, Islam was a religion that spoke to his need for a faith that addressed the practical problems of black life. "Before hearing the teachings of the Honorable Elijah Muhammad, I could have been classified as an agnostic," he wrote. "I did not rule out the existence of God; I believed rather the Christians' concept of god did not relate to my conditions and was powerless to change it." The Messenger, according to Hiram X, taught people how to live and how to meet the everyday needs of life, including food, clothing, and shelter.[15]

For many believers, Islam was not held responsible for white racism and black internalized oppression, much of which was associated with slavery and the legalized system of segregation in the South called Jim Crow. Charlene M. Whitcomb, a sixty-eight-year-old believer from Oakland, California, said that "Islam is a religion of life, while Christianity is a religion of death. . . . Now I see why Christianity is called the 'opium of the masses.' It's used to keep men enslaved."[16] Or as another former minister, Elder L. Hinis, of Elizabeth, New Jersey, said, Christianity was slave religion, and "we have slaved long . . . enough."[17] Some also called Christianity a hypocritical religion, criticizing church members for failing to practice the values of integrity that they preached.[18] Islam met the spiritual needs of those who still thirsted for religion but wanted nothing to do with Christians. "My fear," said John 11X of Miami, Florida,

> was that after seeing the hypocrisy of Christianity, religion was dead inside
> me. Yet, when I thought of the complexity of the human body, the existence
> and precise movements of the planets, and the wonders of nature, I knew that
> deep down inside I was religious and believed in God, whose proper name is
> Allah. . . . Islam taught me to reach the identity I unconsciously sought; an
> identity free of the slavemasters' name, of the slavemasters' language, of the
> slavemasters' flag, of the slavemasters' culture, of the image that the slavemaster and their children presented and present of me to the world.[19]

Sister Ann 3X echoed this criticism of Christianity, proclaiming that Christian "religion is based on a lot of unrealistic ideas given to the slave by his slavemaster to keep him a slave. Christianity satisfied neither the Blackman's material nor spiritual needs."[20]

Many former southerners also tied the religion of Christianity to their lives in the South, and constructed Islam as a religion that brought them new hope in the North. For example, Sister Beatrice X of Washington, D.C., remembered that "my people were farmers and devoted church-goers" in South Carolina. "There was plenty of religion in the family. My uncles were preachers. Looking back, I think of what a shame it was to see them glorifying the white man and preaching his religion with so much fervor."[21] From the late nineteenth century to 1960, millions of African Americans left the South in what historians have called the Great Migration, a movement of persons that had a profound impact on the cultural, social, political, and economic life of the United States as a whole.[22] In northern cities like Detroit, Chicago, Cleveland, Philadelphia, and New York, among others, African Americans sometimes joined established churches. In many other cases, however, they began to experiment with new religious traditions and communities. As Albert Raboteau summarizes,

> Besides increasing the size and number of urban black churches, migration
> also increased the variety of black religious choices. Accustomed to deciding
> between Baptist, Methodist, and perhaps Holiness-Pentecostal churches back
> home, migrants to the cities encountered black Jews, black Muslims, black

Catholics, black Spiritualists (people who believed that the living could communicate with the dead), and black disciples of charismatic religious figures like Daddy Grace, the founder of a church called the Universal House of Prayer for All People, who believed that their leaders could exercise divine power to heal their problems in this world as well as the next.[23]

In choosing to become Muslims, African American members of the NOI often self-consciously divorced themselves from their southern roots and proudly claimed allegiance to a new religious community where they could find what they described as more dignity and happiness. For example, Jerry Wilson of Chicago, Illinois, was born in 1940 in Clarksdale, Mississippi. When he was a boy, his family moved to Memphis, Tennessee, and he was "happy, happy to leave Mississippi." Wilson remembered with regret that his father had taught him as a small boy "to accept any treatment given us by the white folks," a necessary survival measure in the Jim Crow South, but one that left Wilson feeling wronged and ashamed. "Poor dad! Those white shopkeepers used to make him pay several times over for everything he bought from them. With dad losing money on every purchase, it really wrecked our meager family budget. It was not uncommon for us to be forced to walk around with holes in the soles of our shoes," he said. In remembering his life as a black child in the South, Wilson did not directly blame Christian religious doctrine for this discrimination. Instead, he found fault with his church community's lack of true brotherhood. His mother, he said, was very religious, and he sang in the choir. In fact, he admitted, "I really felt a strong attraction for the church and its activities. Our pastor was highly dramatic, seeming to breathe life into all the Biblical characters. I found his sermons exciting, but they filled me with superstition and fear." Then, Wilson was struck with rheumatic fever, and experienced chronic health problems, "both real and imaginary." He felt abandoned by his friends and by God.[24] But he soon heard the teachings of Elijah Muhammad, and eventually converted to Islam. The result was nothing short of amazing. "For the first time, I learned from the teachings of Mr. Muhammad that God really loved His people and wanted us to be happy. I learned that Allah, God, was owner of the earth and all things on earth submitted to Him. I learned to fear only Allah, the Lord of the worlds, and to trust His power to protect me." Wilson also decided to abandon the South and move to Chicago, where he could be close to Elijah Muhammad. "I felt a need to get closer to this great man of God who saved my life and gave purpose and meaning to my existence."[25]

While many believers thought of their adherence to the NOI as a religious alternative to Christianity, they did not always frame their devotion to Islam in rejectionist terms. For example, in 1969 Ronnie X Shorter of Chicago offered this account of his belief in Islamic religion:

> Islam is the natural religion of the Black man. Islam means freedom, justice, and equality. Islam is the true nature of the Black man. Allah, which is the proper name of God, is the author of Islam and the originator of the entire universe. The entire creation of Allah is of peace. When you reject Allah and His Messenger, the Most Honorable Elijah Muhammad, you reject yourself. When you submit to Allah, you submit to peace. Islam is a religion that can be found in the universal order of things. . . . A religion whose origin and roots cannot be found in the universal order of God, cannot be said to be the religion of God. . . . Allah is the truth, and that which others call upon besides Him is false.[26]

There may be an implicit critique of Christianity in this brother's description of his Islamic faith, but his account clearly emphasized the positive reasons for joining Islam.

In a similar vein, Marlene Karriem did not mention Christianity in her explanation of why she came to believe in Islam:

> The central doctrine of all religions is the existence of God and man's relationship with Him. The religion that succeeds in establishing a true relationship between God and man must be true. And the truth of a faith is surely a sufficient reason for believing in it. As Messenger Muhammad teaches us, Islam claims that the creator of this universe is a living God and that He reveals Himself to the creatures in this age in the same manner which He used to reveal Himself in the ages past. This claim can be tested in two ways: Allah may either manifest His signs direct for a seeker after Him or we may come to believe in Allah by studying the life of a person whom Allah has revealed Himself. And we do know that Messenger Elijah Muhammad was missioned directly from the mouth of Allah himself. I believe in Islam for it does not compel me to accept all those matters, the sum total of what is called religion, merely on authority, but furnishes convincing proof in support of its doctrine. . . . I believe in Islam because it teaches us there can be no conflict between the word of Allah and the work of Allah. Islam does not ask me to ignore the laws of nature and to believe in things contrary to them. On the contrary, it exhorts me to study the laws of nature and derive the benefits from them.[27]

Once again, one might say that Sister Marlene's testimony is an implicit criticism of what she perceived to be Christianity's impractical, irrational, and unnatural doctrines, but she does not offer such comments in an explicit way. Instead, she stressed that any true faith must meet the test of nature and rationality, and explained how Islam met that litmus test for her.

Other believers wrote in to *Muhammad Speaks* to praise the rationality of Islamic religion as well. For example, Minister James 3X of Muhammad's Temple No. 2 in Chicago said that "Islam, as taught by Messenger Elijah Muhammad, has given me a different conception of faith, and that conception is, that faith in Islam means knowledge of a thing with a conviction concerning it so strong as to compel to follow its dictates in my daily life. Messenger Muhammad teaches me that it is absurd to demand from an intelligent person belief in things no one can accept in the face of reason and logic." For Minister James, Islamic religion represented a practical and sensible guide for daily living, and he testified that Islam had taught him physical and moral discipline, the order of things, patience, perseverance, and a thirst for knowledge of history and nature.[28]

Yet another believer who expounded on the practical benefits of Islam without also explicitly criticizing Christianity was James D. X:

I can state that Islam—to begin with—has raised my sights above attempting to seek equality in another people's society, and that has made me realize that I must try to help re-establish the society of my own. Islam has made me conscious of true freedom, justice and equality—and the need for one to enjoy these blessings among those who appreciate a high moral civilization and the best of life. Islam has made me desire unity among my own kind, with true brotherhood, so that the strength of our beings can be united behind one divine leader and teacher for the greater good of our own. Through Islam, my efforts have been mobilized, stabilized and directed toward the path that leads to peace and happiness while we live. Further, it has pointed out the road to everlasting life in the hereafter. I now have a clear, clean-cut understanding of God, the Supreme Being—an understanding that is not cluttered up with mysticism and superstition. And God's enemy, the devil, is made manifest. The religion of Islam fills the void in my life by giving me black history, religion and achievement. It makes one think creatively and completely on plans for fulfillment—with hope for the future. Islam has saved me from hell.[29]

This rich narrative anticipates many of the themes that will be explored in the following chapters. For Brother James, Islam was a vehicle for black communalism, or unity of kind; black pride and historical identity; self-improvement; and personal well-being. But Islam also clearly offered Brother James certain religious truths, doctrinal understandings of the nature of God, good and evil, and heaven and hell. In constructing Islam not only as a set of theological suppositions, but also as a practical guide for living and a solution to the challenges of racial discrimination and internalized racism, Brother James shows how "Islam" became a multidimensional framework that promised answers to the most nagging and difficult questions of his life. Islam, in his view, was certainly a religion, but it was also much more than that, as the testimonies in the next sections illustrate.

## Islam as Salvation, Self-Improvement, and Safety

As much as Islam may have served as a form of religious expression and affiliation, however, believers defined and described their allegiance to their new religion in several other ways as well. In their testimonies of "What Islam Has Done For Me," most believers offered personal narratives about what life was like before conversion to Islam, how they came to convert, and what happened to them as a result. These moving tales often included the stories of how ex-convicts, drug addicts, and sexually promiscuous men and women came to find pride, self-esteem, dignity, good health, a sense of peace and security, a happy marriage, and gainful employment as a result of their conversion to Islam. These stories also frequently included themes of escape—either from the Jim Crow South, racism, ill health, or from a ghetto life of vice and crime.[30] The most famous conversion narrative of this sort in the NOI is undoubtedly *The Autobiography of Malcolm X*, which depicts this remarkable man's transition from what he described as a life of hedonism and crime to his life as an NOI leader and eventually an orthodox Muslim.[31] Malcolm's story was only one of many, however. Less famous figures underwent what can be seen as equally inspiring journeys. For example, Robert 24X of Paterson, New Jersey, was in prison for the seventh time when he heard about the NOI. "I was a young drug addict who had spent too much time in the hells of Harlem's East Side and the equally notorious dens in Paterson, New Jersey," he wrote. Reading Muslim literature in prison, he was at first fearful and then "everything came into focus for me, and six months later I had made up my mind to become a follower of the Messenger." As a result, "I stopped smoking, using profanity and eating improper foods. And I've passed my biggest acid test—no more needles in the arm."[32]

Another former convict and drug user, Edward 4X, told *Muhammad Speaks* editor Sylvester Leaks that what he really desired in converting to Islam was forgiveness: "What really won me over to the Messenger's program is his philosophy that regardless of what you did yesterday, if you come in here and act like a man today, all of that is forgotten. That's why I came in. I wanted somebody to forgive me for what I did." Edward 4X, according to his own admission, had been a thief at age nine and a pot smoker at age eleven. "By the time I was 23 years old I was a dope addict, and had been arrested six times and had served more than five years in jail for stealing, dope and picking pockets," he recounted. Then, one day on the corner of 125th Street and 7th Avenue in Harlem, he was preparing to lift someone's wallet when he heard the preachments of an NOI missionary. After visiting the local NOI temple the next night, he began to listen to the words of Elijah Muhammad. At first, he was not impressed. "When I first heard Mr. Muhammad speak, my impression was not what I thought it would be," said Edward 4X. "I was sort of disillusioned. I couldn't understand him. I had expected an articulate speaker, since most of his ministers were articulate." However, the would-be Muslim persevered and over time gained a better understanding of the Messenger's words. He saw Elijah Muhammad speak in Boston, and then "everything suddenly came clear to me." Becoming a Muslim, however, did not translate into a total reprieve from past hardships. Brother Edward still experienced depression and other problems. But the NOI helped him to "face up to my problems." He entered rehabilitation for his drug habit, married, and learned to cook. "I am so happy with being a follower of Mr. Muhammad that even if, by some stretch of the imagination, it could be proved wrong, I would still keep the Islamic faith," he concluded.[33]

Not all believers were former convicts and drug addicts, however. Nor was the movement exclusively the domain of poor or "under-class" African Americans. As Cynthia S'thembile West has pointed out, "It would be dishonest to suggest that blue-collar and white-collar African Americans, like bus drivers, teachers, doctors, lawyers, insurance brokers, entrepreneurs, and menial workers were absent from the ranks of the Nation. Indeed, the Nation turned around the lives of thousands of Blacks addicted to drugs, alcohol, violence and exploitation, but it also benefited from the moral stability and financial consistency of Black people who came from identifiably middle-class homes with middle-class values, Christian backgrounds, and educationally sound settings."[34] Any comprehensive account of the NOI must incorporate the voices of such believers, and I proceed with an awareness that members of the NOI had several different motivations for joining the movement and that they came from many different life circumstances.[35]

For example, some members, never involved in a life of crime or drugs, said that before joining the NOI, they had suffered from a lack of self-esteem, and found that Islam offered a way out of a psychological state of depression or alienation. Theodore 4X noted that he was never a "drunk, dope addict or a complete failure" before joining the NOI, but he did suffer from "self-pity, self-excuse, [and] self-deprecation." In becoming a Muslim, he said, "I have achieved what the therapists call self-acceptance. Islam has removed the roots of emotional confusion and constant conflict from my presence. Misery and uncertainty have gone and been replaced with happiness and sureness." Brother Theodore came to understand that internalized racism had caused him "to accept a false image of myself. . . . I believed that a person born black would always be degraded." Islam, he said, had cured him of that, and the resulting isolation of such thoughts. He had found a community that dispelled such notions.[36] Several other converts echoed this idea that the community of believers and its deep sense of brotherhood and sisterhood had made them feel valued and loved, which in turn helped them to succeed in life.[37]

The theme of self-improvement, defined in various ways, can be found in many of the narratives published in *Muhammad Speaks*. While some believers looked to the NOI to help them find their first gainful employment, others peered beyond mere economic survival, and found in Islam the strength to dream about greater material wealth.[38] They often testified that Islam had made them efficient and confident workers, even when working for white employers.[39] Others were inspired to create new businesses.[40] Chicago resident Clyde X Smith, for example, was a former high school track star who had turned down the offer of an athletic scholarship at Ohio State University after what he described as an early marriage. Working at a meat packing plant, he said, he first felt "elated . . . at the feeling of earning my own living." Eventually, however, he developed an "uneasy feeling that I was somehow not fulfilling my destiny. At that time my wife and I had no aspirations above our immediate needs. We always felt secure in the knowledge that I was working and too I had enrolled at DuSable for a night course in one of the printing trades. The truth of the matter was, however, I had no ambitions or goals." After joining the NOI in 1962, Smith said, he was inspired to seek self-improvement through career and material advancement. "Today," he wrote, "we have our eyes set on definite goals. There is no end to progress and we plan to achieve it by following Messenger Muhammad. May the Peace and Blessings of Allah be with him, for he is leading us to greater and greater degrees of success and progress. Islam offers hope, success, progress, happiness, respect and a life filled with the creature comforts we all love so dearly."[41] This was a theme echoed by other believers, who interpreted Islam as the source of economic success and the passport to a bourgeois lifestyle. As Sister Hattie C. 3X of Washington, D.C., put it, "Islam, as taught by Messenger Muhammad, makes it possible for us to enjoy the finer things of life on earth, money, good homes, luxury, [and] friendships in all walks of life."[42]

One housewife also looked to Islam to give new meaning to the labor she was performing as a wife and mother. Mrs. Grace X Peoples of Springfield, Massachusetts, said that her duties as a housewife took on added urgency as a Muslim: "As a black woman doing the routine homemaking chores with my husband and children, taking care of my family, sewing, cooking and housecleaning, etc., I found that Islam lifted all of these things out of the routine. They suddenly took on more meaning and they actually became easier. Further, I found that I had time to investigate the arts and sciences and obtained even greater satisfaction." Mrs. Peoples did not offer a detailed explanation of how her identity as a Muslim had changed the meaning of domestic duties, but she did testify to the peace of mind and pride that she felt as a member of the NOI. "I thank the Messenger," she said, "for making me a citizen of the greatest nation on the planet: the nation of Islam. Within that nation I have received freedom, justice and equality. Before that time I had a restless, gnawing emptiness. I would sometimes cry with frustration and I could not find relief. I felt wasted, even though I pretended at living, trying to have a social and religious life, trying to make reality out of the falsehood of my existence." All that changed, she said, after entering the NOI. "Now I have obtained dignity and peace and also great purpose and responsibilities. I am in accord with nature and I contribute to the whole of life."[43] By bringing new meaning to the same old domestic tasks, Mrs. People's version of Islam gave her a sense of accomplishment, communal belonging, racial pride, and personal fulfillment.

Many believers also associated Islamic religion with what might be called proper etiquette, clean living, and the care of one's body. Sister Anne 3X, only fourteen years of age in 1963, said that since she "accepted the teachings of the Most Honorable Elijah Muhammad, I have wanted to try to do everything right. One way is by taking care of my body, eating the right foods instead of just eating anything to satisfy my hunger. Another way is by reading labels on food to see what the food consists of. A third way is by eating one meal per day. Since it takes about eight hours for your food to digest, that leaves the stomach about sixteen hours a day to rest. A fourth way is by fasting. That is, taking a three-day fast once a month to clean up my mind and clean out my stomach." In addition to seeing Islam as a mode of dietary control and purification, Sister Anne testified that Islam had caused her to "walk right, talk right, look right and try to be right."[44]

Similarly, boxer Louis X Carr also testified that the bodily disciplines of the NOI helped him to be a better boxer and better human being. His manager, Clint Watford, had originally pointed out "the similarity of the clean living practiced by the Muslims and that [which] good athletes must follow," he said.[45] For another believer, Don X Slaughter, who attended both West Virginia State College and Northeastern University in Boston, Massachusetts, the clean living advocated by Elijah Muhammad also translated into greater wealth. NOI leaders had taught him "not to lie, cheat, smoke, drink, gamble or commit adultery. That enables any businessman to save his few pennies. Before I was a follower of Elijah Muhammad, I was not even able to take a yearly vacation. Now, I am able to do so," said Brother Don. In addition, he said, the NOI's program of moral uplift eliminated "the squalor found in the majority of Negro communities." In the NOI, he said, "a man's home is his castle and cleanliness is next to Godliness."[46] Sister Gwendolyn X Warren of Providence, Rhode Island, said that the clean-living guidelines of Islam had done more than just provide her with wealth— they had literally saved her life and given her back her health. Sister Gwendolyn credited Elijah Muhammad's dietary guidelines with helping her heal from a radical mastectomy.[47]

Members frequently framed the NOI's program for moral renewal, clean living, and bodily discipline in decidedly gendered terms. For women in the NOI, these articulations of Islamic faith often expressed a belief that "respectability"— defined as female modesty, etiquette, and sexual restraint—was synonymous with moral righteousness.[48] For example, Sister Marilyn A. X of Springfield, Massachusetts, described in a testimony how Islam transformed her from an immoral to a respectable woman:

> Before I became a follower of the Honorable Elijah Muhammad, my life was nothing. All the vices the white man had, I had. I would swear, smoke, drink, fornicate and do everything that was unclean and indecent. Many times I had wanted to lead a clean and decent life, but I had nothing I could cling to. . . . One Friday, I was walking down the street, just coming from the nearest bar, when the assistant minister and the captain [a man in the FOI, the all-male organization of the NOI] saw me. They invited me to come to one of their meetings. The next Sunday I went. . . . The minister who spoke that night said, "the reason the black woman in America is leading a life of indecency and low morals, is because this is the way the slave masters taught her." He said "those who follow the Honorable Elijah Muhammad become upright respectable women." This is what I was seeking. . . . Allah has blessed me and I have become a clean, respectable, decent upright woman. . . . Everyday there is something new to be learned, and the women of Islam have a big role, they are the "queens of civilization." . . . Islam has made me put down that cigarette, that bottle and all the vices I once possessed. Islam has cleaned me up, and made me respected.[49]

Another woman, Margaret J. X Mayes from Flint, Michigan, testified that her husband and children had come to respect her as a wife and mother "who has changed her ways and does not smoke nor drink."[50] But women also noted how the NOI had changed their men folk. In at least one case, a woman who had no luck convincing her husband to attend church with her said that she became a Muslim after noticing that her husband would willingly attend the temple.[51] Many men also praised Islam for teaching them to respect women, financially support and protect them, and behave faithfully toward them in marriage.[52] Married men often credited Islam with the happiness they had found in the home partly because it restored them to a place of honor and responsibility as head of the household.[53]

Another common theme in the conversion narratives is that of safety and protection, defined in various ways. For example, at least one believer thought of Elijah Muhammad's ethical commandments as a form of protection against a coming apocalypse. Sister Hilda X of Elizabeth, New Jersey, encouraged others to become righteous by seeking the Messenger's protection: "He will lead us to safety like a hen does her little chicks when the rain begins to fall," she proclaimed. "She shields them with her wings. If a hen's chicks obey her when she clucks for them, how much more should we run to our dear leader and teacher, the Honorable Elijah Muhammad when he is calling us! We must answer to his calling while we can—because it's later than we think."[54] One assumes that this last comment is a reference to the coming end of the world. Indeed, the talk of the apocalypse was quite prolific in the movement. In 1973, Elijah Muhammad published *The Fall of America*, in which he described how white American decline was a necessary precursor to the eventual restoration of black greatness.[55] Like other American religionists, from the mainstream to the marginal, many members of the NOI were millennialists, those who associated the destruction of the world with a renewal of divine justice and the realization of God's will for humanity.[56]

But other NOI members framed the protection afforded by Islam in less eschatological ways, referring instead to the NOI's ability to shield believers against racism and failed attempts at racial integration. One believer, for example, came to Islam after feeling alienated from the "white, collegiate world" where she was courted by a white sorority. "How could I form a sisterhood with pale-faced girls who wore forced smiles and downcast eyes," Pamela X asked. "My taste in clothes, music, etc. was vastly different."[57] Others, like Ruby X Thompson of Fort Lauderdale, Florida, came to Islam after experiencing discrimination in her workplace. She admitted that before she converted to Islam, she thought that the solution to racial inequality was integration. She thought that "all we had to do was qualify ourselves and we would be totally accepted by the white race." This is what her high school teachers had taught her, she said, and she had to learn the futility of this approach the hard way. As a licensed practical nurse, Ruby discovered not only that her white coworkers were paid more, but they were also expected to do less work. When she complained to her supervisor about the situation, she became known as a troublemaker, and even her black coworkers "seemed afraid to talk to me in the presence of whites." During this period, her husband had been attending a local NOI mosque, and after hearing about the NOI from him, she decided to become a Muslim. Though it is not clear whether she quit her job, joining the NOI was liberating. "No matter how many colleges or universities you have attended," she wrote, "or how many degrees you may own — without having a true knowledge of your God and yourself and following the teaching of the Honorable Elijah Muhammad, you never will attain freedom, justice, or equality."[58]

Sister Arnetta X of Monroe, Louisiana, the wife of an NOI minister, also came to the NOI after attempting to work for integration and voting rights in the South. A holder of two college degrees, she worked with potential black voters in Louisiana, but was frustrated by white backlash. "I saw the reprisals suffered by those who attempted to exercise their so-called right to vote. In a small town very near here, a black man is living a life of misery ever since he dared to vote. He was shot, threatened and had his property burned to the ground," she wrote. The Justice Department had done nothing to protect black voters, she said, and she "saw some of our educators fail to speak out for freedom because they feared the loss of jobs." In addition, Sister Arnetta testified, "some of our ministers completely divorce themselves from the fight for freedom. In our voter registration education projects, we were turned away from some churches." For this NOI member, the lack of voting rights was only one of the problems faced by African Americans in the South. Even after the campaigns for civil rights, she said, "I still saw our children living in substandard houses; I saw our mothers being subjected to the vile language and gestures of the white beasts. I saw the good brains of our youths being wasted on the streets for lack of opportunity; I saw our social clubs, service organizations and fraternal groups fail to contribute to the betterment of the community." Islam offered a solution to all of those problems. But her conversion to the NOI, she said, was not immediate. "I listened to the truth of Islam many years before fully accepting it." Over time, she came to realize that "the way to freedom was not to dine with the wolves, but to separate yourself from the beast. . . . I became completely awed with the character of its adherents and overjoyed to find black men who were men — fearless, righteous men — and not jelly-spined, weak-kneed excuses for men." Sister Arnetta came to define Islamic religion as both a refuge from racism and a gendered system of ethics. Rejecting the drive for integration and voting rights as a form of emasculation, she praised the racial separatism of the NOI as a path to the establishment of dignity for black men. After converting, she felt protected and "proud to be a woman; [Islam] made me take joy in performing feminine tasks." She no longer felt a need to fight for full citizenship in the United States, because Islam had made her "into what I was born to be—a queen, respected and admired by those who know who they are, who God is and the identity of the devil."[59]

Finally, many believers thought of their Muslim lives as an expression of their true nature as black people. Being Muslim was a way to express one's authentic identity. One woman, for example, testified that Islam "is a beautiful religion because it is the nature of the black man and woman." Through the teachings of Elijah Muhammad, she had come to realize that "black is beautiful and every black man, woman, and child should be proud to be black."[60] In 1972, Henry 15X argued that "to become a righteous Muslim is 'blackness' to the fullest."[61] Sister Clara E. 4X Bell described this conflation of black and Muslim identities a bit differently, using a metaphor from the theater. She compared Elijah Muhammad to an all-knowing theatrical director, saying he possessed "the script of life and salvation for his people." The line between real life and the theater was thin, the sister commented. Paraphrasing Shakespeare, she wrote, "The whole world is a stage and everyone on it is an actor." You could play the part of a "Negro," the sister argued, or you could follow Elijah Muhammad and his stage managers, the ministers, "who under his guidance, keep the Muslim actors and actresses all in active roles." The key to a good life for black people was to lose themselves in their real roles. "When you read from the script of life, you will really be in character," she wrote, "because you will be acting the part of self."[62] To play the role of oneself, one needed to convert to Islam.

## Islam as a Total Way of Life

In practice, believers came to associate the meaning of Islam with several different kinds of behavior. Their narratives help us understand the many strands of meaning that they attached to the word "Islam." Up to this point in the chapter, I have generally highlighted, for heuristic purposes, those narratives in which believers stressed one or two reasons for becoming Muslim and living a Muslim life. But it is also important to point out that many believers combined various interpretations of Islamic religion in explaining why they valued their commitment to Islam. In some conversion narratives, NOI members defined Islam as a religion that shaped nearly every aspect of their lives. In one case, a believer also made a distinction between Islam as a "religion" and Islam as "a way of life," as Gail Green of Baltimore, Maryland, put it.[63] In a similar vein, Amos Bradford, an African American follower of Elijah Muhammad who lived and taught in Mali during 1965, said that Islam was not only a religion, but also "an elaborate social order, a self-contained culture, and a full-fledged civilization." Islam assimilates "three basic concepts—namely, man, society and God—into a harmonious whole."[64] Many of these narratives thus combined various understandings of what it meant to be Muslim. In order to capture the spirit of conversion narratives that cited multiple reasons for becoming a Muslim and practicing Islam, I reproduce the narrative of Sister Jean X Reynolds of Nashville, Tennessee:

I have been abundantly blessed, since the Divine Messenger, of Almighty Allah, opened my eyes to the truth; when I say blessed, I mean mentally and physically, not in the material wealth of this world, for that is not essential, nor will it long endure.

I was searching for truth. I was out of the Church two years, when I was blessed to hear and accept my God Almighty, and His religion, Islam. Christianity did not answer my questions about life and death. It did not clearly define God to me and how I could be close to Him. The Christian way of life only taught me to live, to die, before I could find God and heaven. I did not want to die and go to some "Fairytale Land." I did not know who to pray to when I needed Divine guidance. The preacher taught me to pray to Jesus, the holy ghost (whatever that is?) and God the Father.

Christianity was pure confusion for me, that is why I was tired of the Church. I could not find true brother and sister love there. It was an empty "ice box" to me.

The Messenger of Allah taught me about a real heaven and hell. He took my mind out of the sky and directed my mind and body to communicate with the One and Only True God, Whose proper name is Allah.

Allah hears me. He shows me how to help myself. The religion, Islam, taught me how to be civilized. It taught me I am an Original Blackwoman, Queen of the Universe and Mother of civilization. I know about the right foods to eat, so that I can live and enjoy a long and healthy life, to have heaven now, not after I die.

I am taught how to sit, walk, and dress the way a civilized and respected woman should. How to love my own kind, to stop worshipping my enemies and his religion, because it was harmful to me and against my true nature.

The Messenger of Allah taught me not to smoke or drink or curse. He told me to stop eating pork or hog, no matter what form it comes, because it is a "dirty killer," not a food. Christianity taught me I could eat it or anything else I wanted to eat. Allah (God) forbids the eating of this filthy animal, but Christians eat it for breakfast, lunch, and dinner.

Allah has given me a clean slate to begin life anew. I have been forgiven for my sins that were committed in ignorance. I have been in the Nation three years now and I pray Allah, I die a Muslim. I have been blessed with a wonderful and industrious husband, who is a young Minister here in Nashville, Tennessee, trying to help our Beloved Leader and teacher, the Most Honorable Elijah Muhammad, to raise the dead, from their mental death.[65]

Sister Jean's narrative offered several understandings of what it meant for her to be a Muslim. Sister Jean felt lost in Christianity, which seemed to offer pie-in-the-sky solutions to her problems. The experience of being Muslim, however, gave her a more immanent sense of a God, who, through the leadership of Elijah Muhammad, had helped her to feel forgiven for past mistakes and readied her for a practical path toward self-improvement. After converting to Islam, she discovered self-esteem and respectability. For her, Islam was a convincing theology, a set of rules governing gender roles, an ideology of racial separation and self-determination, and a set of ethical directives concerning food and etiquette. In short, it was a total way of life.[66]

In this chapter, I have presented an overview of believers' definitions and descriptions of what it meant to be Muslim. In so doing, I have foreshadowed the themes that will be discussed in the rest of this book. But the following chapters employ a heavier analytical hand in explaining how and why practicing Islam was a meaningful and multilayered phenomenon that included the creation of religious doctrines and theologies, the making of imagined communal identities, the performance of ethical imperatives, and participation in ritualized activities. In a sense, then, the burden of these chapters is to illuminate how all of this religion worked, and why it is important to understand the impact of this religion not only on the believers themselves but also on the larger cultures and networks in which the believers operated. Using the interdisciplinary tools of religious studies, I analyze further the process of Islamization for members of the NOI, and outline the importance of this complex phenomenon to African American and American history more generally. The testimonials above, however, act as guideposts for the rest of our story and provide a corrective to past studies that have too easily interpreted black culture, especially ghetto culture, as dysfunctional political expression.[67] These narratives show that while human beings are invariably influenced by the political contexts of their lives, they do not always respond to such contexts in explicitly political ways. For those that believed in Allah and His Messenger Elijah Muhammad, the desire for social and political liberation was often expressed in religious terms. That fact should not come as a surprise to millions of Americans, of whatever confession, who have articulated their greatest hopes for social change in religious language.

## CHAPTER 2

# Making a Muslim Messenger
## Defending the Islamic Legitimacy of Elijah Muhammad

Silently he comes with the multitudes of history, /
Treading upon the royal battleground, receiving salu-
tations from the Kingdom of the persecuted. / Souls,
ageless, restless, weary, awakening!!! / Wounded
gladiators of the lost, whose blood paints the face
of the cross. / The black rose of civilization weeping
from centuries of peril. / Muhammad tills the fields of
damnation, ignorance, suppression, and laziness. /
Tenderly he plants the seed in the fertile valleys of
love. / The sacred rays of Islam replenish the followers of / Death with Life, revealing Love!! Freedom!!!
Justice!!! / From the bowels of our America we bloom,
among the gardens we strive. / The fields of the dead
give forth a fragrance as truth and peace unfold. /
Throughout this nation of bondage, the essence of
souls rise to give praise to our Savior.
— Joan X Bennett, *Muhammad Speaks*, 23 April 1965

I n 1963, the Rev. Dr. Martin Luther King Jr. penned his famous "Letter from a Birmingham Jail." In this moving and dramatic plea for support from white Christian clergy, King warned that the failure to bolster the nonviolent civil rights struggle would only strengthen the hand of extremism, in all its forms. He cited Elijah Muhammad's NOI as a primary example of the dangers inherent in doing nothing to change the inequities of Jim Crow. The NOI, according to King, was an expression of "bitterness" and "hatred" that was "nourished by the contemporary frustration over the continued existence of racial discrimination." He offered to stand between the forces of complacency in the black community and "the hatred and despair of the black nationalist." If it were not for the nonviolent civil rights struggle, King said, southern streets might be "flowing with floods of blood" and all of America might be heading for a "frightening racial nightmare."[1]

That Martin Luther King Jr. could reference the NOI as a primary example of hatred and despair speaks to its emergence as a potent symbol in American national discourse during the 1960s.[2] But his criticism, as outlined in the introduction, was but one of the assaults against the movement during this period. Journalists, government officials, and Muslims, including both immigrant and indigenous Americans, also criticized the NOI. Rather than framing the NOI as an example of poor race relations, many Muslims questioned the Islamic authenticity of the group, arguing that Elijah Muhammad's teachings violated basic Islamic theological tenets and preached black nationalism rather than Islamic universalism.

Throughout the 1960s and the first half of the 1970s, the NOI sought to counter such criticism by defending the Islamic legitimacy of their Messenger of Allah. Like other new religious movements, the movement relied upon the support of established mainstream religious authorities, especially foreign Muslim leaders, to accredit their movement and their leader as genuinely Islamic.[3] The deployment of these foreign endorsements in the official discourse of the NOI shows the extent to which religious and political voices from Africa and Asia had begun to compete with domestic voices like that of Martin Luther King Jr. for the ear of black America. The era of decolonization and the rise of newly independent states after World War II only accelerated a transnational exchange of liberation discourses that, since the nineteenth century, had linked the domestic struggles of African Americans to those of other persons of color around the globe.[4] As the psychological, political, and cultural impact of African and Asian voices on black American consciousness continued to increase during this era, leaders of the NOI drew on the expertise of foreign Muslims to buoy the religious claims of their leader.

But many homegrown African American Muslim intellectuals in the NOI also mounted a defense of Elijah Muhammad. Generally speaking, these figures were either directly employed by or closely associated with Elijah Muhammad himself. I have called them intellectuals not only because they devoted significant energy and time to articulating reasoned arguments about Elijah Muhammad's religious thought, but also because they were a professional class of persons who were recognized at a public level for producing speech and other forms of intellectual expression. Most of the intellectuals referred to here were either ministers who spent countless hours interpreting Elijah Muhammad's message to devoted followers and potential converts or columnists who offered interpretations of Muhammad's message on a frequent basis in the *Muhammad Speaks* newspaper. Most were also close to the center of power in Chicago, either through kinship ties or other social networks. Of course, there are exceptions that become obvious below.

Contrary to the images presented by some previous scholarship, I argue that these figures were greatly concerned with the Islamic identity of their leader.[5] These intellectuals employed a variety of genres, including public speeches, newspaper articles, and cartoons, in imagining, constructing, and defending Elijah Muhammad's Islamic legitimacy. Frequently, they used allusions to the Qur'an to defend their prophet's authenticity. Their defenses varied in substance and style, and show that intellectuals in the NOI held differing notions of what it meant that Elijah Muhammad was a Muslim messenger. Some of these thinkers sought a theological rapprochement with their Muslim critics; most, however, rejected the outside criticism as plain ignorance. *Almost* all these intellectuals held fast to the idea that they followed the Messenger of God, an Abrahamic prophet who had been commissioned by God to lead African Americans toward Islam. In making this claim, they reconfigured African American Christian traditions of black messianism within an Islamic framework.[6] And even when they occasionally questioned the messianic claims of the Messenger, they still defended the idea that Elijah Muhammad, whoever he was, was central to becoming a Muslim and practicing Islam.

## Citing the Authorities: Outside Muslim
## Endorsements of Elijah Muhammad

Movement intellectuals, and especially the editors of *Muhammad Speaks*, which began publication in 1961, frequently cited the endorsements of Asian and African Islamic authorities to establish Elijah Muhammad's Islamic bona fides. An examination of these endorsements offers a helpful contrast to the kind of support that Elijah Muhammad received from his followers, those who actually believed him to be the Messenger of Allah. Most of Muhammad's external supporters praised the exemplary moral behavior of NOI members and stressed the need for unity among Muslims worldwide. But they did not lend much support to Muhammad's claims on prophecy or his teachings about the white devil. They argued, instead, that the question of Muhammad's Islamic legitimacy should be viewed by taking into consideration the lack of a strong and authoritative Islamic tradition in the United States, essentially asking many of Muhammad's critics to be more patient with him and his erroneous beliefs.

While these foreign and immigrant supporters had differing motivations, the struggle against neocolonialism provides one of the essential contexts in understanding why they praised a fellow Muslim with whom they often disagreed over the most basic theological questions. After World War II, many intellectuals and politicians from the "third world" shared the view that they should unite with other formerly colonized persons in what would come to be called the nonaligned movement, which supported neutrality in the midst of the Cold War between the Soviet Union and the United States. This movement's most important inaugural event was perhaps the 1955 Afro-Asian Conference in Bandung, Indonesia, which attracted press coverage not only in Africa and Asia, but also in black America.[7] Malcolm X saw Bandung as a major turning point not only for the Africans and Asians, but also for people of color everywhere.[8] After this point, he said, many activists, leaders, and intellectuals of color also became advocates of the decolonization of consciousness—that is, they argued for the need to shun colonialist culture and develop a more authentic sense of self.[9] Many of Elijah Muhammad's foreign supporters from Africa and Asia utilized this vocabulary of self-determination and solidarity to explain their approval of the Messenger. Others couched their endorsements more in terms of moral and religious affinity, although they, too, were willing to put aside their theological disagreements with Elijah Muhammad in order to emphasize Muslim unity in the face of neocolonial threats to Muslim self-determination.

In 1962, for example, *Muhammad Speaks* included coverage of the NOI that had appeared the previous month in *Muslimnews International*, an English-language monthly published in Karachi and London. The *Muslimnews* reporter, Abdul Latif Qaisi, emphasized the NOI's success in "social rehabilitation." Asking his Muslim audience to reject criticism of the NOI, Qaisi said that the NOI "can only be appreciated if the position of the Negroes and the psychological state of the United States are kept in mind." Instead of stressing creedal differences with the NOI, argued Qaisi, all Muslims should work for unity and harmony. "Judging them solely by their character and behavior, honesty, personal and public morality, fearlessness and faith in God," he wrote, "one would be led to hail them as excellent Muslims."[10] For Qaisi, there were issues more important than creed, especially given the NOI's success in recruiting African Americans to a godly and moral lifestyle.

In 1964, *Muhammad Speaks* correspondent Sylvester Leaks interviewed Pakistani native S. Muhammad Tufail, then imam of the Shah Jehan mosque in Surrey, England. Leaks asked the Pakistani leader, who had stopped over in New York on his way to Trinidad, whether he considered Elijah Muhammad to be a true Muslim. "This question is very simple to decide," said Tufail. "The Qur'an says: 'And say not to anyone who offers you salutation, As-Salaam – Alaikum, Thou art not a believer." If someone greets you with these words, according to Tufail, "I must accept him as a Muslim." To make his position perfectly clear, Tufail also said that he had read "the writings of the Honorable Elijah Muhammad. He clearly accepts that God is one and that Muhammad is his Prophet and the Qur'an is his holy book." Moreover, Tufail asserted that Elijah Muhammad's movement "will do a great service not only to their people but to Islam as a whole." He also introduced the idea that Elijah Muhammad may represent the fulfillment of a prophecy made by Muhammad of Arabia that the "Sun of Islam will rise in the West." When Leaks responded to this suggestive comment by asking Tufail to clarify whether Elijah Muhammad is a "sign of the fulfillment of the Prophet," Tufail said that "only the future will decide." Leaks also asked, in a rather remarkable moment, whether Tufail had any disagreements with the teachings of Elijah Muhammad. Tufail answered: "We think that God is the creator and Lord of all the nations, communities, and peoples of the universe. So, the criterion of judging people is their character, and not their color, race, class, or family."[11]

Here a reporter employed by Elijah Muhammad invited criticism of his employer; the interviewee, a foreign supporter of Elijah Muhammad, stated a fundamental disagreement with him over who could be a Muslim; and perhaps most important, the exchange was printed. In the first few years of publication, *Muhammad Speaks* continued to act as an arena in which both subtle and obvious disagreements about the meaning of Elijah Muhammad's prophecy and criticism of the movement were aired. In the case of the interview with Tufail, a foreign Muslim leader expressed his support of Elijah Muhammad, while also outlining his disagreement with one of his best-known teachings—namely, that only blacks (a label that included all nonwhites for Elijah Muhammad) are real Muslims. It was a remarkable moment in a movement that officially revolved around the authority of a prophetic figure: in this case, dissent was not only tolerated, but welcomed.

Despite the many foreign endorsements published in the newspaper, there were few explicit declarations of support for Elijah Muhammad's claims to be a prophet. But at least one foreign supporter did register his enthusiasm for the teaching that all white people are by nature devils, a teaching that resonated with the sympathies of third-world liberation activists. In a 1966 article, Pakistani native Abdul Basit Naeem, who wrote dozens of regular columns for *Muhammad Speaks* from the middle 1960s to the early 1970s, discussed Muhammad's prophetic and mythological teaching about the genetically engineered white devil in the light of neocolonialism. Agreeing with Muhammad that the "Caucasian Devil—more commonly known as the white man—is a constant menace to the original (black) people everywhere," Naeem argued that the white man "imperils the order and well-being of our (righteous) society in different regions of the globe." How? "In politically-independent Asia and Africa, he dominates our trade, industry and commerce—our economic lifelines. In colonial territories, which he prefers to call 'overseas provinces' or 'protectorates,' he literally bleeds us 'white'—by completely depriving us of all means of human sustenance and survival. In the 'New World,' he simply continually thwarts the legally-emancipated ex-slaves' efforts to rise above serfdom." None of these problems, Naeem argued, was more "complex," "enigmatic," or "urgent" than the "so-called 'Negro' problem of this country." Naeem did not propose political revolution or any other challenge to the structures of neocolonialism as a solution to the oppression of black Americans. Rather, he advocated the practice of an Islam focused on the moral and social reform of black individuals. The solution to the "problem" was not "silly politics and inconsequential church led activities," he wrote; it was "Islam—the manifest content of the Honorable Elijah Muhammad's 'message.'" Elijah Muhammad's Islam "aims at and is destined to secure for the (so-called) 'Negroes' what they most want: Immediate end of their centuries-old suffering, depravity, and humiliation. If pursued in earnest, it will do even more for the black man—it will set him up in 'heaven' (good jobs, good clothes, good family life) overnight!"[12] Interestingly, Naeem did not stress the separatist elements of Elijah Muhammad's Islam, nor did he cast this Islamic program of black uplift as an explicitly political platform. Instead, he saw gainful employment and moral reformation as the means to salvation in an earthly heaven that sounded quite bourgeois.

Naeem also called on members of the NOI to fight for their integration into the Islamic world and to argue more forcefully on behalf of Muhammad's teachings. In 1967, for instance, he encouraged members of the NOI to study Arabic so that they could (1) read the Qur'an in its original language; (2) communicate and unite with other Muslims across the globe through this shared lingua franca; (3) "enlighten" other Muslims "on the wondrous Mission and unique wisdom and philosophy of" Elijah Muhammad; and (4) do business with Arabic speakers. But he also reminded his audience that a "Muslim is not obliged to learn it [Arabic]; nor does the knowledge thereof automatically make anyone of us a 'better Muslim.'"[13] In fact, he argued in a 1969 article that many "Eastern Muslims" could learn some essential lessons from the followers of Elijah Muhammad: "Whereas the foreign ('Eastern' or orthodox) Muslims have *already* had the Supreme Wisdom (of Almighty Allah) available to them — via the Holy Qur'an and other ancient Islamic scriptures — for nearly fourteen hundred years, the veritable 'dry bones' of these parts remain strewn about in history's worst dungeons of darkness (continued mental slavery to former slavemasters' children) . . . and [Muslims] are still trying to find the path to the 'Promised Land.'"[14] For Naeem, Elijah Muhammad's program of self-help was an excellent antidote to the colonized mind; with it, "Eastern" Muslims might be able to empower themselves economically and politically.

In this same article, Naeem blamed the foreign criticism of Elijah Muhammad's religious teachings on the "devil-devised" news media, a lack of good information about the NOI in the Islamic world, and Orientalist interpretations of Islam. He noted, for example, that some foreigners rejected Elijah Muhammad's teachings as additions to Islam, ostensibly referring to the idea that Elijah Muhammad had engaged in *bid'a*, or impermissible religious innovation. Orthodox Muslims, he countered, were the real religious innovators. "Eastern Muslims," he claimed, "(especially those exposed to and influenced by non-Muslim Orientalists' view of Islam) commonly — albeit erroneously — attribute the founding of Islam to the (Arabian) Holy Prophet Muhammad's advent just fourteen hundred years ago." They were wrong, according to Naeem: "the Honorable Elijah Muhammad's teachings consistently — and correctly — identify Islam as the 'first, most ancient and original' (hence ageless) faith." As for the critics' claim that Islam is "raceless" or "color-blind," Naeem asserted that the foreign critics were being disingenuous. If orthodox Muslims were so committed to a race-less Islam, he asked, then why did white folks receive so much scrutiny when they went to Saudi Arabia for the *hajj*? Elijah Muhammad "advances — on irrefutable authority—that the ORIGINAL (RIGHTEOUS) MAN and the universal evil-doer or mischief-perpetrator (i.e., the DEVIL-MAN) are not one and the same and that is why the latter must not be permitted to 'defile' the righteous (Muslim) ranks."[15] Naeem's references to Orientalist interpretations of Islam and his defense of Elijah Muhammad's racialism seemed to indicate Naeem's commitment to the NOI as an ally in the struggle against neocolonialism. In their heart of hearts, he suggested, Muslim critics knew that Elijah Muhammad was right about white people. If members of the NOI would defend their teachings abroad, Naeem argued, they might convince others that Elijah Muhammad was right, and in so doing make powerful links to the rest of the Islamic world community.

A few other foreign Muslims also criticized Muslims in the "old country" in the pages of *Muhammad Speaks*, although it is difficult to confirm the authenticity of these endorsements. For example, Yessef al Murwar, a student from Saudi Arabia, wrote, "One of the most refreshing, heart-warming and enlightening revelations made clear to me during my visit to the United States as a student at the University of Chicago, is the great work done here by the Honorable Elijah Muhammad. His militancy, his dedication, his insistence upon pursuing the true path of a Messenger of Allah, leads me to believe that I have been misled by my teachers in Riyadh, Saudi Arabia." Murwar added that "it is not easy to admit a revelation such as this, believe me. But I am convinced that the paths to Mecca are not the only ways to godliness." Elijah Muhammad, he explained, offered a path of self-love, brotherhood, and moral righteousness, whereas many of the "Muslims of the East" were plagued by corruption and chicanery. Elijah Muhammad's "teachings, I am convinced, are the true teachings of Islam. His mission is more noteworthy and honorable than those of many so-called leaders of the East." Elijah Muhammad, he said, was "the most profound, articulate, and meaningful leader of Islam in the world, and I give great thanks to mighty Allah for sending this great man of God." Murwar also promised to "tell my people of this great man of God" when he returned to Saudi Arabia, hoping that "such a man would come to us of the near East, that we, too, may rise out of ignorance and poverty to unite among ourselves as Mr. Muhammad is encouraging the black people of this continent to do."[16]

Murwar's use of vocabulary and cadence indicate that he was profoundly influenced by the rhetoric of NOI officials and intellectuals. He used the term "so-called leaders" in the same way that other NOI members did—that is, to question, at the basic level of definition, the legitimacy of leaders outside the NOI. He also adopted phrases that frequently appeared elsewhere in the newspaper, including "Muslims of the East" and "unite among ourselves." And he praised

Elijah Muhammad with the same words that other members did, calling him "profound" and "articulate." In fact, Murwar sounded so much like a member of the NOI that it is worth considering his article as a forgery. Neither I nor an official at the University of Chicago has found any record indicating Yessef al Murwar's attendance at that university.[17] But whether or not Murwar was a real human being, his article is still an important record. The fact that the NOI newspaper published the piece shows that some NOI leaders regarded the authority of foreign Muslims as a significant element in their efforts to legitimate Elijah Muhammad's status as Muslim leader.

Another foreign "convert" to Elijah Muhammad's version of Islam, also impossible to confirm, was Zahid Aziz al-Ghareeb, a naturalized citizen of the United States. In a 1971 article, al-Ghareeb promoted Elijah Muhammad's Islam as a solution to the social ills of the Muslim "East." He identified himself as an Eastern "orthodox" Muslim who became familiar with the NOI through its publications and its business activities. In fact, al-Ghareeb attempted to join the NOI, but was told that for now only those born in the "wilderness of North America" could do so. That barrier notwithstanding, al-Ghareeb expressed his full support of the movement. Acknowledging the criticism of Elijah Muhammad among some orthodox Muslims, he wrote that the "US Muslim leader's teachings actually contain much that is fundamentally ORIGINAL – ISLAMIC and has long been lost on the foreign Muslims." He argued that if Muslims of the East followed Elijah Muhammad's program of uplift, they might be able to eliminate social ills like poverty and corruption. For al-Ghareeb, the fact that Muslim countries flush in oil wealth could not eliminate illiteracy or defend themselves against "a rather small and insignificant enemy (the Zionist State of Israel)" is "tragic." He contrasted impotent "Eastern" Islamic society with the NOI, which he called a "busy-busy beehive" full of members who work long hours and lift up their nation through their economic activities.[18] His comments indicated that for yet another foreign Muslim, the NOI and Elijah Muhammad offered an impressive model for the social, economic, and political liberation of the newly independent states of the developing world. Like others, al-Ghareeb seemed to support the NOI as part of his search for allies in the struggle against neocolonialism. For him, it was the NOI's focus on liberation that evidenced the truth of Elijah Muhammad's claims to Islamic legitimacy.

At times, such support of Elijah Muhammad could raise the ire of other Muslims outside the NOI. In 1972, for example, Dr. M. Abdul Rauf, director of the Islamic Center of Washington, D.C., faced calls for his ouster when he joined the NOI in a protest against police violence in New York. At a rally, Rauf reportedly said, "We have come to express our admiration for your work and the great achievements of the beloved leader, the Hon. Elijah Muhammad. I would like to assure you that the whole Muslim world, which includes 700 million people is behind you." In response, the Islamic Party of North America, a group founded in Washington during the early 1970s by an African American convert, attacked Rauf for giving aid to the "organization and activities of the heretical 'Black Muslims.'"[19] But prominent figures like Rauf, Tufail, and Qaisi never framed their endorsements as testimonials to the prophetic truths of Elijah Muhammad's mythological and theological teachings—that kind of support came only from Naeem, who had a business relationship with the movement, and from random "orthodox" Muslims whose letters and articles may or may not be authentic. It is important to distinguish between the two groups of external supporters. In the end, Elijah Muhammad found few Muslims outside the movement who recognized him as a real Abrahamic prophet, which is how he wanted to be seen. "I have been risen to tell you the truth," he reminded followers in a 1966 article. "And have been given the truth from the mouth of God, as Moses and Jesus prophesied that I would be given the truth from God's mouth."[20] Support for these assertions would not come on the whole from external allies, but from true believers who understood Elijah Muhammad as the Messenger of Allah.

## Scriptural Legitimations of the Messenger

Many past interpreters of Elijah Muhammad and his followers have assumed or argued that the members of the NOI had little true interest in Afro-Eurasian Islamic traditions. I argue, however, that the attempts on the part of NOI intellectuals to defend their Islamic legitimacy through a particular and novel interpretation of traditional Islamic sources and traditions belie that claim. Rather than assuming a theological wall between the admittedly novel mythologies of Elijah Muhammad and the rest of Islamic tradition, my analysis begins by scrutinizing the historical engagement of NOI intellectuals with Afro-Eurasian Islamic traditions. It must be remembered that almost all NOI members were confronting Islamic sources and traditions for the first time, without the filters of *shariʿa*, or Islamic law and ethics; *tafsir*, or Qurʾanic commentary; or any other historically Islamic institution. It was not until the 1950s and 1960s that movement intellectuals, including those who wrote and published treatises, speeches, and theologies, began to be familiar with these sources and traditions. During the 1950s and 1960s, Jamil Diab, a Palestinian Arab, introduced the study of Arabic at Chicago's University of Islam, the movement's primary and secondary school.[21] Wallace D. Muhammad, one of the Messenger's sons, was among his students, and reportedly took great interest in his teaching.[22] During the early 1960s, Akbar Muhammad, another of Elijah's sons, enrolled as a student at Cairo's al-Azhar university, where he studied "Islamic jurisprudence and political science."[23] Akbar Muhammad also learned to write in an elegant Arabic script, as shown in a picture reproduced by E. U. Essien-Udom that depicts Akbar Muhammad at a blackboard, teaching Arabic letters and basic Arabic verbs to a group of NOI members.[24] During the 1950s, however, most students of Arabic in the movement did not possess proficiency in the language. Essien-Udom reported, for example, that he encountered no students of Arabic at the University of Islam who could speak the language. But he did note that, like many non-Arab Muslims around the world, many of the school children had memorized their prayers in Arabic.[25]

By the late 1960s and early 1970s, the number of persons who studied Arabic seemed to have increased in various venues throughout the country. For example, an August 1968 picture that appeared in *Muhammad Speaks* shows Brother Maceo X at a chalkboard writing, in Arabic, "Elijah (Ilyas) Muhammad is the Messenger of God." The Arabic script appears, to my eyes at least, to be from a nonnative writer or a beginning student of Arabic. According to the article that accompanies the picture, Brother Maceo had recently completed an Arabic seminar at Columbia University in New York.[26] In New Jersey's Trenton State Prison, NOI member Robert 49X Jones and other Muslim inmates began Arabic lessons under the direction of Rafiyq Ahmad A. Hamiyd and the "Al-Hamiydiyyah Academy of Arabic."[27] During this period, Sister Brenda 4X introduced her students at the NOI's primary and secondary school in Washington, D.C., to the sacred tongue.[28] And in Chicago, Ali Baghdadi, another Palestinian, taught Arabic to several NOI members. By 1972, according to Baghdadi, twelve members of the NOI, including males and female, had completed at least one or two courses in Arabic.[29] Several students praised Baghdadi's abilities as an instructor. Brother Lee 3X, for example, said that Baghdadi was "a beautiful instructor. He not only teaches the mechanics of language, he also teaches the spirit—the culture of it."[30]

Despite the increasing number of persons who studied Arabic, however, there is little evidence that NOI members read the Qur'an in the original. In fact, it is extremely difficult to determine how many NOI members read the Qur'an in English translation. Elijah Muhammad himself encouraged members to do so in the *Supreme Wisdom* (1957), *Message to the Blackman in America* (1965), and in a 1970 article in *Muhammad Speaks*; the Qur'an, he said, was "full of wisdom."[31] But many members thought that reading Elijah Muhammad's books was more important than reading the Qur'an. As Sonsyrea Tate recounts, "Elijah Muhammad said we had to learn Arabic because in the future we would need to be able to read the Holy Quran . . . in its original Arabic. For now, the Honorable Elijah Muhammad did all of our reading and interpreting for us. We read books he wrote: *Message to the Black Man, How to Eat to Live,* and others in which he told us what he thought we needed to know from the Quran and the Bible."[32] Several of my informants in St. Louis, San Antonio, and Durham, North Carolina, have echoed this sentiment.

At the same time, it is clear that several NOI intellectuals, that professional class of persons who explained Islam to the rank and file and defended the religious legitimacy of Elijah Muhammad, quoted and interpreted dozens of different verses from over a dozen different Qur'anic chapters in their literature and artwork during the 1960s and early 1970s.[33] At least one of them, Brother Maceo of New York, also listened to recordings of Qur'an recitation, an art practiced and enjoyed by Muslims around the world.[34] As these intellectuals came to know more and more about the Qur'an and other Afro-Eurasian Islamic traditions, many of them attempted to interpret the meaning of Elijah Muhammad's mission by adopting the terms of various Islamic textual discourses. In most instances, the Islamic texts that they quoted were translations and commentaries produced by the Ahmadiyya movement, a South Asian Islamic missionary group that had successfully converted hundreds if not thousands of African Americans to Islam in the 1920s.[35] The Ahmadiyya were the first Muslim missionaries to engage in the mass distribution of English-language translations and interpretations of the Qur'an and other Islamic texts in the United States and United Kingdom, where founder Ghulam Ahmad hoped the movement would convert westerners to Islam.[36] Before the proliferation of Saudi-financed Islamic English literature in the 1970s,[37] it was an Ahmadi translation of the Qur'an with which many African American Muslims, whether practicing Ahmadis or not, became familiar. Members of the NOI, including Elijah Muhammad himself, quoted Ahmadi religious literature in their writings and religious ceremonies. *Muhammad Speaks,* for example, regularly featured a column in which both translations of and commentaries on the Qur'an by Ahmadi scholar Mawlana Muhammad Ali were reproduced without acknowledgment.[38] And Elijah Muhammad explicitly cites Mawlana Muhammad Ali's text in *The Supreme Wisdom* (1957) and *Message to the Blackman* (1965), in which he asks readers to study two of Ali's footnotes.[39]

Some NOI intellectuals were also clearly influenced by Ahmadi interpretations of the Qur'an. In order to understand how, it is necessary to say a bit more about the Ahmadiyya. The Ahmadiyya movement, which was established in 1889 in the Indian Punjab, claimed that a man named Ghulam Ahmad was both the Messiah of Jewish, Christian, and Islamic traditions and the Islamic

Mahdi, a figure understood by many Muslims to be the person who will restore divine justice to the earth during the end time.[40] The Ahmadiyya eventually split, however, over the nature of Ghulam Ahmad's mission. One group, called the Qadianis, maintained that Ghulam Ahmad was indeed a prophet. Another group, called the Lahoris, said that Ghulam Ahmad was merely a *mujaddid*, or religious reformer—literally, a renewer of religion. It is important to note that Mawlana Muhammad Ali, the translator of the Qur'an used by many in the NOI, was a Lahori who maintained that Ghulam Ahmad was a *mujaddid*, not a prophet.[41]

One NOI intellectual, who was familiar with Lahori Ahmadi literature, seemed to have understood Elijah Muhammad to be a *mujaddid*, or renewer of religion, rather than a prophet. In 1963, Jamil Muhammad, the grandson of Elijah Muhammad, wrote a newspaper article in which he explained the difference between a prophet and a *muhaddath*, or "one to whom God speaks though he is not a prophet." The young author began this article with a *hadith*, or an account of what the Prophet Muhammad of Arabia said or did: "Surely Allah (God) will raise for this community at the beginning of every century one who shall revive for its faith."[42] He then added an exegesis of this *hadith*, quoting directly from Lahori Ahmadi literature: "generally at intervals of a century divinely inspired people shall be raised among Muslims and they shall revive the faith of the Muslim community." This individual, in "our Arab-tongue," is called a *mujaddid*, he wrote. Again quoting directly from Lahori Ahmadi literature, Jamil Muhammad noted that the *mujaddid* is "raised up by God to remove errors that have crept in among Muslims and to shed new light on the great religious truths of Islam in the new circumstances which Muslim[s] may have to face in every age."[43] And just who is the right *mujaddid* "to shed light on the great religious truths of Islam" for African Americans, according to Jamil Muhammad? It was his grandfather: the "social needs, peculiar to the Negro race" can be "managed by the help of Allah (God) and his Messenger Elijah Muhammad through love, social orderliness, social legislation, social needs, and social control of our youth—Islamic society for a better social rule in our Islamic Youth Community." His grandfather, the "Messenger," was a *mujaddid*, not a prophet, according to Jamil Muhammad.[44]

Of course, this interpretation did not reflect how Elijah Muhammad saw himself, and it did not parallel Elijah Muhammad's style of textual exegesis. Elijah Muhammad, who generally never discussed the *hadith*, certainly quoted passages of the Qur'an in his writings, but he also maintained a privileged role for his prophetic voice in the teaching of Islam. Elijah Muhammad was no typical *mufassir*, or Islamic exegete. His Qur'anic exegesis did not refer to and indicated no knowledge of the Islamic tradition of *tafsir*, or Qur'anic commentary, that Muslims developed throughout the classical and middle periods of Islam. There were also few stylistic parallels between the exegesis of Elijah Muhammad and that of most Islamic exegetes. "At a more technical level," writes Herbert Berg, "of the exegetical devices typically used by *mufassirs*: variant readings, early and pre-Islamic poetry, lexical explanations, grammatical explanations, rhetorical explanations, periphrasis, analogy, abrogation, circumstances of revelation, identification, prophetical tradition, and anecdote, only the last four are employed" by Elijah Muhammad.[45] On the whole, the "Qur'an was always subsumed under the framework of his mythology of racial origins and the eschaton."[46]

Elijah Muhammad often referred to the Qur'an in order to bolster the legitimacy of his prophetic claims—a practice that he and his followers used from at least the 1950s until his death in 1975. According to his reading of the sacred text, he understood God's intentions better than his orthodox critics. For example, in excerpts reprinted in *Muhammad Speaks* from a 1962 speech in the Philadelphia Arena, Muhammad admitted that he had "lost a lot of friends among the orthodox Muslims, who were not able to agree that the nature in which we [blacks/Muslims] are created is different from the white race." But he asserted that these orthodox Muslims were the misguided ones: "I am sorry for your lack of knowledge of self and others. But, if we can listen to and try to hover over the truth that is being taught, you should bear witness that I'm seeking good for you, not evil—but good." His orthodox critics, he explained, failed to understand that they, too, were created differently from non-Muslims, and that Islam was a constitutive element of their very being. "Islam is as old as God himself," Muhammad explained. "Islam is not an organized religion. It is the religion that goes to the very nature of God and his people [who are black/Muslim]. It is the natural religion of God and his people, so says the Holy Qur'an 32:30."[47]

M. A. S. Abdel Haleem translates the verse to which Elijah Muhammad referred as "Say, 'On the Day of Decision it will be of no use for the disbelievers to believe; they will be granted no respite.'"[48] This passage, which comes at the end of the Qur'anic *sura*, or chapter, called as-Sajdah, the "prostration," advises Muslims to turn away from those who decide at the last minute, on the Day of Judgment, to honor God's revelations. In his commentary on the verse, Elijah Muhammad did not explain how the passage supported his claim that Islam was the natural religion for blacks/Muslims, but by using this verse, he seemed to prophesy what would happen to those who, at the last minute, decide that he was right after all. It was a claim that Muhammad would repeat at various times throughout the 1960s. "Some Orthodox Muslim[s] mock us for the sake of being accepted as a friend of their and our enemy," he said in 1969. "They are spooky minded and believe that Allah (God) is some immaterial something but yet He made a material universe and a material man. . . . The Washington Orthodox Muslims call us a 'cult.' This is an absolute insult to us to be called a 'cult,' when there is such a Show of the Hand and Power and Wisdom of Almighty Allah (God) in the Person of Master Fard Muhammad, to Whom Praises are Due Forever. . . . They will come to a naught [sic] and they will be confounded and ashamed of themselves."[49]

Like most of his followers, Muhammad used an English translation of the Qur'an when referencing the holy book. By critiquing English translations of the Qur'an—despite his lack of Arabic—the Messenger was able to show how essential his prophetic pronouncements were to a proper understanding of the text. In 1970, for example, he published an article discussing translations of Qur'an 30:30 by Mawlana Muhammad Ali and Yusuf Ali. He noted that, on the whole, both of these men "have done very good jobs of translating the Holy Quran into the English language." But he quickly added that "they did a good job but they did not do a complete job." Yusuf Ali's problem, he explained, was that he does not understand the difference in the Qur'an between references to white "mankind" versus references to black "man." *Mankind* was the creation of the mad scientist Yacub, according to Elijah Muhammad; *Man* was created by Allah God Himself. Elijah Muhammad did not blame Yusuf Ali for the bad translation, however, noting that white scholars of Islam were at fault for obfuscating and corrupting the real meaning of Islam.[50] As for Muhammad Ali's translation, Elijah Muhammad complained only that it did not make abundantly clear the truth of Islam, namely, that when God created human beings—and remember, only blacks were the original and authentic human beings for Elijah Muhammad—God was, in essence, re-creating Himself. Or to put it differently, in the terms of Muhammad's metaphysics: "Allah, Being the First of the Creation—Self-Created or Self Made and we being of Him,—that makes us Self-Created." The Messenger acknowledged that this interpretation may contradict that of the translator, but defended the need to teach the truth. "I cannot help it if the translator does not bear me witness," he wrote. "I am only bringing you that of the truth that has been revealed to me and taught to me by Allah (God) in the Person of Master Fard Muhammad."[51]

Despite his differences with his Muslim critics, however, Elijah Muhammad also insisted on the notion of pan–Muslim unity: "We are the brothers of not only the Muslims of Arabia, but all over the entire world." In a 1963 statement, the Messenger answered claims by the *Chicago American* newspaper that orthodox Muslims rejected his teachings, specifically the idea of "the white race as being a race of devils." The paper's real goal, he implied, was to discredit him in order to promote an agenda of racial integration. "Orthodox Muslims," he wrote, "are gradually coming over with me in the understanding for the first time in their history; the realization of the devils. It is in the Holy Qur'an that these people are the devils, and the scholars of Islam know it." Muhammad also claimed that no representative from the Muslim world had come "to tell me and my followers in America to stop teaching that [which] I have received from Allah." But he also reminded his readers that his authority did not come from Mecca or Jidda, but from God. "Neither Jeddah nor Mecca have sent me!" he said. "I am sent from Allah and not from the Secretary General of the Muslim League [probably referring to the Saudi-led Muslim World League, established in 1962]. There is no Muslim in Arabia that has authority to stop me from delivering this message, . . . anymore tha[n] they had authority to stop Noah, Moses, Jesus, and Muhammad."[52]

Most NOI intellectuals supported the notion that followers should read the Qur'an exclusively through the lens of Elijah Muhammad's prophecies, especially Muhammad's magnum opus, *Message to the Blackman in America* (1965). According to these intellectuals, NOI members should not attempt to interpret the text by themselves: "The Holy Qur'an that we have today is an instruction to a Messenger," advised Minister Abdul Salaam. "That Messenger is amongst us today in the person of the Honorable Elijah Muhammad. It is he who is best qualified to give us the true meaning of that which we find in the Holy Qur'an."[53] Louis Farrakhan, who became Elijah Muhammad's chief spokesperson in the middle 1960s and later reconstituted a version of the NOI in the late 1970s, also argued that using Elijah Muhammad's exegesis in reading the Qur'an was imperative. "There have been many wonderful scriptures revealed for the good and the guidance of man during the last 6 thousand years," he wrote. "[T]he most powerful are the Torah–Old Testament brought by Moses, the Injil–New Testament brought by Jesus and the Holy Qur-an brought by Muhammad Ibn Abdullah." But each of these scriptures required "proper" and "clear" interpretation, of which only Elijah Muhammad was capable. "Neither Moses, Jesus nor Muhammad interpreted the scriptures which they brought," Farrakhan asserted. Moreover, while "many sincere, dedicated and religious men have arisen . . . who have shed some light on the word of Allah . . . it is also a certainty that many irreligious, uninspired, and unscrupulous wonderlusts [*sic?*] have also risen to add their wicked and false interpretations to the holy word." The resulting confusion, he argued in a riff on the Babel theme, has "done much to cause bloodshed, division, hatred and war among the people and nations of the Earth." It is interesting to note that Farrakhan did not cite the Sunna, or the traditions of the Prophet Muhammad, as a prism through which the Qur'an might be interpreted, despite the fact that the Sunna is the first source to which many Muslim interpreters have turned for help in understanding the Qur'an over the centuries. He simply said that the Qur'an was "in need of better interpretation than those offered by all of the religious scholars and scientists of the world of Islam and Christianity who have boldly attempted to interpret this book to its many readers and seekers of truth." Elijah Muhammad, the "greatest leader, teacher and educator of all times," offered that guidance, concluded Farrakhan.[54]

While most movement intellectuals never questioned the basic premises of Elijah Muhammad's Qur'anic worldview, however, they still rendered original interpretations of the holy book, sometimes quoting verses that Elijah Muhammad himself did not cite. The Qur'an also became a symbol in the movement's visual as well as literary discourses. For example, Eugene XXX or Eugene Majied, who was the organization's most prominent newspaper cartoonist, frequently used the image of the Qur'an and various Qur'anic verses in his artwork. In a 1962 line drawing entitled "The Great Physician," the artist depicted Elijah Muhammad dressed in suit, bow tie, and fez, Qur'an in hand, walking past a hospital bed where a convalescing black man stretches out his hand to the Messenger. A sign hanging on the bed reads: "20 million sick, made deaf and dumb 'Negroes.'" Below the bed lay an abandoned crucifix, a handgun, and a pornographic magazine called "Lust." On the other side of the bed, opposite Elijah Muhammad, stands a grinning white man who wears a string tie and holds a whip. The sign above his head reads: "310 years of American Chattel Slavery & 100 years of Free Slavery." Below the entire drawing, Majied quotes Qur'an 62:2: "He [God] it is who raised among the illiterates a Messenger from among themselves, who recites to them the book and the wisdom. . . . Although they were before in manifest error."[55] For most Muslims, and for most traditional Qur'an commentators, this verse refers to Muhammad of Arabia, whose lack of literacy is often said to be evidence of the miraculous nature of the Qur'an.[56] But in the hands of Majied, this verse becomes proof of Muhammad's miraculous mission to modern African Americans. The drawing employs the Qur'anic verse to frame, interpret, and verify Muhammad's prophetic mission, which is designed to help black people recover from the moral and religious illnesses contracted through their centuries-old oppression at the hands of white American Christian slaveholders.

Throughout his tenure as a semi-official artist for the NOI, Majied often depicted Elijah Muhammad as a man protected and sanctioned by the Qur'an. His drawing "As It Was in the Days of Daniel, So It is Today" portrays Elijah Muhammad in the middle of a pride of lions. The Messenger tucks away the Qur'an in his left hand, while his right hand extends in a peaceful gesture toward sheep lying at his feet and toward the unusually calm lions that encircle him. Outside

# Our Great Physician

"Our Great Physician." Cartoon by Eugene Majied. *Muhammad Speaks*, June 1962, 14.

this circle, snakes with human heads and with the word "hypocrite" printed across their bodies slither toward the Messenger, saying, "I want his office."[57] In this scene, the Qurʾan might be interpreted as religious accoutrement and talisman, an object that affirms the Islamic identity of the Messenger and signifies his power to keep away the hypocrites, tame the fiercest beasts, and protect his vulnerable flock of sheep.

But to appreciate the meaning of this drawing more fully, it must also be analyzed in terms of its larger historical context. This artwork depicting Muhammad as the Biblical Daniel appeared in May 1964, only months after Malcolm X had been silenced by the NOI and had announced his intention to form the Muslim Mosque, Inc., which he said would act as a "religious base" for his political and social activism.[58] In response to what they saw as a direct challenge to the Messenger's authority, various movement intellectuals cited the Qurʾan in a coordinated campaign of criticism against Malcolm X. Articles in *Muhammad Speaks* warned Muslims to "beware of false prophets," offering verse after verse of the Qurʾan that condemned hypocrites and disbelievers.[59] In an article that explicitly discussed the dispute between Malcolm X and Elijah Muhammad, NOI Minister James from Chicago's Temple No. 2 argued that the Qurʾan was on the side of his prophet, not Malcolm X. "The Holy Qurʾan teaches us," he wrote, "that the angels cannot say anything after Allah makes His choice of an Apostle." Human beings may find this person unfit, said the minister, but God knows better. And no human being can choose him/herself for such a role. "You cannot force yourself on God for such a office," Minister James declared, using the word "office," just as Majied did, to describe Elijah Muhammad's divine appointment.

In offering proof for his assertions, Minister James also cited Qurʾan 75:37–40 and 76:1–3, recounting the tradition, well known in Abrahamic traditions, that God often chooses unlikely candidates to be God's prophets. "Moses complained of not being able to speak plainly or eloquently," the minister said. "But that did not make God choose Aaron for His Apostle because Aaron was a better speaker." In this passage, Minister James equated the Biblical and Qurʾanic figure of Moses with Elijah Muhammad. Like Moses, Elijah Muhammad was never known, even to some of his followers, as a brilliant orator, and he often spoke haltingly, especially when suffering from an apparent asthmatic condition. For example, Sonsyrea Tate writes that when she heard Muhammad's voice broadcast to her temple in Washington, D.C., on the fourth Sunday of the month in the early 1970s, she thought that "his speech was broken and his grammar was bad compared to the grammar we learned in his schools."[60] Louis

Martin, a non-Muslim and editor of the *Chicago Daily Defender*, stated that "Elijah Muhammad . . . is one of the few, if not the only, mass leaders in the national Black community who is not regarded as a great orator. He talks softly with almost none of the eloquence one traditionally associates with Black leadership and especially Black religious leadership. Some reporters claim that the Muslim leader literally drives them up the wall when they try to catch his words in a formal speech."[61] Malcolm X, on the other hand, was always lauded for his rhetorical skill, but his efforts to establish Muslim Mosque, Inc., showed, according to Minister James, that he had rejected God's will, and, even worse, had set out to compete with the Messenger. "This mosque," James wrote, "is mentioned in the Holy Qur'an 9:107: 'They build the mosque to cause disunity and to s[o]w dissension among the Muslims and to afford shelter to the enemies of Islam.'" God destroyed this mosque, James reminded his audience, and in Qur'an 9:73 instructed "the Apostle to strive hard against the hypocrites and be firm against them." Throughout his article, Minister James cited the Qur'an as a source of religious authority and authenticity, making analogies between the Qur'anic narratives and the contemporary mission of Elijah Muhammad.

Like Minister James, the artist Majied also compared Elijah Muhammad to Moses. Depicting the story of the plagues in Exodus, Majied drew on a narrative well known to his primarily African American audience while also recasting Elijah Muhammad as a Muslim Moses, who wears a fez and holds on to the Qur'an.[62] In the drawing entitled "As It Was With Pharaoh So It is Today," Elijah Muhammad wears a black suit, bow tie, and fez, and holds onto a copy of the "Holy Qur'an" in his left hand. He stands serenely on the periphery of a horrible scene in which locusts attack men who are dressed in ancient Egyptian garb. Pointing to Elijah Muhammad, Pharaoh cries, "He has the truth . . . God (Allah) plagues us!" Pharaoh braces himself against the onslaught of locusts and raises his clenched left fist across his forehead in a gesture signifying great woe. Pharaoh's face is none other than the face of President Lyndon Baines Johnson.[63] Tellingly, just fifteen days before this drawing was printed in *Muhammad Speaks*, President Johnson signed into law the Civil Rights Act of 1964, which sought to create equal rights for citizens in public education, voting, public accommodations, and federal programs, regardless of race, color, religion, or national origin.[64] In Majied's view, this bill seemed to have represented a Pyrrhic victory for black Americans. Elijah Muhammad, not the false promise of federally guaranteed civil rights and integration, offered his followers true freedom. Like Moses, the drawing implies, Elijah Muhammad was chosen by God to lead his people away from the oppressors.

Columnist Tynnetta Deanar, frequent contributor of a women's column to

*Muhammad Speaks*, also referred to the Exodus narrative in her explication of Elijah Muhammad's mission. Like the children of Israel, she wrote, "we are . . . a wandering, vagabond people in the midst of our captors, without a land of our own; and the Honorable Elijah Muhammad is the only one speaking in the exact spiritual context of securing land for the lost and found nation of so-called Negroes." Just as Moses led the Jews and Muhammad led the Arabs, according to the author, Elijah Muhammad appeared among the "so-called Negroes." She explained, ostensibly referring to Qur'an 10:47 or 16:36, that his mission was "in fulfillment of the Qur'an statement to all nations and people we sent a messenger." Moreover, she claimed, Elijah Muhammad's advocacy of racial separatism was similar to the views of other prophets: "And as all bona fide divine spokesmen of the past, the Honorable Elijah Muhammad is carrying out the divine work of separating our people from the nation and people responsible for our captivity." She also asserted, like many of her peers, that Elijah Muhammad had special knowledge of the Qur'an, which was "perhaps the most enviable position of all." He possessed "great knowledge and wisdom and interpretation of the Qur'an, for it is in this area where the Honorable Elijah Muhammad has no eligible candidate, competitor or equal in all the earth."[65]

The casting of Elijah Muhammad as a Qur'an-sanctioned prophet and modern-day heir of the Abrahamic prophets was a trope employed frequently in movement discourse. In addition to comparing Elijah Muhammad to Daniel and Moses, Majied's "As It Was in the Days of" series of drawings juxtaposed the trials of Elijah Muhammad with the persecution of other prophets. In an August 1964 drawing, Majied depicted the faces of prophets carved in the side of a mountain, just as the faces of certain U.S. presidents are reproduced at Mt. Rushmore. In Majied's drawing, the location of these mountain carvings is not the western United States, but the Near East, as indicated by the Muslim man riding a camel at the base of the mountain. From left to right, the tribulations of the prophets are catalogued as follows: Noah, accused of drunkenness; Lot, accused of having relations with his daughters; Moses, accused by his own sister; David, "accused of Uriah's wife"; Solomon, accused of bringing the downfall of his own kingdom; and Jesus, accused of being a sinner and devil. The last figure on the right is obscured; underneath is written the question, "And Today?"—an obvious reference to Elijah Muhammad. Below the image, Majied included the image of a scroll whose title reads, "Why are the righteous accused?" The answer, from Qur'an 6:112, is: "And thus did we make for every prophet an enemy, the devils from among men and jinn, some of them inspiring others with gilded speech to deceive (them)."[66]

Majied's drawing further evidences the hybrid nature of an African American Islamic religious culture that utilized Afro-Eurasian Islamic traditions to reinterpret many of the black Christian symbols and narratives with which NOI members were already familiar. In his artistic use of Qur'an 6:112, which announces God's will to "make for every prophet an enemy," Majied indicated that all of the figures under consideration were *Islamic* prophets, which is also how each one is discussed in the Qur'an and other Islamic sources. Their Muslim identity seems to be confirmed by Majied's inclusion of Jesus, who is not considered a prophet in most Jewish or Christian traditions. But Majied's drawing also showed the continued salience of Christian traditions in the religious culture of the NOI. Many of the accusations against these men reproduced in the drawing are not derived from the Qur'an; they are based mainly on accounts in the Old Testament/Hebrew Bible, which indeed accuses Noah of drunkenness (Gen. 9:18–29); Lot of (unintentional) incest (Gen. 19:31–36); Moses of marrying a Cushitic woman (Num. 12:1); David of murder (2 Samuel 11:1); and Solomon of loving foreign, idolatrous women (2 Kings 9–11). Most of these charges were not made in the Qur'an, although Solomon seems to forsake his prayers (38:30–40) and David asks to be forgiven for some unnamed sin (38:24). On the whole, the Qur'an praises the character of these prophets, who are models of human goodness. Likewise, the accusations against Jesus of being a "sinner" and "devil" seem to be derived more from the New Testament than the Qur'an. In John 9:16, for example, Pharisees accused Jesus of violating the Sabbath, and some observers asked how such a sinner had the requisite power to perform miracles. In addition, Pharisees and others constantly criticized Jesus for associating with sinners and tax collectors (see Matt. 9:11, 11:19; Mark 2:16; and Luke 5:30, 7:34–39, 15:2, 19:7). And they claimed his power was from Beelzebub or some other unnamed devil (Matt. 9:34, 12:24; Mark 3:22; Luke 11:15; and John 8:48, 8:52, 10:20). Jesus suffers the enemies of truth in the Qur'an as well, but it is mainly because of those who plot against him and reject his prophetic call (see, for example, 3:50–55).

In placing Elijah Muhammad in this pantheon of persecuted prophets, Majied attempted to show how opposition to Muhammad was but further evidence of his prophetic authenticity. Such a defense was much needed in August 1964, especially in light of the fact, made public just weeks before, that Muhammad had committed adultery with several women, including his secretaries.[67] While many outside the movement condemned Elijah Muhammad for violating his own strict code of sexual ethics, many NOI intellectuals defended their Messenger's character even more zealously. Minister Isaiah Karriem of Baltimore, like Farrakhan and Majied, called on followers to view the false accusations against the Messenger as the trials of a Muslim prophet. He asked fellow members to pray to God for the success of Elijah Muhammad:

> Bless Muhammad, Thy message, the best of Thy creatures, the chosen one of Thy servants, the harbinger of mercy, the prosecutor of goodness, they [*sic*] key to blessings. He exerts himself for thy purpose and exposes himself to pain for Thy sake, and faulted Thy enemy till his mission was accomplished; and what was planned for his friends was achieved. . . . Therefore, O' Allah, exalt him for his exertion to Thy cause to the highest rank in Thy paradise till his position may not be equaled by any angel or prophet. Endow him with effective intersection [*sic*] for sacred members of his house and true believers.

In this prayer, Karriem not only alluded to God by God's Arabic name, Allah, he also asked God to grant Elijah Muhammad the power of intersession for his "house," a term that usually refers in Islamic traditions to the family of the prophet Muhammad of Arabia. Confronting accusations of embezzlement and adultery made against Elijah Muhammad, Minister Isaiah also wrote that his twenty-year association with Elijah Muhammad had shown the Messenger to be nothing but "a righteous man." Elijah Muhammad's accusers, according to the minister, were "disbelievers and hypocrites"; Elijah Muhammad's mistresses were "prostitutes who accused the Messenger of getting babies." They should "hang their heads in shame for putting out such lies on the Honorable Elijah Muhammad," Karriem wrote. "Here the Messenger has been ill for the last 2 or 3 years, sometimes too weak to get out of bed, and yet they accuse him." As for "that no good Malcolm Little, who the Messenger of Allah took out of the garbage can, . . . the only thanks he gave the Messenger was lying, scandal, and trying to pull followers away from the Messenger to follow him to his own selfish end." All of those who oppose Elijah Muhammad, continued the minister, must "know that Allah is with His Messenger."[68]

Absolute devotion to the prophet was necessary, and even members of the Messenger's immediate family would be banished if they did not obey. During this period, the Messenger's son Akbar, who had studied the Islamic religious sciences in Cairo, Egypt, returned home to question his father's teachings. Akbar aired his disagreements in public, which led to his ouster from the NOI. According to a declassified FBI telex from Cairo dated 25 August 1964, and information from an FBI informant in Chicago, Akbar decided to break with his father sometime during that month. Elijah Muhammad's subsequent ban of Akbar was announced in November 1964.[69] "On Sunday, November 29, 1964," proclaimed a "decree" in *Muhammad Speaks*, "at Muhammad's Temple No. 7, New York City, a speech was made by Akbar Muhammad containing statements and views which were not in keeping with the teachings of the Honorable Elijah Muhammad, the Messenger of Allah." The decree went on to declare Akbar a hypocrite, a person who was no longer a follower of his father, the Messenger. Nothing, including family ties, could prevent Elijah Muhammad from fulfilling his mission: "The Honorable Elijah Muhammad in the tradition of all great spiritual leaders of modern and ancient times, will forever defend the truths entrusted to him by Almighty God, Allah, and neither kith nor kin nor defectors of any kind will be allowed to alter the obligation of the divine mission the Messenger is destined to accomplish for his people."[70] Another son who fell in and out of favor with his father during this period was Wallace D. Muhammad, known today as W. D. Mohammed. As he attempted to become more "orthodox" in his practice of Islam, he spent much of the 1960s and early 1970s estranged from his father and the NOI.[71]

But Malcolm X posed a special risk. In 1964, Malcolm's growing stature as a spokesperson for "orthodox" Islam threatened the NOI's campaign to establish the Islamic legitimacy of Elijah Muhammad. Malcolm's famous *hajj* to Mecca and his sponsorship by the Muslim World League evidenced his growing bona fides as a "real" Muslim and a potentially powerful spokesperson for "orthodox" Islam.[72] Prominent American newspapers like the *New York Times* covered Malcolm's activities throughout 1964, including his return home from a trip abroad in November.[73] NOI leaders took note of this coverage, and attempted to dismiss the support that Malcolm had gained from the Muslim World League.[74] Louis Farrakhan, then minister of an NOI mosque in Boston, called Malcolm "Muhammad's biggest hypocrite," comparing him to the Biblical and Qur'anic figure of Korah and the Christian Judas. "Korah thought he was playing the game well, claiming to be an aid to Moses," Farrakhan wrote. But he "turned out to be Moses' deadliest hypocrite. Korah was successful in getting a few to follow him, but Allah caused an earthquake to open its mouth and they all were dropped to their death into a crevice of the earth," said Farrakhan (cf. Num. 16 and Qur'an 28:76–82, 29:39/38, 40:25/24). Malcolm was also akin to the New Testament Judas, according to the minister. "Judas had hugged and kissed Jesus many times. . . . So has Malcolm hugged and kissed Muhammad many times . . . though Muhammad knew Malcolm's hypocrisy."

In addition to citing sacred scriptures to defend Elijah Muhammad against Malcolm's newfound power as a Sunni Muslim missionary, Farrakhan used other sources to draw parallels between the life of Elijah Muhammad and the history of early Islam. Farrakhan urged followers to "give special attention to the Messenger's history here in America as it compares almost 100 per cent with the history of Muhammad and his followers, hypocrites, and enemies almost

1400 years ago." He argued that "Malcolm's defection from Messenger Muhammad compares so completely with the hypocrites of the Holy Qur'an that it does not take a scholar's eye to detect it."[75] Rather than referring to the Qur'an to make the comparison, however, Farrakhan cited narratives recounted in Washington Irving's nineteenth-century biography of "Mahomet."[76]

Farrakhan mined Irving's book to recount the story of Moseilma (Musaylima b. Habib), a charming "false prophet" who "held a kind of regal and sacerdotal sway" over a certain region of Arabia in the seventh century A.D. Like Malcolm X, Moseilma had the gifts of rhetoric and poetry, Farrakhan pointed out in a section entitled "Malcolm Repeats Moseilma's Work." But these talents did not save Moseilma from death at the hands of a great Muslim army that came in the name of God and the true prophet, Muhammad. In the aftermath of the false prophet's death, recounted Farrakhan, the survivors of this region converted to the real Islam.[77] It seems clear that Farrakhan was warning of a similar fate for Malcolm and his followers. In retrospect, it is a chilling story, since Malcolm would be gunned down less than three months after its publication.[78]

For some scholars who narrowly define Islam as a tradition characterized by a historical engagement mainly with the Qur'an and Sunna, or the traditions of the Prophet Muhammad, Farrakhan's use of Irving as an Islamic source may represent yet more evidence of the NOI's Islamic marginality and its distance from Afro-Eurasian Islamic history. Indeed, it is safe to say that most Afro-Eurasian Muslims have not learned about their prophet by reading Washington Irving's biography, which is a classic Orientalist work. But it is also true that most Muslims, even the learned 'ulama, have relied on sources other than the Qur'an and the hadith in their quest to understand and emulate Muhammad's life example. Afro-Eurasian Muslims have composed and listened to poems and stories about Muhammad, created and viewed artistic images about his life, and even sought mystical union with him.[79] How one learned about the Prophet Muhammad in the Afro-Eurasian landmass depended upon several factors, including one's gender, domicile, class, linguistic group, religious orientation, and ethnicity.[80] It so happens that in the United States, many African Americans have learned about Islam and its prophet through Orientalist sources. In the 1920s, for example, Noble Drew Ali's Moorish Science Temple borrowed its Muslim symbols not from the Qur'an, but from the black Shriners and the Masons.[81] Though Farrakhan clearly knew more about Afro-Eurasian Islamic traditions than did Noble Drew Ali, he, too, relied on some Orientalist sources to craft an Islamic apologia for Elijah Muhammad and a rhetorical assault on Malcolm X.

## Debating Orthodoxy

By the middle 1960s, then, the lines of ideological battle between Muslims inside the NOI and those outside the movement were more clearly drawn than ever. In light of the Messenger's harsh criticisms of Malcolm X and his banishing of sons Wallace and Akbar Muhammad, NOI intellectuals knew all too well what was at stake in rejecting the Honorable Elijah Muhammad's religious and moral authenticity. And yet, at the beginning of 1965, at least one family member and burgeoning NOI intellectual attempted to fashion an ideological compromise between the teachings of Elijah Muhammad and the arguments of his "orthodox" critics. Jamil Muhammad, the grandson who had called Elijah Muhammad a *mujaddid*, or religious renewer, now wrote that Elijah Muhammad was indeed "Allah's holy apostle." But he also insisted on qualifying what it meant that his grandfather was a messenger, and in so doing offered an interpretation of Elijah Muhammad's religious mission that differed slightly from that of Ministers Farrakhan and Cross: "We recognize the Honorable Elijah Muhammad as the center of Allah's authority," wrote Jamil Muhammad, "and as the head of the Nation for freedom, justice, and equality. The whole of this earth is a Mosque; therefore, whatever is in heaven or on earth, must submit to the Glory of Allah, regardless of its status." Rather than leaving well enough alone, however, he added that "we should not argue who is the real and final Messenger of Allah's, his [H]oly Apostle. Allah sent into the nation of mankind many prophets, apostles, or messengers with the 'real' truth."

On the one hand, Jamil Muhammad now clearly confirmed a belief in his grandfather as a man of Godly authority in charge of a "Nation," a special mission indeed. On the other hand, he implied that the arguments over Elijah Muhammad's status as Messenger were a waste of time. Referring to ideas found in Qur'an 10:47 and 16:36, the same verses that Tynnetta Deanar cited in her defense of Elijah Muhammad's prophetic status, he made the case that God has sent messengers to every people in every era. Critics and defenders alike should focus on his accomplishments as leader, and leave moral judgment to God, he argued: "There should be no point to the arguments and questions about the Most Honorable Elijah Muhammad's personal or public affairs. He has the keys to every scientific field of life, to prove the Islamic principles of Allah's authority. Allah is the Supreme Judge in this court (world) and has the ethical code and has regulated its guidance to His Messenger, Elijah Muhammad, the great signer and warner."[82] God chose this man as a warner and a leader, Jamil Muhammad claimed. If one desires proof, he said, examine how his teachings, or "scientific" knowledge, evidence "Islamic *principles*" (emphasis added). Perhaps this was Jamil Muhammad's plea to focus on the positive aspects of a program of uplift imbued with Islamic principles and to cease bickering over the finer points of religious doctrine. If so, Jamil Muhammad echoed the comments of foreign Muslim religious leaders who had endorsed Elijah Muhammad's mission while also noting some of their theological and ideological differences with the Messenger.

Other NOI intellectuals largely ignored Jamil Muhammad's request. In fact, it is hard to find evidence of movement intellectuals who negotiated, in explicitly theological terms, the difficult contradictions between the religious thought of Elijah Muhammad and that of his Muslim critics. Rather than attempting to reconcile Elijah Muhammad's teachings with some of the basic theological precepts of Sunni or Shi'i Islamic traditions, some NOI intellectuals instead turned to theological relativism in order to defend Elijah Muhammad's theological particularism. Dr. Leo X McCallum, a dentist and frequent contributor to *Muhammad Speaks*, stressed, like some foreign Muslims, the importance of historical context in understanding Elijah Muhammad's teachings. In 1965, McCallum wrote that he would "like to explain one or two things so that our brothers of the East born in Islam . . . will understand our position." He began his arguments by pointing out that "one Muslim is the brother of another. . . . Islam is their religion and Islam is our religion. Allah is their God and Allah is our God." However, "and this is necessarily a big However," he declared, "it is vitally important that one understands the difference in the conditions imposed upon the Muslim *back home* and those who have accepted Islam under the Honorable Elijah Muhammad [emphasis added]." Muslims "in the East," he continued, hear the call to prayer five times a day and are exposed to Islam from birth, while the "so-called American Negro not only has no idea who Allah is, he doesn't even know who he, himself is." The African American context, McCallum said, is so radically different that "our brothers in and from the East should recognize immediately that trying to reach us with the traditional Islam taught in the East is like trying to drown a fish. It just doesn't work!"

McCallum did not make any exclusivistic claims to the truth on behalf of Elijah Muhammad. In fact, rather than emphasizing the uniqueness of Elijah Muhammad, he stressed the similarities between Elijah Muhammad and Prophet Muhammad of Arabia: "I should think that the so-called 'orthodox' Muslim would understand very quickly the need for the approach of the Honorable Elijah Muhammad simply by having knowledge and history of earlier prophets." Both Muhammads, McCallum argued, faced persecution, scorn, and unpopularity. Like Majied and so many other movement intellectuals, McCallum also asserted that their rejection by the powerful interests of their times was a sign of these prophets' legitimacy. Lot, Jesus, and Moses, he claimed, were all radicals in their time, too. "They were considered extremist, hate teachers and everything, but what they were—messengers and prophets of Allah."[83] McCallum's appeals were patient in tone and seemed to be sincere efforts to engage Muslim brothers and sisters outside of the NOI in a reasoned discussion about Elijah Muhammad's prophetic mission.

Similarly, Minister James Shabazz of Mosque No. 25 in Newark, New Jersey, wrote in 1968 that Muhammad's critics had not applied the proper hermeneutic in understanding Elijah Muhammad's Islamic teachings. "Some charge distortion of Islam, or a new brand of Islam, or self-styled teacher of Islam," he observed, "but in the presence of facts they themselves will be found to be the distortioners." If one wants to know the truth about the NOI, he continued, "it will take a Muslim, who has benefited from the teachings of self-knowledge by Messenger Muhammad to testify to it." Shabazz then turned to a parable to illustrate his meaning: "When a carpenter uses his augur, instead of a hammer, it does not mean he does not use a hammer too, nor that he is not a carpenter; you would have to look in his tool box. I believe, a divine man is correct when he addresses himself to the time and condition of the people to whom he is sent."[84] One plausible interpretation of this passage is that Elijah Muhammad may indeed have different Islamic beliefs and practices than his orthodox critics, but there are many ways of being Muslim. As a divine man and a leader, Muhammad's approach to Islam was one that was relevant to those whom he had come to serve, according to the minister. "The fruit of his work justifies his method," Shabazz argued.[85] Shabazz thus pointed to several interpretive keys in unlocking the truth of Muhammad's Islamic mission: he privileged the first-person voice of those humans who actually followed the Messenger; he insisted that the historical context in which Elijah Muhammad was operating be considered; and he argued for the use of different "tools" in order to meet the particular needs of particular believers in particular contexts.

On the pages of *Muhammad Speaks*, however, most movement intellectuals took a far more rejectionist view toward outside Muslim criticism of Elijah Muhammad's theology. They refused to cede any ground to their critics, and tried to beat the critics at their own game. In a series of articles published throughout the fall of 1965, columnist Tynnetta Deanar rejected Jamil Muhammad's pleas for a moratorium on the discussion of Muhammad's status as prophet. She asserted that Elijah Muhammad, not Muhammad of Arabia, was the seal of the Abrahamic prophets—a teaching that most Muslims in the United States and abroad would have considered heretical. Directly addressing the "criticisms entertained and often voiced by some members of various Islamic Schools of

Thought in their attitude towards the Divine Position of the Honorable Elijah Muhammad," Deanar argued that Elijah Muhammad's life signaled the end of the "old world" and the "beginning of the new." Adapting millennial themes commonly found in many American religious traditions, Deanar submitted that the rise and fall of Euro-American power was the harbinger of a new age.[86] Muhammad of Arabia was a man of the old world, and thus could not be the last prophet, who would come to usher in a new age, according to Deanar.[87] The old world, she argued, had persisted for fourteen hundred years after the Prophet Muhammad of Arabia. Only after the rise of European and American power, she said, would a new age and a new prophet appear.[88] Of course, Deanar reminded her audience, "the great flourishing of Islamic Culture, spiritual values, and scientific genius" that developed with the "advent of Islam [in Arabia] . . . was undeniably of great import." But Muslims around the world had become too defensive in their posture toward this old version of Islam: the "effort to safeguard and protect that sacred history of Muhammad and Islam by the masses of devout believers has hindered their understanding of its vital significance in this day and time." Many Muslims had simply missed the "many traditions and scriptures" that testified to the "advent of a Muhammad . . . whose work would bring about a conclusive victory of Islam in the entire world." They also failed to understand the scriptural traditions that pointed to twentieth-century America, the new Babylon, as the place where the prophet would do his work. Deanar attempted to explain why so many Muslims had not recognized the truth: "The answer," she wrote, "comes from the Messenger, himself, who explains that the actual coming of the Mahdi (God in Person), and the raising of His Last Messenger had to remain as a concealed truth and as a well guarded secret."[89]

In the final installment of her series, Deanar explained the utility of this concealment, arguing that "the power of the enemy to interfere was made impossible due to the Supreme Wisdom and Superior Planning of the God, Himself, Who Came in the Person of Master Fard Muhammad." According to Deanar, Muhammad of Arabia may have warned his followers about the coming of the Day of Judgment, and may have prepared them to face it in righteousness, but Muhammad of America was the prophet whose presence would signal the actual coming of the end of the old world. "Muhammad of 1400 years ago did not live at the time of the end expressed in the Holy Qur-an," she stated, "but the Muhammad who speaks today is in the time of the end to be witnessed by this generation. Muhammad [of Arabia] gave reference to the Coming of God, as did all his Divine Predecessors; and Muhammad, today, teaches us of the presence of God." She concluded her article by calling on Orthodox Muslims to "stop clinging to the past." "Wake up, Orthodox Muslims! Wake up, so-called

Negroes! An announcement of mighty significance has been made to the peoples of the entire earth. Only those who have knowledge will abide!"[90]

In another article, published four years later in 1969, Deanar further supported her view of the millennial Messenger, Elijah Muhammad, by offering an analysis of certain Qur'anic proof texts *and* the epistle of Barnabas, an apocryphal Christian text that was "sometimes quoted as Scripture in the early centuries of the church."[91] Her source for Barnabas was the 1926 edition of *The Lost Books of the Bible*, which she claims was "kept hidden until its first general publication in the 1920s."[92] Through a proper interpretation of these books, Deanar argued, one could understand some of the mysteries of Elijah Muhammad's mission. Take, for example, Muhammad's teaching that the six days of creation described in Genesis 2:2 symbolically refer to the six-thousand-year rule of the demonic white man. She quoted Barnabas 13:3–5 as proof of this teaching: "The meaning of it is this; that in six thousand years the Lord God will bring all things to an end. . . . For him one day is a thousand years. Therefore, children, in six days, that is, in six thousand years, shall all things be accomplished."[93] According to Deanar, these teachings are confirmed in Qur'an 32:5: "He orders the Affair from the heaven to the earth; then it will ascend to Him in a day the measure of which is a thousand years as you count." It is important to note that she used the Qur'an as a source of authority to interpret both the text in Barnabas and the teaching of Elijah Muhammad, claiming that the Qur'an also equates a day in divine time to a thousand years of human time.

Deanar then argued that the seventh day, which represents the millennium of divine intervention on the earth, was also prophesied in these texts. Again quoting from Barnabas, she claimed that the epistle foretells the mission of Elijah Muhammad, who will come to lead at the end time: " 'And he rested the seventh day'; he meaneth this; that when the Son shall come, and abolish the season of the Wicked One, and judge the ungodly; and shall change the sun and the moon, and the stars; then he shall gloriously rest in the seventh day." Elijah Muhammad, she implied, was the prophesied Son who will end the wickedness of white rule on earth and alter the very fabric of the heavens. According to Deanar, the Qur'an "reveals in this same language" the truth of this prophecy: " 'On the day when earth will be changed into a different earth, and the heavens (as well), and they will come forth to Allah, the One, the Supreme.' (Holy Qur'an 14:48)." Deanar did not elaborate further on this verse, suggesting that the connection between the apocalyptic language of Barnabas and that of the Qur'an was self-evident. She ended her article with a simple question: "Who can now read such proof and still deny the Presence of God's Messenger in our midst?"[94]

Unlike Jamil Muhammad, Deanar argued for the legitimacy of her prophet by privileging her access to special, ultimately esoteric knowledge. She expressed little interest in engaging the theological presuppositions of Elijah Muhammad's critics, and used apocryphal Christian texts to help make her case. In so doing, Deanar chose confrontation as a strategy to deal with the cries of Elijah Muhammad's critics.

## Conclusion

This chapter has shown how a professional class of NOI ministers and newspaper columnists responded to Muslim criticisms of Elijah Muhammad's Islamic legitimacy from the late 1950s until his death in 1975. Citing the endorsements of Asian Muslim authorities and verses from the Qur'an, most of these intellectuals defended Elijah Muhammad as a true Islamic prophet. A few intellectuals, like Jamil Muhammad, sought a rapprochement with Elijah Muhammad's critics, though most simply rejected the criticisms of their prophet as unholy and plain wrong. In either case, the increasing engagement with other Muslims had important, sometimes unforeseen consequences. As they considered the views of other Muslims, these intellectuals turned their gaze outward toward Muslims who were not members of the NOI. Those outside Muslims could be allies or they could be enemies, but in either case, they became points of focus for the construction and negotiation of African American Muslim identity. Just as important, the increased use of Islamic texts, especially the Qur'an, meant that NOI intellectuals now read the same sources as their critics. In some cases, this deeper engagement with Islamic texts and traditions led to dissension and outright rebellion among NOI intellectuals. During the 1960s, Malcolm X and brothers Akbar and Wallace Muhammad left the movement to practice what they believed to be a more authentic form of Islam. But most of the intellectuals discussed here, including Minister Lonnie Cross, Minister Louis Farrakhan, and columnist Tynnetta Deanar, stayed in the movement through the 1960s and into the 1970s, privileging Elijah Muhammad's esoteric interpretations of the Qur'an in their readings of the holy book. All these intellectuals, card-carrying members and defectors alike, had something in common: they referred to the Qur'an as an authoritative source. They had become part of an old Islamic tradition —a transnational conversation about the meaning of the Holy Qur'an.

## CHAPTER 3

# Black Muslim History Narratives
## Orienting the Nation of Islam
## in Muslim Time and Space

From the Land of the Hot Sun

The Tigris and the Nile

From the Sun Baked Valleys of Egypt

To the Faraway Himalayas

Down Again into Tibet

And China

And then Pygmy Country

Where Tiny Black People Grow Very Tall

In their Smallness

Of Stature

Black Man!

Turkey, Iran, Iraq and Persia

Lands of Splendor

And the Prayer is to Allah

And the Tongue is Arabic

Sometimes Different

But the Melodic Beauty

Is One and Same

Black Man!

Black Man

Giant of Giants.

— William E. X, "Poetry Corner: Black Man,"
   *Muhammad Speaks*, 7 July 1967

Thⁱs chapter illustrates how NOI members, including both intellectuals and the rank and file, produced historical narratives that linked the destiny of black people to the religion of Islam. Many of these narratives incorporated Afro-Eurasian Islamic figures, place names, texts, events, and themes; others utilized African American Christian symbols, black secular traditions, and novel mythologies popularized by the NOI's intelligentsia. These stories about the past sometimes focused on Elijah Muhammad and his role in history, but many did not. This is an important fact, since it suggests that no matter how central the Messenger was to the life of the movement, he was not the sole focus of its religious culture. This chapter further complicates our picture of the NOI, since it challenges any one-dimensional view of the NOI as a "cult" solely focused on the meaning of Elijah Muhammad's mission and the power that he held over believers' lives.

Instead, we turn our gaze toward men and women who entertained various notions of what it meant to be Muslim, including historical interpretations of their Muslim identities. In creating and sustaining these historical narratives, members of the NOI constructed and contested the meaning of their collective identity as Muslims. The content, form, and even functions of these narratives differed, but taken as a whole, they help to explain how African American Muslims came to see themselves as part of what Benedict Anderson has called an "imagined community."[1] In using that term, Anderson did not mean that the group identity to which individuals ascribed was somehow fake. An imagined community, as Gupta and Ferguson put it, is not *imaginary*.[2] Rather, Anderson argues, "communities are to be distinguished, not by their falsity/genuineness, but by the style in which they are imagined."[3] Anderson's seminal study on imagined communities, which focused on the origins of modern nationalism, sought to understand how people who never knew each other personally came to see themselves as members of a common nation. He showed how this collective identity was often rooted in particular notions of a community's history.[4] In the case of African American Muslims, it will be demonstrated that NOI members saw themselves not only as a "nation," but also as a transnational community rooted in Islamic religion and history.[5] This reorienting of African American mental geography toward the Muslim world had important implications not only for NOI members' sense of religious community, but also for their political identities. In seeking to identify political struggles of liberation worthy of African American

Muslim attention, some NOI members began to see Asians and other nonblack Muslims as important allies and comrades.

My focus on the role of the historical imagination in the construction of collective identity is also useful in understanding the relationship between the religious culture of the NOI and African American culture more generally. For over two centuries, African Americans have been producing what might be called black history narratives. As historian of American religions Laurie Maffly-Kipp has observed, these narratives constitute a distinct "textual genre" in African American religious history that features "reference[s] to a community beyond the self, be it defined by African descent, Christian communion, or most commonly, both; and a more or less explicit linear chronology that situates the community in a wider history." Maffly-Kipp notes that most historians of the African American experience in the United States have paid more attention to slave narratives, conversion accounts, and autobiographies than to this genre, which focuses on "collective stories" and includes "tales filled with histories of ancient people, fraternal orders, individual churches, national denominational bodies, Protestant nations, and eventually, racial histories in the modern sense, that is, stories of people united by a shared biology, history, and sacred purpose."[6]

The making of African American *Islamic* history narratives is an important chapter in this larger story, since these narratives attempted to sever the links between Christianity and persons of African descent, instead touting the connections between black people and Islam. According to Melani McAlister, the popularization of these black Islamic narratives had important repercussions outside the NOI since they helped to reorient aspects of African American politics and religion toward the Middle East more generally. She argues that "between 1955 and 1972, a potent combination of religious affiliation, anti-colonial politics, and black nationalist radicalism turned claims upon the Middle East into a rich resource within African American communities."[7] For African American Muslims inside the NOI, it was not only a collective reorientation toward the Middle East, but also toward other places and times where blacks/Muslims had lived. African American Muslims in the NOI located the story of their people, the black/Muslim people, in many epochs and locales, including ancient Egypt, Muslim West Africa, Asia, a mythical Arabia, and the classical period of Islam during and immediately after the time of Prophet Muhammad of Arabia. These black Muslims "moved across" time and space, constructing their contemporary identities by imagining who they had been in the past.[8] They also mapped their identities *beyond* time and space, positing a primordial origin for the black man, who had no beginning and has no end. In both cases, narrators and readers created and entertained differing notions of what it meant to be Muslim.

# Negro History Week versus the Black Man's History

By the 1960s, Negro History Week, which would become today's Black History Month, was celebrated by an increasing number of black and in some cases non-black educators, intellectuals, and organizations. Founded in 1926 by Carter G. Woodson, one of the first black men to receive his Ph.D. from Harvard University and the father of the *Journal of Negro History*, Negro History Week focused attention in black schools, civic organizations, and other institutions on important events and personages in the history of "Negroes" in the United States, and to a lesser extent in Latin America and Africa. Originally observed during the second week of February to mark the birthdays of both Abraham Lincoln and Frederick Douglass, Negro History Week gained in popularity throughout the twentieth century and often featured elaborate parades, high-profile lectures, library events, and school essay contests in the United States and abroad.[9]

Despite the fact that Carter G. Woodson's view of black history included the great achievements of precolonial African civilizations and the revolutionary history of African American men like Toussaint L'Ouverture of Haiti, some figures in the NOI rejected Negro History Week as the misguided and compensatory celebration of a shameful past.[10] As a 1962 article in *Muhammad Speaks* put it, "Muslims are taught by Messenger Elijah Muhammad to ignore the annual hue and cry over so-called 'Negro History Week'" because "so-called Negro history is all slave history. . . . According to the Messenger, the black man's American history will begin only and when he stops groveling, begging, cringing in fear before the white man, still his master, and stand on his two feet as a full-fledged man with pride of self and race." According to this unattributed article, which bears the rhetorical imprint of Malcolm X, "there is nothing in it [Negro History Week] that would inspire a black child to want to be like the characters in this history. Muslims extol, in place of Booker T. Washington, Richard B. Allen [a founding father of the African Methodist Episcopal Church], etc., the fighting men and women of the black man's past such as Hannibal of Carthage and King Menelik of Ethiopia whose small army in 1866 inflicted a resounding dedfeat [*sic*] on the mighty forces of Imperial Italy." That black intellectuals would hail slave history as a proud history, the author writes, only shows how much they have been "brainwashed" and "demoralized" by their white overseers.[11]

Similarly, member Priscilla 2X of Mosque No. 2 in Chicago argued that the history of black women in America was a shameful story that had lingering effects on contemporary black women. "For four hundred years (400) the Black Women here in America has been under a physical, mental and spiritual slavery, to its highest degree," she wrote. "The Black Woman's very body was used to build a Nation that was not her own. In the slavemaster's field, in the slavemaster's kitchen, raising the slavemaster's children, breeding more slaves for the slavemaster. Can you understand the mental and spiritual effect upon this Black Women?" For this writer, and others in the NOI, the living memory of rape and abuse during slave times still affected contemporary African American women. "After being free from physical slavery for a little over 100 years, the Black Woman's brains were completely dead when it came to knowing her real self. She has only known the life of being under the slavemaster." In fact, she claimed, the black woman lost the ability to love fully and "naturally" during slave times. "During slavery everytime she showed or expressed her true love for other than the slavemaster the slavemaster took that love. She had no children to love. She did not even love herself. She could only express love for the slavemaster and this was false love."[12] In an ironic twist, Sister Priscilla's views echoed the conclusions of sociological "ghetto literature" that identified the cause of African American social deviance in lingering pathologies developed during slave times.[13] One can simultaneously view her instrumental use of history as a call for greater self-love and love of others. This was only possible, she said, if women "get behind" Elijah Muhammad, who will teach them to internalize the following sentiment: "My sister you are the Queen of the Universe, the whole earth belongs to you."[14]

These historical narratives about the wounded black woman in need of Muhammad's healing continued to be articulated well into the 1970s. Sister Edna Mae 2X, for instance, called on the "degenerate and lost" black woman "to come to Islam." Like Priscilla 2X, she blamed slavery for the "degeneration" of the black woman, focusing on the utter "destruction" of her morals: "Prior to being brought to America, her character was that of dignity, self-respect and high morals: her garments were modest; her hair was covered in public places; also she veiled her face to hide her beauty from strange men. Being flirtatious, laughing loud and using vulgar language was not her conduct; she was found in her home caring for her children, husband, herself and performing duties of a civilized woman. Her way of life was that of Islam: entire submission to the One God, Allah." *Where* did the black woman lead this life? Although her description of the place makes it sound like an idealized Victorian America, Sister Edna Mae says only that it was a "highly civilized Nation in the East."[15]

While NOI intellectuals agreed that the history of slavery was shameful and that Elijah Muhammad could heal the slave mind, at least one NOI intellectual saw the history of certain slaves as heroic and worthy of historical chronicle. In a 1962 comic strip, for example, Eugene Majied depicts four men—two whites, two blacks—discussing various events in U.S. history. Three of them recall important military events in the history of the United States, shouting out the names of Pearl Harbor, San Juan Hill, the Alamo, Bunker Hill, and Vicksburg. One proud black man, by implication the only sane man in the group, also calls out the names of Gabriel, Vesey, Nat Turner, and Garvey. Majied adds in a footnote at the bottom of the comic strip that "Gabriel, Denmark Vesey, Nat Turner were famous black leaders of slave revolts during slavery."[16] Marcus Garvey, who is not identified, was the leader of the Universal Negro Improvement Association, an organization popular with African Americans in the 1920s. For Majied, there were real heroes in U.S. history, but they were the black men who resisted slavery, or in Garvey's case, led a popular black nationalist movement.

*Muhammad Speaks* also included in its news sections positive representations of African American history. During the middle 1960s, the paper featured several articles chronicling African American historical events, figures, and achievements. Noting how black history had become a commodity, one 1966 article claimed that the "immutable law of commerce [ap]pears to be finally winning out over the law of White Supremacy in the field of black man's history, as businesses gingerly begins to supply a new and hungry market seeking information on the lives and deeds of black men in America and Africa." This article described various publications on black history and featured a likeness of Benjamin Banneker, who helped to plan the nation's capital.[17] Another article in early 1967 featured a review of Margaret B. Young's *The First Book of Negroes (American)*, which the paper hailed as a "new book full of vital Black American history."[18] In all of this increased coverage, one sees the influence of non-Muslim editor Richard Durham, winner of a Peabody award for "Destination Freedom," a radio series on a Chicago station about famous figures in African American history.[19] It is worth speculating, based on the print evidence, that Durham found more meaning in slave history than did many of his regular Muslim columnists. To be sure, he was committed, like many advocates of Negro History Week, to telling the courageous stories of African Americans in slavery.

Just because Durham included more coverage of topics related to African American history did not mean that NOI intellectuals suddenly became unqualified supporters of Negro History Week. Columnist Tynnetta Deanar, for example, worried in 1968 that the new interest in black history was presenting "only fragmentary impressions of the past accomplishments of the Black Race." Furthermore, she claimed, much of this history was "projected through [a] Western lens . . . which by no means . . . touches upon the source of Black Creativity or History in the aeons of uncalculated time of our existence in this—the Universe of Black Man." While she did not aim to "underrate the noble attempt by black men and women of all ages for their leanings in a right direction," she wanted to "emphasize [that] the proper scaling of black history . . . requires the teaching of Islam as a prerequisite." The "Islam" to which she referred could be found in the teachings of Elijah Muhammad about the origins and destiny of black people.[20]

Similarly, Minister Angelo 3X of Pensacola, Florida, reminded readers that the history in which black people should take the most pride is that taught by Elijah Muhammad. "So-called Negro history is on the lips of many partially awakened Black people today," he wrote. "But what is 'Negro history?' Where does this history take a Black child in the past? Only as far as the plantations of the white slavemaster. 'Negro' history is only a little more than 310 years old." Instead of studying that history, said the minister, black people should look to the historical teachings of the Messenger: "What young and old Black people need today is the 'knowledge of self,' which is more than 66-trillion years of history; this is the history of the 'Original Man.'"[21]

Sister Anna Burks Karriem of Mosque No. 5 in Cincinnati, Ohio, explained this idea further in a September 1968 article. For three years as a student at Tuskegee University in Alabama and later as a resident of Cincinnati, Karriem had been a member of the Student Non-Violent Coordinating Committee (SNCC), an arm of the Southern Christian Leadership Conference (SCLC) that became one of the most vocal proponents of the black power movement. Karriem left SNCC "after experiencing bitter frustration in all my attempts to help my beloved Black brothers and sisters in this country, and watching Black men cry 'Black Power' at the top of their lungs by day and sleep with white women by night." She found relief from the "depths of despair" in becoming a follower of Elijah Muhammad, who gave her "life . . . and a new sense of direction."[22] In advocating Elijah Muhammad's doctrine of the original man, Karriem noted the dissonance between her teachers' narratives of "Negro History" at Tuskegee and the Messenger's teaching of the black man's true identity. First, she said, instructors incorrectly referred to this history as Negro or Afro-American. "I am neither an Afro-American nor am I a Negro," she wrote. "As Muslim followers of the Honorable Elijah Muhammad who is a competent teacher, we know that we are members of the original Asiatic Black nation of the universe." Unlike many voices in the black consciousness movement, Karriem insisted that our "boundaries are not those of Africa." It is not clear from Karriem's comments exactly how she mapped the territorial boundaries of Asia, but she did indicate that for her Asia includes or was originally called Africa. Such an assertion made sense in light of Elijah Muhammad's teaching, which echoed the claim made by Noble Drew Ali in the 1920s, that all nonwhite humans — that is, those people not from Europe — are black Asiatics. The important and larger point that Karriem makes is that "Afro-American and Negro are not expressive of the Black man's true identity — because he is universal, the God of the universe, the original Black nation of the universe."[23] In other words, wherever one might place the homeland of black people on a world map is less important than the knowledge that blacks are part of the very being of the *universe*. Sister Ann 3X echoed Sister Anna's views in a 1970 article in which she complained of the lack of educational institutions that teach true black history. "How many of these 'learning institutes' teach young black children where they come from (and I do not mean Africa)," asked Sister Ann. "I can tell you they are far and in between."[24]

In offering a mythological reading of black origins, this strain in African American Muslim historical narrative adopts a *supralocative* perspective, meaning in this case that it maps the origins of the black man beyond the boundaries of this-worldly space.[25] The supralocative nature of some black Muslim history narratives can be seen not only in stories about the origins of black people, but in visions about their ultimate destiny as well. For example, "Holy City," a poem written by Sister Kris X of Temple No. 7 in Harlem, describes the promised city of black salvation more as a state of mind than a geographical location:

In the Holy City
Where the Righteous doth abode.
To ever hear the name Allah and walk in silken robes.
Oh, to sail the streets of justice,
Allah's breath the guiding wind.
Your ship is safely anchored;
Bow and stern are free from sin.
Once again, as time afore, You sit upon the throne
And sing the songs of Zion.
Silenced — is Babylon.
Riches, fame and power
Will never send you there.
Belief in Allah and His Messenger
Reserves the seat and pays the fare.
Hurry! Quick! Take flight
Lest ye be left behind.
The hour glass of judgment
Has always been on time.
The trial is almost over;
Harvest time is nigh.
The tried have shed their grave clothes;
There's no heaven in the sky.

Oh, to see that Holy City
Where Islam rules supreme;
Greeted with the holy names:
Shabazz—Hassan—Karriem.
If Allah should will
To take His law of life from me,
And I would not be here
To see her end, the eagle flees.
Brother! Sister!
Take my remains with thee.
Perhaps 'twill make a flower bloom,
Or fertilize a tree
That grows within the gate of
The Holy City.[26]

The hermeneutical key indicating that the Holy City is a state of mind rather than a specific spot on the map is the line "There's no heaven in the sky." This formulation repeats Elijah Muhammad's teaching that heaven and hell exist only on the earth, not somewhere in the sky, and that true salvation for black people requires their recommitment to Islam and the establishment of political and economic self-determination.[27]

Many NOI members regarded the telling of this supralocative black history narrative as essential in creating the conditions necessary to achieve this earthly salvation. Dr. Leo P. X McCallum, the semiofficial dentist of the NOI and frequent contributor to *Muhammad Speaks*, noted that the history taught by Elijah Muhammad had a different purpose than what was commonly thought of as history. He argued in a 1969 article that history, as it is usually defined, "attempts to find past actions of the human beings and proceeds by the interpretation of evidence to get answers to the questions one asks about the past." But Elijah Muhammad "goes even further than this," revealing the "specifics of history as they reflect the needs of the present." McCallum claimed that this instrumental history, or what some professional historians call presentism, was vital to people who have been "robbed of their history." Like other NOI intellectuals, McCallum cited the history of the original man and the origins of the universe as essential to the project of recovering black identity and pride. "And why is it so important to have a knowledge of one's self?" he asked. "Most civilized people agree generally that it is of importance that one should know himself so that first of all he will know those personal peculiarities and things that distinguish him from other men and his true nature as a man." History, then, is one way of classifying, in a kind of genus-species model, the identity of individuals as members of a group. But having this knowledge, according to McCallum, could also lead to great accomplishments: "Knowing yourself means knowing what you can do and since nobody knows what he can do until he tries, the only clue to what man can do is what man has done."[28] Ultimately, then, the myth of black origins not only distinguishes black people from nonblack people, but also inspires blacks to achieve greatness (since they discover that it is in their very nature).

Eugene Majied framed the myth of black origins in similar terms, showing that it could be an important weapon in the battle against poor self-esteem among black children.[29] In a 1969 comic strip, Majied depicts an African American boy, called Tommy, crying as he gets off a public school bus. Another black boy, who greets him, asks what's wrong.

"I . . . I . . . I was tryin' to be f-friendly with a couple of white boys at school . . . a-and they pushed me away from them!" responded Tommy. "T-they s-said they was *better'n* m-me!"

"Poor Tommy!" answers Tommy's friend. "You wouldn't be cryin' if you were being taught their true history. Our teacher said the white man spent 2000 years in the caves of Europe. He lived a beast's life, walking on all fours and eating raw meat! Moses was sent to civilize him!" As the two boys walk together, Tommy's friend puts his arm over Tommy's shoulder to comfort him.

"Boy!" exclaimed Tommy. "They sure don't teach that at the school I go to."

"You and I are from the original people—the Asiatic Black Man, the Maker, the Owner—Cream of the Planet Earth, and God of the Universe! We have no beginning nor ending. Our people built civilization millions of years *before* white people were made!"

"Wow! We come from a great people! I wish I could study such history," said Tommy.

"You can at the University of Islam! Join the Muslims and follow Mr. Muhammad! We're taught the knowledge of ourselves and others! We learn more than just the '3-Rs'!"

"Okay!" shouts a now smiling Tommy.[30]

In this comic, Majied, like others, seems to have recognized the psychological value of such a legend for children, whether or not he believed it to be true. This rendition of Elijah Muhammad's myth of black origins dramatically inverts common American stereotypes of blacks as "beasts," instead claiming that white men were the truly uncivilized animals. The comic strip also reiterates the importance of separate and independent black schools, implying that only institutions like the University of Islam put black history and black children first. Finally, it employs the image of a crying black male child to show how "white-dominant" education and integrated schools could deeply wound black children. This supralocative narrative is constructed as a therapeutic device, or what Leon Forrest somewhat pejoratively called "Muhammad's miracle drug," meant to heal the wounds of internalized racism.[31]

## Afro-Asian Sitings of Black Muslim History

Not all black Muslim history narratives were supralocative in nature, however. African American Muslims in the NOI also produced *translocative* and *trans-temporal* narratives, stories that sited the history of blacks in specific times and places, most often in Asia or Africa, and then moved forward to show how that past could fuel black renewal in the present.[32] These narratives varied dramatically in content and form, sometimes vaguely referring to historical periods of past black glory, and at other times offering very specific discussions of particular historical personages, events, or themes. Throughout the 1960s, for example, the editors of *Muhammad Speaks* offered an interpretation of Elijah Muhammad's myth of black origins in scientific terms, relying on modern archaeological and anthropological evidence to prove that blacks were the first human inhabitants of the earth. For example, a 1962 issue of *Muhammad Speaks* devoted its front page to a story entitled "Who is the Original Man?"[33] White supremacist scientists, it claimed, had long been engaged in a "super-secret project" to officially "establish earth's 'Original Man' as white." However, the article continued, Louis Leakey's recent discovery of the remains of a fourteen-million-year-old man in Kenya had proven conclusively that humankind's birthplace was Africa. The article juxtaposed his discoveries with other academic efforts that challenged white supremacist arguments. Included in the discussion were a Smithsonian exhibit of a basalt sculpture from La Yenta, Mexico; the "fictional" Peking Man and Java Man; and the Southeast Asian digs of Tom Harrison. In addition, the article featured several pictures, one of which depicted a slovenly Neanderthal, and referred to him as the "hairy, dumb, brutal, . . . [and] idiotic creature . . . [that] could very well be the forbearor [*sic*] of any of today's proud caucasians." Similar articles in at least ten different issues of *Muhammad Speaks* attempted to prove the scientific authenticity of the doctrine of the original man throughout the 1960s.[34] In these discussions, the origins of black people are not said to be in the "universe," or in primordial space and time, but in every inhabited continent outside of Europe. This mapping of the world asserted that, in the beginning, all human beings were black.

But just how, then, did lighter-skinned peoples, not quite white or black, arise? Sister Tynnetta Deanar answered in poetic terms, explaining in "Black Beauty" how whites overtook the pristine world of blacks, and how they produced mixed groups of human beings:

The days have passed and we have seen
The manifestation of man's dreams,
From early Mesopotamia to the Kingdoms of the Nile,
To the ancient sands of Arabia to the Polynesian Isles.
Then there came the rise of Europe and with her mighty quake,
The pillars of black kings began to tremble and shake.
How suddenly it seemed to happen
That yesterday's Black Beauty was reshaped,
But the stiff gown of Queen Victoria
And the powdered whig [*sic*] of Marie Antoinette can[n]ot compare
To the silken garb of an Asiatic woman,
Nor to the ancient Egyptian's long black hair.
Today's fair skinned Asian knows full well
What the white man has failed to tell;
Of how white chiefs met with black chiefs,
Took their women and their girls,
And what one calls the Hamitic and Semitic unfurled.
Who is more proud of skin so fair
Thank the Black Race of America who wish to share
Their children and generations to come
With this white race of infidels,
Who from the Holy Lands were run.
All people admire their Black Queens
But the 20,000,000 in America who have their Kings.
Little black sheep who have lost their way
Who were once the greatest shall be again![35]

This version of the "fall of man" is a cautionary tale about racial integration and miscegenation. It attributes the loss of black power in the Afro-Asian world of Mesopotamia, Polynesia, Arabia, and the Nile to the forcible seizure of black women by white men. It also offers a critique of contemporary African American men who no longer act like "Kings," who do not treasure and protect black women, and it urges black women to recognize their own beauty.

The poem is also similar to "Black Man," the epigraph cited at the beginning of the chapter, in that it imagines black/Muslim geography to include Asia. Brother William's poem recognizes the diverse linguistic, phenotypical, and geographic roots of blacks/Muslims, but insists that on the whole blacks are still one and the same. In his poetic romp around Asia and Africa, Brother William sees the Muslim "black man" as possessing a common god, language, and character—all of which are constructed as Islamic. Whether the black man lives in the Middle East, China, or even Tibet, he is, at heart, a Muslim.

Both "Black Beauty" and "Black Man" offer sweeping historical views of black/Muslim experience in Africa and Asia. But other black history narratives circulating in the NOI presented far more detailed and narrow views of blacks/Muslims in time and space. In fact, some NOI intellectuals relied on canonical Afro-Eurasian Islamic sources to establish historical parallels between Afro-Asian Muslims and American Muslims. In "Muhammad's Message," a series of weekly comic strips that appeared in *Muhammad Speaks* during 1965 and 1966, Eugene Majied depicted the classic tale of the conversion of Umar ibn al-Khattab, the second caliph of Islam. His retelling of the story legitimizes the mission of Elijah Muhammad in terms of classical Islamic history while also showing the relevance of Umar's story to contemporary African American Muslims. While Majied does not identify his source for the story of Umar's conversion, it was likely one of the many English pamphlets and books on classical Islamic history circulating in the movement.[36] The setting for Majied's narrative is a classroom in the University of Islam, the movement's primary and secondary school. Majied depicts a black male teacher, dressed in the requisite dark suit and bow tie, who teaches a lesson in black history. Appearing before a group of boys and girls, the teacher explains the importance of history to his students. Elijah Muhammad, he says, "is giving us the knowledge of ourselves, and our true history. Our black fathers had many civilizations before the whiteman had come out of Europe's Darkness."[37] In the next installment, the teacher reminds students that "as Mr. Muhammad teaches us, the root of civilization is in Arabia, at the Holy City of Mecca." Identifying Mecca as the birthplace of the Prophet Muhammad of Arabia, the fictional instructor links the Prophet's mission to that of Elijah Muhammad. "Just as Muhammad of Today is opposed by unbelievers, and hypocrites in establishing Islam in the Wilderness of North America, so was the Messenger of that day opposed."[38] Once again, Majied uses the trope of the persecuted prophet to describe the similarity between the two figures.

In the next installment, Majied uses flashbacks to illustrate the story of how Muhammad of Arabia, whose message was initially rejected by many inhabitants of Mecca, asked God for someone to help him. In response, God sent an unlikely candidate, Umar: "Having been born in the 'upper class,' Omar was at first *opposed* to Islam [emphasis in the original]."[39] By calling Umar a member of the upper class, Majied implicitly compares him to "elite" African Americans, like Martin Luther King Jr. and Roy Wilkins, who had criticized Elijah Muhammad and the NOI. Like these critics of Elijah Muhammad, Umar harshly reacts at first to the mission of the Muslim messenger. He even beats a servant who converts to Islam.

At this point in the narrative, Majied interjects that Islam could not be stopped, even by such violence. Islam, the cartoonist explained, offered converts "meaningful salvation . . . salvation from ignorance, from spooky and superstitious idol-worship."[40] In making these comments, Majied is able simultaneously to reference Muhammad of Arabia's famous iconoclasm while also reiterating Elijah Muhammad's critique of African American Christianity, which he said encouraged blacks to delay their quest for this-worldly freedom and wait for other-worldly salvation.[41]

The Prophet's success, according to Majied, infuriated Umar, who pledged to silence the Message, even if it meant killing the Messenger himself. As Umar "whirled toward the Safa Hills, vowing to kill the Holy Prophet," a man cried out to him.[42] "Omar! You ride like a madman! Where to?"

"To kill that meddling Prophet! . . . Before he snares another follower!"

"Perhaps," the man screamed, "you should start at your own house! Your sister, Fatima, is now a follower!"

Umar rushed to his house, where he found his sister, Fatima, in prayer. He struck her. Then, filled with regret, he paused to question himself. "Have I lost my senses—attacking my own flesh and blood?"[43] The cartoonist emphasizes the great regret that Umar feels when he hits Fatima. The act is understood as unnatural, an attack on his "own flesh and blood." It jars Umar's conscience and prompts him to ask for his sister's Qur'an, which in turn leads to his conversion. Pleading the forgiveness of his sister, he asks to see the book that she holds in her hand. "Surely there must be some great truth in the book Muhammad has given to you." He then "retreated to a corner of the room . . . and as he read pages of the Holy Qur'an, the Divine truth and beauty of Allah's word gripped his heart."[44] After this epiphany, Umar rushed once again to the Prophet—not to harm him, but to embrace Islam. The story demonstrates that even a most unlikely figure can be redeemed, if he or she will only trust the innate instincts of familial, and by implication, racial bonds.

The last of the series on Umar appeared in December 1965, when the cartoonist concluded his work with what might be seen by a movement outsider as a rather anticlimactic gesture. Pointing to a picture of Elijah Muhammad, the classroom teacher counsels that "we must remember, children—this history of the Prophet of 1400 years ago was a foreshadow of what was to come today. . . . But Muhammad of today is doing a greater work than Moses, Jesus,

"Muhammad's Message." Cartoon by Eugene Majied. *Muhammad Speaks*, 19 November 1965, 27.

and Muhammad of 1400 years ago! He is raising a dead nation to become the guiding star of the nations! . . . From a people that has been crushed beyond recognition!"[45] The story thus ends as it begins—by explaining the importance of classical Islamic history in relation to Elijah Muhammad's claims to prophecy and by emphasizing the irresistible power of Islam to transform the lives of Muslims both in the past and present. At least one reader of *Muhammad Speaks* testified to its effectiveness. In a narrative explaining how her membership in the

NOI had made her life happier, Sister Aaronetta X Anderson from Milwaukee wrote that "the history of Islam in Muhammad's Message is very interesting, and made me more aware of the bravery of brothers and sisters. I am proud to be a Muslim."[46]

NOI leaders offered other proud examples of black heroism in classical Islam, including, for example, the contributions of Bilal ibn Rabah, an Abyssinian slave turned Muslim convert who became the first *muadhdhin*, or prayer-caller, in Islamic history. In November 1966, Elijah Muhammad sponsored the showing of an Egyptian film about Bilal, whom *Muhammad Speaks* dubbed "the first black man to embrace the truth of Islam," at the Rhodes Theater in Chicago. Muhammad Ali, the heavyweight champion, was on hand to shake hands with the Arab promoters of the film outside the theater.[47] The press release touting the film explained that Elijah Muhammad was sponsoring the event "as part of his unrelenting drive to bring knowledge of self, culture, and history to the American black man." The article included transliterations of Arab names based on Egyptian colloquial Arabic, indicating that much of its content was taken from the Egyptian promoters. It explained that Bilal, upon hearing the message of Islam, was "so impressed by it, he embraced it." His "employer," however, "so hated the Muslim religion that upon learning his friend had adopted the faith, became so enraged that he set out to do bodily harm to Belal by having him whipped many times and tortured." Fortunately, Abu Bakr, the man who would become the first caliph of Islam after Muhammad of Arabia's death, took pity on Bilal, manumitted him, and allowed him to practice the faith freely. According to the press release, Bilal went on to become one of the great companions of the Prophet Muhammad.[48]

This discussion of Bilal defined black Muslim identity in terms markedly different from those in Muhammad's myth of black origins. Unlike Majied's retelling of the Umar story, this narrative does not refer to Elijah Muhammad at all. It is also noteworthy that Bilal is called the "first black man to embrace the truth of Islam." That idea directly contradicts Elijah Muhammad's teaching that all Muslims, based on their very ontology, are black, including Muhammad of Arabia and all the Muslim prophets who preceded him. Instead, the press release frames Bilal in terms that would be familiar to many modern Arab and other Afro-Eurasian Muslims, especially African Muslims who have proudly claimed Bilal as a black ancestor.[49] For these Muslims, Bilal was indeed one of the first (perhaps black-skinned) Africans to convert to Islam; one might add that he was also one of the first *persons* to convert to Islam, according to many Islamic traditions.[50] One should not overemphasize the importance of one press release in characterizing the forms of black history narratives in the NOI, but its presence indicates that NOI members were exposed to several different Muslim history narratives, not all of which necessarily adopted Elijah Muhammad's readings of black history.

Artist and writer Eugene Majied, as we have already seen, was one major source for black history narratives. In addition to illustrating the conversion of Umar, Majied also retold the story of Khawlah bint Azdar, a heroine of the campaign to conquer Damascus in 634–35 C.E. The likely source for Majied's narrative was Syed Sulaiman Nadwi's *Heroic Deeds of Muslim Women*, a book later offered for sale in *Muhammad Speaks* by Books and Things, a Muslim bookstore on Lenox Avenue in New York City.[51] Though advertisements for the book actually appeared a few years after Majied had published his comic strip, it seems that Majied had already obtained a copy of Nadwi's text, which was published in English in 1961 and 1964. Majied's transliterations of Arabic names and his recounting of the story parallel the Nadwi version in precise fashion.[52] If Majied did indeed rely on Nadwi's text, it helps to illustrate the diversity of Islamic sources used by some NOI members to construct black history narratives. In the last chapter, we saw how many of the sources used by NOI members, including translations of the Qur'an and *hadith* manuals, were published by the Ahmadiyya movement. But Nadwi was no Ahmadi. He was a prominent Sunni Muslim scholar from India.[53]

Majied's recounting of the story of Khawlah is also important in that it offered an explicitly gendered reading of black Muslim history. While many of the historical narratives produced in NOI circles associated Muslim manhood with black political and psychological self-determination, the story of Khawlah offers a slightly different view. Addressing veiled female students in a history class at the University of Islam, the same male teacher who recounted the Umar story proclaimed that "no woman of the Caucasian West can compare in bravery, valor, or martyrdom with our Muslim sister[s] of that time!"[54] Women, according to the teacher, followed men into war and tended to horses, weapons, and the wounded. They buried the dead and fed the living.

But in the siege of Damascus, the teacher explained, women were forced into a more aggressive role. "The people," the teacher said, "were under the heels of the Romans, and were being fed Christianity (much like the American so-called Negro today)."[55] Abu Bakr, the first caliph of Islam, "directed Khalid Bin Walid [a general] to lay siege on Damascus—and remove the death-grip of Christianity." Muslim forces had effectively sealed the ancient city, when another "Roman" army of 90,000 marched on Muslim forces in a place south of Damascus called Ajnadayn. The Muslims, only 24,000 strong, were outnumbered. In response, Khalid ibn al-Walid ended the siege on Damascus and turned his forces toward Ajnadayn.

The Damascenes, however, saw a chance for revenge and attacked the contingent's rearguard, the section in which Muslim women were traveling. One particularly brave woman, Khawlah bint Azdar, swore in the name of God to fight the "infidels" unto death. Under attack, Khawlah grabbed a tent pole and subdued one of the assailants, crying "Allah is the Greatest!"[56] Soon her comrades followed suit. By the time they had finished, thirty Damascenes were dead and the honor of the Muslim women was saved. "Thus," the teacher announced, "the names of those brave women of Islam—Khaula . . . Afira . . . Afara . . . Salmah—will live in history." He added that "by following Messenger Elijah Muhammad, today's black woman will make history!"[57]

That said, the teacher turns to address the boys sitting in the classroom at the University of Islam. "However," he declares, "we must remember it was the men of Islam who carried its banner to astounding heights of glory."[58] This comment reflected the official NOI approach to gender. Though the movement encouraged black men to show respect toward black women, it also attempted to limit women's participation in the public sphere. Women were encouraged to raise and educate their children, be helpmates to men, and to work toward their own spiritual growth. In turn, it was promised, Islam would bring dignity, strength, and respect to black women.[59] To encourage women in their roles as nurturers, the movement required its female vanguard to attend Muslim Girls' Training (MGT) and General Civilization Class (GCC). Class activities and subjects included prayer, sewing, art, English, penmanship, refinement, beauty, hygiene, and cooking.[60]

On the one hand, Majied's closing comment about men's primary role as the historical defenders of Islam echoed the official gendered ideology of the NOI. He implied that only in social emergencies, like the one faced by Khawlah, should women enter the public sphere. Otherwise, they should cultivate the more "natural," nurturing aspects of their gender's psyche, as directed by Elijah Muhammad. On the other hand, most of Majied's cartoon portrayed Muslim women in a much more public and aggressive light than did Elijah Muhammad. Given the vigor and drama with which the women's military actions are depicted, it is tempting to read Majied's comment to the boys as insincere, and to wonder whether some women in the movement did not do so as well. In fact, as we shall see in chapters 4 and 5, the separate and gendered spheres provided spaces where women in the NOI could assert their public selves and, in so doing, craft an African American Muslim woman's culture that, at least implicitly, subverted the male dominance of the NOI's public face.

Khawlah was not the only historical heroine praised in the NOI. NOI intellectuals presented other examples of strong Muslim women from Islamic history. Columnist and sometime poet Tynnetta Deanar also drew on the classical age of Islam to locate the past greatness of women and to inspire black women of today. Citing an Orientalist work of scholarship by Dorothy Van Ess, Deanar briefly chronicles the philanthropic work of "Zodeidah [sic], wife of the famous Khalif, Haroun Al Rashid."[61] She was referring to Zubayda, or Zobeidah, indeed the wife of the caliph, Harun ar-Rashid.[62] She notes that Zubayda had a great mind for engineering, and had made available "wells and cisterns . . . for pilgrims along the whole 900 miles between Iraq and the Holy City Mecca in the Hijaz [in Arabia]. She also had the waterworks of Mecca constructed," Deanar wrote. "Another piece of her engineering was a gold tree in her palace with gold birds who sang by automatic devices." For Deanar, Zubayda evidenced the great potential of all black women. "It is indeed sorrowful to hear our people exclaim that the Muslim woman is a backward product of Islamic Society," she argued. "Without historical claim . . . many of our people insist upon reproach in the place of intelligent approach to the subject of the Muslim woman."[63] It seems that Deanar is referring here to the common Euro-American stereotypes about Islam's oppression of women, and attempts to prove them wrong in this short recollection of Zubayda. It is also important to note how Deanar draws on the history of a Muslim woman from the Middle East, once again showing that for many in the NOI, the history of blacks was the history of Muslims, and vice versa. Arabia and Iraq are presented as black territories. They, too, are part of the black Muslim world in Deanar's imagination.

By the early 1970s, when the NOI began to welcome at least dozens of black Latino converts into its ranks, one NOI member argued for the inclusion of black Latinos in the imagined community of blacks/Muslims. Diogenes X Grassal of Temple No. 7 in New York, who established a successful mission to Latinos in the area,[64] blamed the "white" conquistadors for the Christianization of Latin America and called on Latin American persons of color to return to their original faith. "The white man has had us tricked and divided for centuries in order to enslave us," he wrote in 1971. "The Spanish speaking Black brother of the Dominican Republic fights his French speaking Black brother of Haiti; the Puerto Rican Black brother thinks he is different from his Panamanian Black brother." In 1506, he claims, Spain ordered the expulsion of Muslims from Hispaniola, and the colonizers attempted to prevent Muslim slaves from entering Latin America from this point on. European white men, the "Archdeceiver," used missionary Christianity to divide blacks and Indians from one another and to slaughter and enslave people of color. Thus, he says addressing fellow Latinos, "you have not known Islam because Islam was not permitted to enter the Western Hemisphere by the enemies of the truth, the same white people who have enslaved us." Diogenes calls on "Latin Americans—of African and Indian descent—to know our true history, heritage, and religion (Islam) which has come back to us thanks to Allah, Who came in the Person of Master Fard Muhammad, to Whom praises are due forever, Who taught Islam to the Honorable Elijah Muhammad."[65] Like the narratives about Muslims in Asia and Africa, Diogenes' narrative moves back through time and space to establish the true identity of today's black and Native American Latinos, while also explaining why Christianity had become the majority religious tradition of these persons.

## Siting Islam in Africa and the Challenge of the Black Consciousness Movement

The NOI's emphasis on the roots of black identity in African and Asian history anticipated a renewed interest in black history that arose as part of the black consciousness movement in the latter half of the 1960s.[66] The black consciousness movement, an admittedly general label encompassing a number of groups and trends, emerged partly as a response to what some younger black, often self-consciously male leaders perceived to be the failure of the civil rights movements to address institutional racism, poverty, and black cultural self-determination. Many historians have highlighted the role of the 1965 riot in Watts, an African American neighborhood of Los Angeles, in helping to shift the public focus of younger African American activists away from the traditional campaign for civil rights toward a larger array of issues and concerns, including an emphasis on the need for solidarity with third-world liberation movements.[67] As we have already seen, however, African American sympathies with third-world nationalist and radical movements had begun several years before, in part due to the NOI's endorsement of decolonization and its insistence on defining all persons from Asia and Africa as "black."[68]

Nevertheless, it is fair to say that, after 1965, the supporters of black radical politics and black cultural renewal became more prominent in both American and African American public discourse. Advocates of a Marxist-style revolution, like the Black Panther Party's Bobby Seale and Huey Newton, called for a leftist coalition to combat poverty, racism, and other forms of oppression. Others, like Los Angeles's Ron Karenga of the US organization, were suspicious of any interracial coalitions, and repeated Elijah Muhammad's demand for exclusively black cultural, educational, and economic institutions.[69] Maulana Karenga, as he came to be known, also promoted the renewal of an explicitly Afrocentric style of cultural and religious practice among black Americans.[70] Downplaying the historical differences between African cultures, he adapted elements from various African harvest rituals to create the holiday of Kwanzaa, which included an exchange of African heritage symbols, a ritual lighting of candles, and the sharing of the unity cup. He also advocated the practice of seven key African values, which he defined as "*Umoja* (unity), *Kujichagulia* (self-determination), *Ujima* (collective work and responsibility), *Ujamaa* (cooperative economics), *Nia* (purpose), *Kuumba* (creativity), and *Imani* (faith)."[71] Though these principles included implicit references to Africa's Islamic heritage, especially in their adoption of certain Swahili terms, Karenga presented both the holiday of Kwanzaa and the seven principles as pure black African traditions that had nothing to do with Islam.

Like Karenga and other black consciousness enthusiasts, members of the NOI produced historical narratives that established the African roots of black collective identity and culture. Unlike many strains of the new black consciousness, however, these narratives emphasized the Islamic-ness of the black heritage in Africa. In 1966 and 1968, for example, cartoonist Eugene Majied fashioned black Islamic history narratives inspired by the historical achievement of sub-Saharan black Muslims.[72] In one of them, Majied composed a series of comic strips about the Songhay empire of West Africa. This series begins with a picture of a small black male child, dressed in coat and tie, asking his father, who is similarly dressed, about his people's identity: "Daddy, since we arn't Negroes, Who are we?"[73] After hearing an explanation that "we are members of the great aboriginal nation of black man," the son asks, "Did we ever have Presidents, or Kings, Generals and soldiers?"[74]

"Certainly, son!" the father answers. "We are members of the great Black Nation . . . the original owners of the Earth." Even more, he continues, "the greatest rulers and soldiers on Earth were from our Black Nation of Islam! . . . One such ruler was Sonni Ali." The child in the comic is referring to Sunni Ali, who established the Songhay empire in the 1400s and took control of Timbuktu in 1468.[75] "This great soldier-King," the father explained, "conquered almost all of Africa from Lake Chad to Tripoli, stretching to the Atlantic Ocean! He ruled with justice the empires of Ghana, Mali, and Songhay, and was patron of a great center of learning." Majied's construction of the black Muslim heritage in Islamic Africa highlighted the military and spiritual strengths of an exclusively black empire. "You see," the father pictured in the comic strip concludes, "Mr.

Muhammad teaches us the truth! We have a glorious history, and we can only disgrace ourselves by begging to integrate with others!"[76]

For other Muslims in the NOI, ancient Egypt was yet another example of a proud and civilized black nation in Africa. Ancient Egyptian ideas and symbols were constructed not only as black culture, but also, at least indirectly, as Muslim culture. Minister James Shabazz, for example, claimed that "Islam and the many benefits derived therefrom . . . will put [the] Negro back on the road to conquest of the lost arts and sciences that is his birthright. The ancient wonders to behold, the pyramids and the time-tested Sphinx, with broad nose, wise knowing eyes and thick lips so detested by the integration minded. This is some evidence of our connection with these past sciences of which we retain only our musical skills."[77] Minister James associated the practice of Islam with the retrieval of ancient black/Egyptian knowledge only partially retained by contemporary black persons in their musical abilities.

Similarly, Mrs. Betty X West, who wrote a column for *Muhammad Speaks* on home economics, embraced ancient Egypt as a symbol of black Muslim pride. In 1965, she is pictured with her husband, Leroy X West, in her home. They stand next to a statue of an ancient Egyptian guard of King Tut's tomb that she has painted black and gold. Above the statue is a felt wall hanging that features, in Arabic script, the words of what Muslims around the world refer to as the *basmala*, which the newspaper translates: "In the Name of Allah, the Beneficent, the Merciful."[78] This pairing of an ancient Egyptian artifact and the *basmala* might seem odd or even heretical to some Muslims, but not to Mrs. West. For her, these are complementary symbols.

The mixing of ancient Egyptian, Islamic, and NOI symbols can also be seen in naming patterns, especially in the names of businesses associated with the NOI. For example, a 1967 edition of *Muhammad Speaks* features classified ads from the following Cleveland-based enterprises: the Shabazz Restaurant, Barber Shop, Laundry, and Family Shoe Store (named after the lost Afro-Asiatic tribe of Shabazz from which African Americans originally came, according to Elijah Muhammad); the Asiatic Restaurant; the Crescent Sandwich Shop; the Kaaba Haberdashery; and the Omar Ice Cream Parlor.[79] Some prominent black intellectuals and leaders of the late 1960s and early 1970s were also influenced by this combination of Islamic, ancient Egyptian, and African American signs and narratives. For instance, Amiri Baraka's play, *Black Mass*, alluded explicitly to Elijah Muhammad's myth of black origins and incorporated various terms and symbols that evoked a black Islamic synthesis.[80]

At the same time, however, many of these figures, including Baraka, questioned the movement's exclusive focus on Islam as a source for black African

"Muhammad's Message." Cartoon by Eugene Majied. *Muhammad Speaks*, 11 March 1966, 27.

identity and culture.[81] For example, argues Melani McAlister, novelist Ishmael Reed, a well-known figure in the Black Arts Movement, "insisted on a different genealogy, one that challenged the connection to a black Islam and instead constructed a historical, religious, and cultural matrix that privileged Caribbean voodoo (in the United States, hoodoo) as the authentic African American religion." According to McAlister, Reed's 1972 novel, *Mumbo Jumbo*, also identified ancient Egypt "as a black African heritage that provides the site for an alternative vision of black identity as sexual, playful, intuitive, creative, and polytheistic."[82] In 1971, Chancellor Williams went much further, offering a blistering indictment of both Arabs and Islam in *The Destruction of Black Civilization*. As Stephen

Howe summarizes, Williams depicted Arabs as "relentless enemies of Africa, wreckers and traducers of all its indigenous achievements."[83] Stokely Carmichael, the former chair of SNCC and prime minister of the Black Panther Party, portrayed Islam in a similar fashion in a 1971 meeting on pan-Africanism in Newark, New Jersey. Islam, he said, was a foreign religion that had been brought to Africa by Arab conquerors and slave traders.[84] "Islam is not an African religion," he is reported to have said. "It invaded Africa, originating in the Middle East. The Muslim came with the sword in the most barbaric manner."[85]

NOI intellectuals criticized such views, countering with several different arguments. In response to Stokely Carmichael's criticisms, for example, Brother Robert 7X mounted a spirited defense of the notion that "Islam, as taught by the Messenger Muhammad, is the very pivot in the Black man's nature . . . [and] contains the key ingredient that will unite the entire Black world." Citing the *Encyclopedia Brittanica*, *Colliers Encyclopedia*, and *Americana*, Robert 7X dismissed Carmichael's ill-informed views toward Islam, noting that Carmichael's views mirrored some common Christian prejudices against Islam. "Christian dogma usually charges Islam as coming with the sword as a method of justifying and hiding the most atrocious acts of genocide ever performed," he claims. "These acts have been committed by Christian nations, such as the bombing of Hiroshima and Nagasaki. . . . In Viet Nam, it is a Christian government, not Islam, that is waging war against the people. It is a Christian government that has enslaved 30,000,000 Black people in North America and which colonized Africa. Islam has not done these things." Robert 7X also questioned Carmichael's view that pan-Africanism somehow contradicted the message of Islam. Briefly recounting a history of pan-Africanist leaders W. E. B. DuBois, Marcus Garvey, Kwame Nkrumah, and George Padmore, Brother Robert argues that "nowhere do we find in the history of Pan Africanism it denouncing Islam." He also notes, quite trenchantly, that "Mr. Carmichael presently resides in a country that has a population over 70% Muslim — Guinea."[86]

Several months later, in October 1971, Edward L. X Truitt of Ann Arbor, Michigan, offered commentary in *Muhammad Speaks* that took a different approach to the question of Islam's black authenticity, arguing that "it is not important to say that Islam is an African religion." This was the wrong question, said Truitt. While it was true that "Islam does have some roots of origin in the continent which the white man has named Africa, . . . what is important as the Honorable Elijah Muhammad teaches, is that Islam is a religion of the Original people, who are the Black, brown, red and yellow descendants of the Original Black Man, the maker and owner of the planet Earth." Combining elements of both supralocative and translocative black Muslim history narratives, Truitt explains that while the original black/Muslim man's roots lie in the Nile Valley and the holy city of Mecca, an area that is "only a hundred miles or so" from Ethiopia, black men came to rule the entire Afro-Asian world, including the river civilizations of the Ganges, Euphrates, and Nile. The teachings of Islam, as taught by prophets Abraham, Noah, Moses, Jesus, and Muhammad, then "spread throughout the circumference of this geographical area; thus, today Islam is strong in both Africa and Asia." Truitt calls for unity between all of these peoples, whom he identifies as residents of the third world.[87] In sum, Truitt attempts to change the terms of debate, dismissing the exclusive focus on Africa as site of the black man's heritage as misguided and offering an alternate view of black identity that incorporates Asia. For him, the key to understanding black culture is a proud identification with Afro-Asian Islamic history.

Another response to the black consciousness movement's siting of black identity in ancient Egypt and sub-Saharan Africa came from Diogenes X Grassal, who cautioned against "substituting the ways of non-Islamic Africa" for the culture of Islam. Studying Swahili and Yoruba, he asserted, was no substitute for learning Arabic. In fact, Diogenes blamed the white man for this renewed interest in languages that pose "no threat to him." He argued that Arabic, unlike Yoruba and Swahili, is an "unlimited" language of power, "a language full of manuscripts, data and information about our true history and sciences." (It seems that the writer was unaware of the rich literary traditions in Swahili.)[88] "With African languages we can only go so far." The white man knew this, according to Grassal, which is why he tried to prevent the importation of Muslim slaves into the Americas and why he expelled Muslims from Brazil after the nineteenth-century slave revolt in Bahia. "Islam," he asserts, "is the wisdom promised by Allah thru his Prophets to make us the head, and not the tail. . . . Islam means Black Unity."[89]

Diogenes' defense of Islam against the challenge of black consciousness reflected well-established nineteenth-century African American prejudices against the folk, or "primitive," cultures and languages of Africa. His approach constructed Islam as a more authentic source and expression of civilized behavior and black achievement, whether in West Africa, Egypt, Arabia, or Asia.[90] Charles 67X, editor of *Muhammad Speaks* in 1974, also responded to criticisms of Islam by pointing to its great accomplishments as a civilization. He condemned what he called "the sinister movement afoot in intellectual circles which seeks to poison the minds of young Black people against the great work of the Honorable Elijah Muhammad . . . and against Muslims in general, and against Islam itself. The movement," he claimed, "is propagated mostly by a motley collection of Africanists, and Black nationalists," giving Amiri Baraka, Roy Innis, and Owusu Sadaukai as examples. Their assault on the NOI often "takes the form of denouncing Arabs—and Muslims by association—for allegedly exploiting 'Mother Africa.' . . . And it usually includes references to the alleged destruction of African civilization." According to Charles 67X, however, "no amount of flagellation nor braying and complaining will alter the fact" that the first, most cultured, most intellectual, most enduring, most universal, most advanced, most perfect civilization "was and is Islam." He goes on to argue that Islamic civilization advanced mathematics, gave birth to the European renaissance, and sustained African "citadels of learning," including Timbuktu, Mali, Ghana, and the Sudan.[91]

## Conclusion

Charles 67X's opposition to the black nationalists of the early 1970s is significant, since it shows how one prominent member of the NOI pitted Elijah Muhammad and his interpretation of Islam against the mission of certain black nationalists and their version of black nationalism. The evidence presented in this chapter also shows, in a similar vein, how many of the historical narratives produced in the movement by both paid and unpaid contributors to *Muhammad Speaks* questioned, at least implicitly, many aspects of the black nationalist project of the 1960s. This observation flies in the face of many interpreters who classify Elijah Muhammad and members of the NOI as quintessential black nationalists.[92] In a certain sense, the movement was a classic black nationalist organization. It was called the *Nation* of Islam, and in the early 1960s, Elijah Muhammad, Malcolm X, and other NOI members were perhaps the most prominent African American advocates of a separate black nation, or at least a territory, where African Americans could determine their own economic, political, and social future—a nationalistic demand if there ever was one. Moreover, until the mid 1970s, *Muhammad Speaks* continued to print Elijah Muhammad's call for some "land of our own" to be donated by the U.S. government for the establishment of a black territory in the United States.

At the same time, however, Elijah Muhammad and many of his followers did not define the collective identity of blacks *exclusively* in terms of a desire for a separate nation or polity. Black identity for members of the NOI also encompassed more than a shared biology. What these history narratives show, over and over again, is that many in the NOI constructed black identity in terms of a shared history that was defined by its Islamic character. Of course, members offered differing understandings of their shared black/Islamic heritage, and they sited Islam in multiple times and places. Their supralocative narratives, those that defined black identity in primordial terms, saw blacks/Muslims as the universal "original man," and expressed a millennial hope that salvation in the figurative "Holy City" of freedom, justice, and equality would come through a proper understanding of their collective past. Transtemporal and transspatial narratives mapped the heritage of blacks/Muslims in various periods of African, Asian, and even Latin American history, offering tales of black achievement that were meant to inspire contemporary African Americans. Refusing to locate the history of blacks in one country or even on one continent, these stories adopted a *transnational* perspective toward black identity that rested upon its common Islamic roots. In the imaginative time and space of these narratives, African Americans were more than members of a nation. They were a people defined by their relationship to a religion.

This exploration of black history narratives in the NOI reveals how movement followers attached a great many meanings and significances to the word "Islam" during the 1960s. As NOI members defined it, Islam was not just a theology based on Elijah Muhammad's mythological and eschatological teachings. Nor was it merely an identification with the Qur'an, which was so central to the defense of Elijah Muhammad's Islamic legitimacy. Though many believers in the movement did define Islam as such, they also viewed it as a history that determined their ontological and existential identities as human beings of a particular kind. In the discourse of the NOI, Islam came to signify a notion of black communal affiliation that defined who one really was, is, and shall be. These persons constructed their identities in the imagined realms of Muslim time and space. Those historical narratives represented yet another form of Islamization in the NOI.

## CHAPTER 4

# The Ethics of the Black Muslim Body

Islam has made a woman of me —
the woman that was supposed to be.
It has made me respect our men,
It has made me a queen again.
The women in Islam are beautiful to see
Just the way I've wanted to be.
The clothes they wear are neat and clean,
The lengths they are befit a queen.
Beautiful sisters all can tell
Everything they do — is done so well.
When you see them, you know who they are —
Their beauty stands out like a shining star.
I give thanks to Allah every day
For guiding me to the righteous way.
Black women everywhere, hear what I say,
follow the Messenger, you'll get respect this way.
Black women everywhere, reclaim your own,
Ascend onto your rightful throne.
— Sister Linda X, "The Queen of the Earth,"
  *Muhammad Speaks*, 4 March 1966

From slave times until the present day, the care and protection of the black body has been a central concern in the formation of African American culture.[1] For much of American history, persons of African descent have been denied the most basic rights to protect themselves and their families from bodily harm and humiliation.[2] Even today, dramatic events such as the 1998 lynching of James Byrd in Texas or the sexual assault of Haitian immigrant Abner Louima by New York City police in 1997 continue to show how bodily safety can become a key concern of African American life. As a result, the black body has been and continues to be an important symbol of the struggle for black liberation more generally.[3] In the past, some African Americans have responded to the challenge of bodily safety by vigorously asserting the right to defend oneself against violence. Antilynching activist Ida B. Wells, for example, famously declared that a "Winchester rifle should have a place of honor in every home."[4]

But African Americans have also proposed many other strategies for the protection of the black body, as well—some of these have been explicitly political, while others have been more social and cultural in nature. To cite one example from this tradition in African American culture, nineteenth-century female poet and novelist Frances Ellen Watkins emphasized that individual black bodies, including female bodies, could be protected from slavery and other forms of violence through the collective actions of black families, the black race, and the American nation.[5] As scholar Michael Bennett has argued, "Watkins' bodily politics is based on an understanding that freedom can only be won through acts of resistance within the domain of power," including her own racial community and the nation-state.[6] Many of Watkins's late-nineteenth-century black peers took a similar approach, but also emphasized what might be regarded as the social and cultural dimensions of the struggle for equality. Advocates of what Wilson Jeremiah Moses dubbed "civilizationism" called for the disciplining, beautifying, and cleansing of the black body, assuming that a "civilized" black body would command more respect and recognition from whites. As clergyman and missionary Alexander Crummell explained in his 1895 Atlanta and Cotton States Exhibition speech, becoming civilized meant recognizing the "body, with its desires and appetites and passions as a sacred gift, . . . under the law of divine obligation."[7]

Elijah Muhammad and a broad array of NOI members, who might be regarded as twentieth-century heirs of these nineteenth-century African American traditions, shared the goals of protecting and civilizing the black body, which was constructed as a sacred gift from Allah. Like the poet Watkins, members of the NOI insisted that the protection of individual black bodies would only be possible through the nurturing of black families and the uplift of the black race. Unlike Watkins, however, they gave up on the idea that the American nation-state would protect them. Echoing the sentiments of nineteenth-century black predecessors like Crummell, Elijah Muhammad and his cadre of leaders and intellectuals also promoted the "civilizing" of the black bodies, associating civilized behavior with the values of thrift, sexual propriety, industriousness, and temperance, which they found sorely lacking in many of their black contemporaries. They argued that too many black men were emasculated, impure, and lazy, and blamed white supremacy and blacks themselves for the sad state of the black body, and by extension, the black race. In appropriating racist images of the black body, some NOI members also caricatured black women as deviant, promiscuous, and neglectful caretakers of black children.[8]

Both leaders and followers in the NOI argued that Islam could cure the black body of such physical and social diseases. In his 1957 work *The Supreme Wisdom*, Elijah Muhammad claimed that Islam "dignifies the black man. It gives him the desire to be clean, internally and externally. . . . It heals both the physical and spiritual by teaching what to eat, when to eat, and what to think, and how to act."[9] Like other black religious groups formed during the first half of the twentieth century, the NOI condemned various aspects of black popular culture that it associated with the moral decline of the black body, including the polishing of nails, straightening of hair, gambling, and the wearing of short dresses.[10] Black Muslims instead advocated "clean living," like many of their black brothers and sisters who were members of the Church of God in Christ, a black Pentecostal denomination, and other religious communities in which African Americans took part.[11] The NOI also eschewed pork, as did many black Jews, like the Commandment Keepers of the Living God.[12]

One important difference between these groups and the NOI, however, was that members of the movement understood their ethics of the black body to be Islamic in nature. African American Muslims appropriated many older, sometimes explicitly Christian themes of black uplift and recast them in an Islamic mold. Literally hundreds of followers wrote to the editors of *Muhammad Speaks* or contributed articles that explained how Islam, as taught by the Honorable Elijah Muhammad, had inspired them to change their diet, clothes, coiffure, and sexual behaviors. These documents and the available oral historical evidence indicate that for a large number of persons, the practice of Islam not only meant the private conversion of the soul but also the public display and physical reforming of the body, which was to be accomplished through strict discipline and purification. This is why some observers have labeled members of the NOI black Puritans.[13] But the believers understood themselves and their ethics to be Muslim, not Christian. Sometimes, they quoted passages of the Qur'an or utilized other recognizable Afro-Eurasian Islamic symbols in interpreting their ethics of the body as Islamic. For the most part, however, they understood a value or norm to be "Islamic" because it was issued as a commandment by their prophet, Elijah Muhammad, the Messenger of Allah. In either case, their ethics focused on the Islamization of the black body, a site that was depicted as a main battleground for the souls of black folk and the destiny of the black race.

## Diet, Purification, and Health

One area of emphasis for the NOI's official discourse on the ethics of the body was diet. From at least the middle 1950s until his death in 1975, Elijah Muhammad advocated dietary change as a major component of his project to resurrect the black body. In the Chicago temple during the late 1950s, believers received an eighteen-page mimeograph of permitted and prohibited foods issued by the Messenger. Permitted foods included small navy beans, string beans, June beans, white cabbage, cauliflower, eggplant, okra, carrots, mustard greens, turnips, spinach, tomatoes, celery, lettuce, green and hot peppers, white potatoes, fresh corn, radishes, asparagus, whole wheat bread, white fish, trout, bass, and salmon.[14] While red meat was also permitted, Elijah Muhammad encouraged believers to avoid it as much as possible, claiming that it was "not good for us" and difficult to digest.[15] Believers, said Elijah Muhammad, should also avoid processed foods with too many additives. When eating bread, for example, he told them to eat homemade wheat bread—the darker, the better.[16] Foods that were banned outright included lima beans, butter beans, black-eyed peas, green cabbage, collard greens, pinto beans, kidney beans, brown field beans, cornbread, carp, catfish, crustaceans, mollusks, rabbit, possum, squirrel, coon, and especially pig/hog/swine, which was "divinely forbidden."[17] Muhammad associated many of these foods with slave culture, which was uncivilized, according to the Messenger.[18] His prohibition of water scavengers like crab and shrimp may have also indicated the influence of Jewish and specifically Black Jewish kosher laws.[19] In fact, Muhammad permitted believers to eat foods prepared along strict Orthodox Jewish guidelines, arguing that this food was clean and healthy.[20] Moreover, he identified the consumption of pork as one of the worst possible offenses against Muslim dietary laws. Muhammad claimed that whites had bred the poisonous hog from cats, rats, and dogs for the purpose of making medicine, not food.[21] Many believers shared Muhammad's hatred for the swine. In fact, one female prisoner and NOI member in Texas is reported to have paced "up and down the [a]isles in the dining room removing the poison animal from her Sister prison inmates' plates and teaches them why." There is no report of how her sister inmates reacted to her zeal.[22]

In his many teachings on diet, including the two-volume *How to Eat to Live*, Elijah Muhammad also taught that believers should eat only one meal a day. According to Elijah Muhammad, limiting food intake would help believers live longer and healthier lives and save them money.[23] Follower Samuel 25X also said that while the Messenger's teachings may contradict "common superstitions of the type which urge people to stuff themselves with food," it was supported by the latest nutritional research. The writer compared Elijah Muhammad's rule to limit meals to one a day to a scientific study by C. M. McKay, "Effect of Restricted Feeding upon Aging and Chronic Diseases in Rats and Dogs," arguing that limited food consumption was the key to long life in human beings.[24] Muhammad also told his believers to fast as much as possible, since fasting "takes away evil desires."[25] If believers followed these guidelines, said Elijah Muhammad, they could also heal various illnesses. "High blood pressure, diabetes, cold and fevers, ailments of the heart, headaches, stomach aches and all types of ulcers can be cured and vanish under the right food and time that we should eat," he claimed.[26]

Muhammad also cast his dietary guidelines as a path to physical and spiritual purity, saying, to quote the old saw, that "cleanliness is next to Godliness." Believers, he said, should remove anything from their homes that was unclean, including dogs, which were depicted not only as unclean animals, but also as poor companions for black human beings. Criticizing "dog worshippers," columnist Jamillah Muhammad said that dog owners "suffer from a psychological or emotional illness and are really covering feelings of guilt and self-doubt." She argued that these persons needed to develop friendships among other human beings. Dogs carried diseases and they were expensive to maintain, she added.[27] "The Most Honorable Elijah Muhammad has warned us repeatedly to get these filthy disease carriers out of our homes and away from ourselves and our families and at no time should [we] see animals of this sort in the homes of Muslims under the guidance of Messenger Muhammad," she wrote.[28]

Illegal drugs, which were blamed for crime in the black community, were also outlawed. Discussing the violent criminals that plagued black neighborhoods and public housing projects in 1974, *Muhammad Speaks* editor Charles 67X argued that drugs and alcohol could lead to physical disease and a life of crime:

**FROM GOD IN PERSON**
**MASTER FARD MUHAMMAD**

By

**ELIJAH MUHAMMAD**
Messenger of Allah

Elijah Muhammad

**BOOK No. 2**

# HOW TO EAT TO LIVE

Book cover of *How to Eat to Live, Book No. 2*, by Elijah Muhammad. 1972. Reprint, Newport News, Va.: National Newport News and Commentator, n.d.

"Be they bent over with rot-gut alcohol, or nodding from the effects of poison-ous, dusty powders, forced into unwilling bloodstreams from filthy syringes which transmit double doses of death—the drugs, plus the hepatitis, the scars, the abscesses, the infections which come from using those nasty needles over and over, and over . . . whoever these attackers are, they are doing only what they have been taught to do against their own Black kind which is by nature opposed to such conduct."[29] Bad behavior was *learned*, and it violated the code of eth-ics that was, by nature, part of the black man from birth, according to Brother Charles.

Elijah Muhammad also outlawed the use of tobacco and the consumption of liquor, both of which were seen as poisons for the body. By discontinuing their use of liquor and cigarettes, some believers noted that they were able to save money for other purposes. For instance, in 1958 Brothers James 43X, Harvey 3X, and Jesse 3X of Temple No. 7 in New York City "pooled the money they saved from not drinking and smoking, which came to $84. To this they added weekly until the sum totaled $300. With this meager sum they opened a small grocery store." According to *Muhammad Speaks* correspondent Sylvester Leaks, the small store that they established in 1958 later expanded into two stores: "They employ nine people, and two own apartment houses." The three busi-nessmen credited Elijah Muhammad with their success, even though, as Leaks notes, there was a financial cost associated with operating the businesses ac-cording to Elijah Muhammad's ethical guidelines; by refusing to sell liquor and cigarettes, they lost a significant source of revenue.[30] In an effort to educate read-ers, *Muhammad Speaks* also featured medical reports of the potentially harmful effects of using tobacco or abusing liquor.[31]

Members of the movement associated these products not only with physical illness, but also with various social diseases contracted during slave times. Eu-gene Majied, who produced the cover of Muhammad's *How to Eat to Live*, drew cartoons for *Muhammad Speaks* that illustrated the physical and moral evils of bad food, cigarettes, and alcohol. For example, a December 1965 cartoon in *Muhammad Speaks* depicts how African American celebrations of the Christmas holiday encouraged drunkenness, poor diet, and gambling.[32] In this drawing, members of a family, many of whom are drawn as caricatures of Sambo, gather around a holiday table featuring massive amounts of food and alcoholic bever-ages, including eggnog, beer, and malt liquor. An overweight black woman says grace over a pig, which is served whole on a large platter. "We thank you for this food," she prays. The caption below the image declares that she is asking "God's blessing on his own curse!" In the next frame of the cartoon, an African American man unloads a truck of beer. A drunkard nearby declares, "Christmas don't come but once a year—if I get drunk I don't care!" Next, two men begin to throw dice, crying, "Come, Mary! Come, Jesus!"[33] The cartoon questions the religious sincerity of the Christmas holiday and also implicitly refers to the idea that some slaveholders provided slaves with liquor during Yuletide, making it one of the few times when slaves might relax and recreate.[34] In making the participants in the cartoon look like Sambos, Majied illustrates the supposed effects of drink, gambling, and pork on the black body. But he also closes his cartoon narrative by offering his readers a way out of this self-oppressive lifestyle. He depicts two rows of upright, disciplined Muslim men and women who wear, respectively, dark suits and white robes. They raise their hands in a prayer of supplication. The scene's sheer minimalism evokes dignity and honor. The path to such a life, says the cartoon, is available to all those who follow Elijah Muhammad.

Another of Majied's cartoons about the effects of a "slave" diet on the black body shows an overweight black man and woman sitting at a large, round dinner table that is graced by whiskey and large platters of pork, including the pig's head. The man's clothes are made to accentuate his large belly, and as he bends over the table, he seems oblivious to anything but the consumption of large quantities of hog, which he eats with his hands. Sitting at the opposite end of the table is his wife, listlessly smoking a cigarette. Meanwhile, their neglected child, a little girl with picaninny-style braids in her hair, squats on the floor, out of sight, and eats the scraps off her parents' table. The caption above warns, "Read what Allah has revealed of this poison swine! Eating the wrong food. It forms your features, and your characteristics." An explanatory note further condemns the hog: "The meal in this cartoon consist[s] of 100% swine. The gentleman is eating the feet. The swine is eaten by the black man from his snoot to his tail. The intestines (chitterlings) is the prided part of the ugliest animal, the silliest animal, filthy, smelly. He lives and thrives off of filth. Poison has little effect upon him. Lye, snakes, potash, take no effect on him. Allah said this animal was grafted from cat, rat and dog!"[35]

Elijah Muhammad encouraged individual followers and his mosques to establish businesses that would provide healthy food and employment opportunities to the believers. Throughout the 1960s and 1970s, *Muhammad Speaks* promoted and hailed these enterprises, which were established across the United States and in places outside the United States, including Bermuda. Gordon X's Meat Market, for example, located at 327 Blue Hill Avenue in Boston, promised to "deal exclusively in the best cuts of 'prime' and 'choice' kosher meats and poultry," and "to bring to the people the best at the lowest possible cost to them." At the store's opening, Minister Louis Farrakhan was on hand for a ribbon cutting and a celebration of Brother Gordon's accomplishments.[36] In New York, the Harlem-based Temple No. 7 Restaurant on 113 Lenox Avenue encouraged its patrons to "try our original bean pie and whole wheat muffins." Located in the "heart of Harlem," the restaurant also guaranteed its customers "pleasant surroundings."[37] In St. Louis, as in other cities, a whole row of Muslim businesses, only some of which offered food and baked goods, was created along the 1400 block of Grand Boulevard, near the temple. Believers called the area "Little Egypt."[38] There, as in other places, the businesses were often named after the tribe of Shabazz, the Afro-Asian tribe from which African Americans originally came, according to Elijah Muhammad.[39]

In Washington, the Shabazz restaurant was located along 14th Street, "one of the dingy sections of town," according to journalist and former child member of the NOI Sonsyrea Tate. When the Tate family would go out to eat in the early 1970s, they would generally patronize the Shabazz, which strictly followed Elijah Muhammad's dietary guidelines. "The brothers in the Nation who had turned the building into a restaurant with a health food store up front and a fish market on the side had done a great job of carving out a nice, spanking clean place for us to dine," she wrote. "But all around it the streets were ugly." Tate remembers that the restaurant staff "wore white chef jackets and hats," serving food from behind a counter. In accordance with the directives of Elijah Muhammad, the restaurant served "fish loaf instead of meat loaf, brown rice instead of white rice, and brown rolls made from 100 percent whole wheat flour." They also "served carrot fluff, a sweet blend of soft carrots, brown sugar, nutmeg, cinnamon, and enough eggs to make it fluffy like mashed sweet potatoes."[40]

In Chicago, the Salaam Restaurant, located at 83rd Street and South Cottage Grove Avenue, became a place not only where one consumed Muslim cuisine but also where one went to see and be seen.[41] For example, in 1968, Jesse Jackson's Operation Breadbasket met at the Salaam to conduct its weekly planning meeting over breakfast. In one photograph, members of the organization were depicted standing under a large star and crescent sign that towered above the restaurant.[42] In 1970, *Muhammad Speaks* also included a "Notables at Salaam" section, one of which featured pictures of WXFM radio personalities after the taping of their show, which aired each Saturday.[43] This section evoked the society page of the *Chicago Defender* and other newspapers across the United States. At the Salaam, it was said, one could enjoy civilized food in a civilized environment, one that reflected the true heritage of blacks/Muslims. Columnist Margary Hassain bragged that "magnificently colored and gracefully hung drapes, the soft, amber torch-type lights and the many chandeliers, the plush gold wall-to-wall carpeting, which sinks under your feet, the exotic music, the tasteful wall murals

Advertisement for Your Supermarket. *Muhammad Speaks*, 2 August 1974, 16.

depicting scenes of the landscape of the eastern-hemisphere [especially mosques and minarets], place us again in our natural place . . . a palace in paradise." She even equated dining at the restaurant with prayer, ending her article about the establishment with the words of the Islamic *adhan*, or call to prayer: "Come to prayer . . . Come to success."[44]

Elijah Muhammad also purchased several farms, promising to provide both job opportunities and the finest food to his followers. By 1970, the Messenger had bought farms in Georgia, Michigan, and Alabama. He also owned a dairy and a meat processing plant.[45] The NOI supermarket on 8345 South Cottage Grove in Chicago sold meat and produce from these farms, including watermelons from Georgia and chickens from Michigan.[46] In the 1970s, Elijah Muhammad also launched a fish business, first importing various varieties from Japan. In 1974, the NOI began importing Pacific Whiting from Peru, and called the venture Whiting H and G (headed and gutted).[47] The fish, frozen at "12 degrees below zero for longer freshness and more wholesome taste," was imported by ship from South America.[48] Through this enterprise, the NOI employed dozens, if not hundreds of black men to act as distributors, especially in the New York area.[49] For example, Minister Theodore G. X of Temple No. 50 in Oklahoma boasted of his success in selling fish through his local Shabazz Fish Market.[50] And Larry 14X, a staff writer for *Muhammad Speaks*, said that this high quality fish sold for 65 cents a pound, well under the market average of $1.10 to $2 for "comparable quality seafoods."[51]

Not all of Elijah Muhammad's food-related businesses solicited such reactions from followers. As the NOI's business empire began to grow throughout the late 1960s and into the 1970s, there were widespread rumors of corruption among the leaders of the NOI. Though believers were encouraged and sometimes commanded to support these businesses, they did not always do so. When fish sales were sluggish, for example, columnist Bayyinah Sharrieff scolded followers who were not purchasing enough fish. "He [Elijah Muhammad] is in the process of bringing you fresh good clean fish from the unpolluted waters of the Caribbean Sea and you say, 'Um, what kind of fish is this? I never had this before,' or 'I do not know about this fish,' or 'Our people won't want this, can't we get some other kind like we used to eat?'" Sharrieff reminded followers that "Allah and His Messenger well know what foods we need, and are well aware of where to get our food and necessities of life." In fact, she implied, those who refused to eat the fish were supporting his competitors, and in so doing were siding with Muhammad's enemies. "The opposers against the Honorable Elijah Muhammad are a foolish people," she said. "They are asking for death and shall receive it."[52] One might summarize Sharrieff's dead-serious position thus: those that don't eat the fishes may swim with the fishes.

Brother Rachi X of Temple No. 46 in New Orleans, Louisiana, may have also been contributing to the marketing campaign for Elijah Muhammad's canned fish business when he wrote an attack on "scavenger fish" for *Muhammad Speaks*, but his opposition to certain types of fish and crustaceans was not necessarily insincere or even unfounded in scientific fact. He noted that "the eating of such creatures as shrimp, lobster, crab, tuna, catfish, and clam present a danger to us for several reasons. They are either poisonous from their eating habits or they are po[i]sonous by nature." Whatever the cause, Brother Rachi was certainly right that seafood could be dangerous to eat, especially when improperly stored and prepared. His advice, like that of Elijah Muhammad, expressed a certain folk wisdom. At the same time, he also opposed the consumption of these foods for social and cultural reasons. "Many of you will say that my parents and their parents ate these creatures and 'if it was good enough for them, then it's good enough for me,'" he wrote. "You only show blatant foolishness and lack of love for yourself when you make silly rationalizations like this. Your and my foreparents only ate these creatures out of necessity in some cases, and ignorance in most." Scavenger fish were the food, he implied, of poor and uncivilized people, those who did not have the benefit of Elijah Muhammad's guidance. "We cannot use either of these as excuses today for Almighty God (Allah) has raised a Divine Teacher who is giving to us the proper knowledge of 'How to Eat to Live.'"[53]

Still, no matter how hard intellectuals and leaders of the movement defended their enterprises and the ethical directive of the Messenger, some believers ignored them. For another example, take Elijah Muhammad's advice about the consumption of refined sugar. "There is no need to draw sweets out of sugar cane and sugar beets to sweeten other foods that we eat when by nature all foods that we eat have some natural sugar or sweetening in them," he wrote in 1969.[54] "You eat too much sugar," he said in 1970. "That is why we are troubled with diabetes. We eat too much starchy foods [so] lay off all those sugar and starchy foods. . . . Use no drugs to keep blood sugar down. Just eat right. Stop eating sugar and starches and the sugar in your blood will clear up."[55] Nevertheless, Elijah Muhammad Jr., the son of the leader and proprietor of Amena Pastry Shop on 640 E. 79th Street in Chicago, who promised that his "modern," "spic and span" bakery would put "as much accent on health as on taste," seemed to use quite generous amounts of refined sugar in baking beautiful and elaborate wedding cakes.[56] One advertisement for the Shabazz Bakery on 440 East 79th Street in Chicago pledged to use only "nutritional ingredients without coloring, preservatives and other harmful chemicals" in its cakes and pies, but said nothing about sugar.[57] Jamillah Karim, a child of NOI members and now a professor at Spelman College in Atlanta, remembers eating bean pies made with refined sugar in the 1970s: "The bean pie I grew up on in Atlanta, among the best, is made with both refined sugar and white flour."[58] Both of those ingredients were objects of Elijah Muhammad's criticism.

According to Karim's father, Harvey B. Smith or Harvey X, the Baltimore version of the bean pie violated Elijah Muhammad's dietary directives in another way. "Baby, it was the best bean pie I ever had in my life," recalled the former minister of the NOI who is known now as Ahmad Karim. "But Minister Shabazz's [the NOI minister in Washington, D.C.] standards were very high. He wanted the best of natural ingredients with nothing artificial. But I was so crazy about this bean pie that I went on some research of my own." Minister Harvey traveled to Baltimore to visit the local NOI bakery, where he discovered that the bean pie was made with artificial flavoring. Though Minister Harvey tried to convince Minister Shabazz to allow him to make the bean pie using the Baltimore recipe, Shabazz refused. "My father thought it was a loss because he thought it would make more money," Karim recalls. But not all ministers were as strict as Shabazz. Different communities used different ingredients, according to Minister Harvey: "Some didn't use the brown sugar and the 100% whole wheat flour because you didn't get the desired taste. And expense may have been a factor."[59] What this incident helps to show is that the practice of Elijah Muhammad's system of ethics among his followers was not monolithic in nature. Bean pies could be made with white sugar in one city and with brown sugar in another. One could follow certain ethical guidelines while ignoring others, depending on one's own sense of values and the culture of control and enforcement in one's local Muslim community.

No matter which dietary guidelines they observed, many believers testified to the positive effects of following Elijah Muhammad's dietary rules. "The Messenger has given us more love than we have given ourselves," wrote Sister Josephine X of Detroit, Michigan, "because he teaches us the way to prolong our lives while we are steadily killing ourselves by taking into our system the wrong food and liquids."[60] Sister Beatrice X said, "Sixteen years ago I weighed more than 200 pounds. I was sluggish and always was 'down with something.' But today I am vigorous and active. I always have liked to work with food and children, which requires much standing. However, I work with food and children today with relative ease."[61] Sister Lydia Hazziez said that before "accepting Islam . . . I was always sick." But "since the Messenger taught us how to eat properly, my sick spells came to an end. He teaches us that what, how, and even when we eat has a direct effect on our health."[62]

Columnist Bayyinah Sharrieff admitted that when she first joined the NOI, she was "a little skeptical about my being able to limit my eating to one meal a day." Since other members followed this rule, however, she overcame her initial reluctance and began to follow this regime. Later, she learned to fast for one, two, or even three days at a time. As a result, she said, "I found that I reduced my weight to what I desired, I was physically stronger and healthy, and my mind comprehended things very quickly." She was able to avoid illness. In addition, her fasting contributed to what she described as an even greater desire for self-improvement: "I also found myself trying to be more exact about so many things [that] my desire to strive for improvement and perfections of self and work was strong." By controlling her diet, she developed a heightened sense of awareness similar to extrasensory perception. "Sometimes (it may sound strange to you) I would have an idea of what people were going to say and do prior to their saying or doing so," she testified. Sharrieff also became a vegetarian. As of 1971, she said, she had not eaten meat for two years. "Some worry about protein or vitamin deficiency," she conceded. "But if we ate the foods that the Honorable Elijah Muhammad tells us to eat, bean soup, fresh vegetables, brown rice, whole wheat bread, whole milk, we have no worries about protein or vitamin deficiency." She added that nursing mothers need not be concerned about following the NOI's dietary guidelines: "I breast fed my baby during the time that I ate once every other day, for as long as I desired (11½ months) and had plenty of milk."[63]

Allen 3X explained how following Elijah Muhammad's dietary laws saved his life. "As far back as I can remember," he wrote, "I suffered from headaches, heartburn and occasionally, hemorrhoids. . . . I existed on B. C., Stanback, and in later year[s], Dristan tablets. Then in the spring of 1964, the headaches became unbearable. I would take the pills but got little or no relief. One night, while lying in bed restless with a severe headache, something seemed to have burst inside of my head." Brother Allen decided to get X-rays and visited a chiropractor. During the examination, he explained to the chiropractor that it had been two weeks since his last bowel movement. The chiropractor responded by saying that this brother's headaches were related to his constipation. Brother Allen did not describe what treatments he received under the care of the chiropractor, and he did not indicate whether he felt better as a result of this care. Instead, he wrote that his healing began when he joined the NOI: "In August of 1964, something wonderful happened. The Honorable Elijah Muhammad came to Los Angeles. He spoke at the Olympic Auditorium August 9. I went to hear him and came in the Nation the following week. During the processing period, I attended the weekly Orientation classes. There I learned that Muslims eat once a day. So I began this practice at once." As a result, the brother testified, he began feeling better. "I noticed that, occasionally, my system worked naturally. With time it kept getting better. . . . Then one week while reading the Honorable Elijah Muhammad's column on 'How to Eat to Live' I was struck by something he said about eating one meal a day or one meal every other day: 'You will be treating yourself to life, and life filled with sickless days.' At this I began eating every other day. My system began to work perfectly."

Brother Allen 3X reported that his symptoms disappeared: "my head cleared up and felt light, muscles and joints became limber, and I felt energetic and youthful. . . . Though I ate every other day for four months, I had a glimpse of what it feels like to be sixteen again." In a statement indicating that he might have been suffering all along from hyperglycemia, he added that "as long as I stay off pastries and minimize my intake of starches which the Honorable Elijah Muhammad teaches us are not good for us anyway, . . . I don't have any problems." Of course, it is not possible to know for sure why Allen 3X started to feel better. Perhaps dehydration from untreated diabetes had been the root cause of the constipation and the headaches all along. Or perhaps he suffered from a spiritual or psychological ailment.[64] Whatever the cause of his illness, what we can know is that for this believer, following the dietary laws of his prophet made him feel better. "I wrote this article," Allen 3X concluded, "because I know that many Black people suffer needlessly from many symptoms that could be eliminated by putting into practice what the Honorable Elijah Muhammad teaches. . . . This done, they would bear witness that the Honorable Elijah Muhammad, the last and greatest Messenger of Allah, is fulfilling that prophecy, attributed to Jesus, wherein it reads, 'I am come that ye may have life and life more abundantly.'"[65]

In sum, following the dietary rules of the Honorable Elijah, according to many NOI members, was good for body and soul. A Muslim diet purified the black body, kept it morally clean, and made it physically strong. It also contributed to the economic health of the communal body, which was sustained by commercial enterprises that employed believers and added to Elijah Muhammad's personal wealth.

## Dress and Adornment

For most members of the NOI, becoming Muslim also meant changing the way one dressed and adorned oneself. Elijah Muhammad issued a gendered set of guidelines concerning dress, coiffure, and adornment, directing men and women to present themselves in a "civilized" manner. Men were to wear dark business suits. Women were to dress modestly and avoid makeup. Believers were also supposed to fix their hair in an Islamic fashion. "There is no need to conk, fry, process or slick down with 'bear grease' our hair," said Ermine X Lowe. "We find, under the impact of Islam, that it is indeed a divine blessing to be unique—and our hair and color help make us that. As Christians, we feel so ashamed of the blessings God has given us, in His wisdom, that we bleach our skins and suffer any kind of indignity or hardships to make ourselves look like some grotesque caricature of our open enemy. . . . Only through love of self and kind," she said, "can one achieve self-respect."[66] Some men and women also wore jewelry especially made for members of the NOI. Yusuf A. X Gross of Washington, D.C., offered rings, pins, lavalieres, earrings, tie clips, and cuff links made with enamel and gold. Most of them featured the star and crescent, Islamic symbols that were shared by members of the NOI with Muslims from around the world. Elijah Muhammad endorsed Gross's business and wore a "ceremonial Muslim ring, designed and made especially for him by Brother Yusuf."[67]

Much of the discussion on dress code in *Muhammad Speaks* focused on women's dress. Contributors to the newspaper recognized the countercultural nature of Elijah Muhammad's guidelines on women's dress and argued that women faced incredible social pressures to conform to contemporary fashions. According to columnist Tynnetta Deanar, "the Black woman who puts away the short western style of dress and social habits and adopts the Muslims' style of dress and social etiquette becomes an object of mockery and cruel discussion. Likewise, the Black woman who passes by the cosmetic counters and prefers the clean, natural look to the facial makeup worn by her dark skinned sisters . . . she again becomes an object of scorn and ridicule."[68] But Deanar and others attempted to cast women who gave in to such pressures as weak and misguided. In fact, NOI intellectuals devoted significant energy to comparing the civilized and modest men and women of the NOI to unconverted African Americans who impersonated the white slavemaster's fashions and hairdos. African American women who wore makeup were also the subjects of great criticism. In one of Eugene Majied's cartoons, for example, a scantily dressed, high-heeled, buxom, and overweight black woman wearing a fur approaches a Muslim woman dressed in a long white robe and headscarf. She mocks her Muslim sister, crying, "What happened to *you*? No Make-Up!!!"[69] Of course, the cartoon makes clear that it is the uninitiated woman who is truly mocked. Below the scene the caption reads, "The so-called Negro must clean up," associating cleanliness with modest dress and plain adornment. The cartoon links the wearing of heels and makeup with impurity and a loss of dignity.

Several writers in *Muhammad Speaks* associated immodest dress with white people and argued that black women must dress differently in order to be true to their racial identity. Tynnetta Deanar, for example, explained in 1962 that "nothing is wrong with the white woman's dress because it is her dress and she has the right to wear it as short as she desires." But black women, she said, should not follow her lead. "Morally, spiritually, psychologically, internally, externally, ethnically, mentally, physically and technically we have by our appearance gravely retrogressed into oblivion. . . . We are simply playing the part of 'copycats.'" Deanar advised her black sisters to "be yourself" by developing "styles of dress conforming to the personality of your own people. Then you will be loved, respected and admired the world over! Remember that there is as much difference between the white woman and the black woman as night is from day!"[70] Deanar made the same argument about cosmetics, which had been invented, she said, to cover up the naturally "unattractive" white woman. "The so-called Negro woman," she proclaimed, "is naturally beautiful without the agency of the white man's cosmetic industry." She also noted that buying cosmetics was a terrible waste of money, criticizing the advertising industry and capitalism more generally for convincing women that they must wear makeup to be beautiful.[71] Another believer, Sister Wilma, also remarked on what she regarded as the cultural irony of cosmetics, products that were designed to make white women look "black." Addressing black female readers, she asked, "Is it not the desire of the white woman to imitate your beautiful warm skin, full eyebrows, dark beautiful eyes, ample nose and full mouth that makes the cosmetic industry a multi-million dollar business?" Any black woman who used makeup, she concluded, is "attempting to imitate those who imitate her."[72]

The criticism of immodest dress and the use of cosmetics as a betrayal of one's true black heritage had a long life in the movement. Ten years later, Sister Claudine X of Temple No. 26B in Oakland, California, echoed Deanar's comments and argued that the imitation of white women's dress styles resulted from an inferiority complex. In the past, she explained, "we were told that to get ahead, we must pattern ourselves after the social status of the white race, which in reality is designed for the white race's benefit primarily. . . . We as Black women thought the criteria in being dignified, honorable, and respected, was to excel in imitating the white woman. We have in the past gone to extremes in painting our faces with cosmetics, dying and tinting our hair, bleaching our skin to look like her." According to Sister Claudine, such behavior is a denial of one's black racial heritage. "By disowning any qualities of naturalness and the rejection of self trying to imitate the white woman, we became a symbolic image of racial shame, mockery, and pity. . . . Little did we know then that no nation in the world is respected and honored above the respect and honor that a people bestow upon their women." Sister Claudine said that Elijah Muhammad had changed her life and the lives of other women by offering guidance on how to dress: "That once shameless, aggressive, loud, boisterous Black woman now has absorbed the ingredients from Allah's Messenger that enables her to be extremely intelligent, submissive, modest, refined, and well cultured."[73]

Several other writers in *Muhammad Speaks* criticized black women for donning the popular fashions of the day, associating this "artificial" dress with the decline of black civilization and the coming of the apocalypse. In "How to Avoid Divine Chastisement of Modern Babylon," Sister Geraldine of Temple No. 7B in New York criticized the attitudes of the black middle-class sisters who reject "the Message to clean up." She argued that the middle-class woman was "having too good a time being like the women she reads about in the slick paper magazines and watches on TV and in the movies. She is blinded by the razzle dazzle of the fool's gold set forth in the mass communications media." Sister Geraldine compared the middle-class black woman to Pinocchio, Pygmalion, and Trilby, arguing that "all are artificial creations, made and programmed to look and act in a predetermined manner." But she also condemned "the black sister from the ghetto [who] has lived for so long in filth and dirt, in smelly, run-down buildings crawling with rats and roaches, amid garbage covered streets, that she is unable to relate to the idea of a 'clean' life." Both middle-class and poor black sisters, she said, "are locked in a vice which will doom them to be destroyed in the Divine chastisement and ultimate destruction of this modern Babylon which . . . is America." She begged them to join the movement and become "the rulers of the New World of Decency and Righteousness which dawns on your horizon. The choice is yours alone to make, dear sister. You may remain . . . in the mainstream of 'American culture,' or you can, if you have the strength of your convictions, follow the Messenger of Allah."[74] This was an important observation that shows how the thinking of at least one female member of the NOI linked respectable dress and adornment to Elijah Muhammad's teachings about the end of the world. For Sister Geraldine, African Americans who refused to dress and adorn themselves in a naturally black/Islamic fashion would be subject to destruction, right along with white Americans.

In 1972, Dorothy Wedad linked immoral dress not only to the decline of black civilization, but also the decline of black manhood. Her critique of women's fashion and its relationship to gender relations sounds uncannily like some of the reactionary opposition to the Equal Rights Amendment and feminism more generally. While issuing a familiar condemnation of women who wear revealing clothes, she also blamed men for encouraging and allowing such behavior. "[The scantily-clad sister] is a disgrace to civilized society and you brothers who whistle and make suggestive comments are helping to encourage her to wear these filthy garments." Wedad encouraged men to take control of their women.

"If a Black man allows his woman, whether it is his mother, wife, daughter or sister, to wear these styles, he needs to be horse-whipped," she said. "Most Black Women do not know what is good for them. The devil has so destroyed her with his hand-me downs of freedom that she thinks she can do just what she wants. You can't tell her anything. If you try to enforce your will on her, she may call the devil police on you. If she goes into the devil's courts, nine and a half out of ten times she will win." Wedad concluded, as one sees again and again in this genre of *Muhammad Speaks* commentary, by asking men to join the NOI, which will put them "on the road to controlling yourself, your home and your woman."[75]

Many in the NOI were proud that they became associated with conservative dress and "civilized" relations between men and women in the minds of both blacks and whites outside the movement. For example, one Newark, New Jersey, woman said that she delighted in the "respect that you gained from the brothers. When we wore our garments, and covered ourself, there was a different respect from the brothers on the street than you got if you wore a short dress."[76] Sonsyrea Tate also remembers her grandmother dressing for Sunday meetings at the mosque, explaining that "you could tell she was proud by the way she carefully balanced her Nation-issued uniform hat on her head."[77] Many women at the time also wrote to *Muhammad Speaks* to explain how their lives had been changed as a result of following the movement's guidelines on dress and the care of the body. "When I move about the city," said Gertie M. Kirk of Los Angeles, "I feel proud and dignified in my long dresses. I have something that no one can take away from me — Islam."[78] Sister Shirley Moton of San Francisco explained that she "wore the clothes of a civilized people. My dresses are far below my knees and I love it. This makes me respect myself better but it also makes other people respect me. In all the civilized nations of the world, the civilized woman wears dresses down to her ankles. Only uncivilized women feel they have to be half naked. The Caucasian woman is a good example." She added that proper dress is only one component of claiming her natural beauty. "The Honorable Elijah Muhammad teaches us that we, black women in America, are the most beautiful of all women. We have our own natural beauty and we do not have to be made up by using the white woman's makeup. To bring out the best of our appearance, we must eat the right food and live the right (healthful) life."[79]

Sister Edna Mae 2X from Mosque No. 1 in Detroit, Michigan, described how her transition from a party girl to a model Muslim had changed her perception of herself. "I prayed to Allah . . . for cleanliness, because I knew God would not accept me as I was. Allah showed me my nakedness so I gave away my nude party dresses and pants. He made me aware of the poison stick, whiskey, beer and wine. He took away from me the 'cool stick' called 'marijuana.' I cut off my bleached-out hair, pulled off the mask of make-up and found my way to Muhammad's Mosque." For Sister Edna, following the Messenger's teachings about dress and diet was central to becoming a Muslim. "May Allah be praised," she wrote, "for directing the course of my life to the door steps of the Messenger—Islam." Like others, Sister Edna witnessed that she now felt proud of herself. "Now I no longer feel ashamed when I walk the streets of this wicked society, from my head to my ankles are covered. My attire is not up to my 'sit-down part' showing my private places. My face is not plastered with Helene Curtis, Max Factor, or the sort." She encouraged others to join her in the movement: "To you my beautiful black sisters of North America . . . you too have a place in this beautiful garden of paradise where perpetual peace, and love—brotherly and sisterly love—flows forever. Know that you are a queen—queen mother of civilization."[80]

This trope of the modestly adorned black woman as an object to be protected and worshiped also found expression in verse. Sister Beverly 3X wrote:

Years ago, hemlines were not too short, but the clothes fit tight:
I thought I was really all right.
A stone fox? No! An ignorant fool, following the devil's evil rule.
Now, my clothes fit neat and down to my ankle;
To the Messenger of God, I am forever thankful.
The most Honorable Elijah Muhammad teaches us the beauty of modesty.
Cover up, married one; only your husband should see.
Cover up, single one, for your husband-to-be.
Clean, long Muslim clothes, stylish and chic—
Welcome, dear sisters, to our open arms!
Islam will bring out your hidden charms—
Charms of a righteous nature you didn't know you had;
From Wickedness to righteousness will make the devil mad.
Pray to the true and living God; have no fear;
Believe, have faith. Allah (God) our Savior and our leader and teacher
      are here.
They give us backbone to be in this world but not of this world;
The Messenger says "Black woman, you are more precious than any
      genuine pearl."[81]

For Sister Beverly, to wear the right clothes was to follow Elijah Muhammad faithfully into a heavenly state of being in the here and now.

By the late 1960s, the clothing styles and hairdos of some NOI members began to reflect the influence of the black consciousness movement. As we have already

"Whom Shall You Serve?" Cartoon by Eugene Majied. *Muhammad Speaks*, 9 September 1964, 5.

seen, one strain of that movement, symbolized by Maulana Karenga's appropriation of African traditions in creating the holiday of Kwanzaa, emphasized the need for African Americans to claim and practice what was represented as a more authentically African or black way of life. Many African Americans, whether officially part of the black consciousness movement or not, proudly displayed and touted their original black style, often simply called "soul," that indescribable thing that all black people shared. "Soul" might include listening to soul music, eating soul food, getting the right haircut, wearing a dashiki or a caftan, "giving skin," and walking with a certain gait.[82] As various African American "soul-ways" gained in popularity among African Americans, Elijah Muhammad and some leaders attempted to ban their practice in the NOI. In 1968, Elijah Muhammad prohibited "African dress and hair styles." He warned members "against accepting traditional African tribal styles and garments with gay colors," saying that women who wore them "will be dismissed from now on, from the circle of Islam." Though he did not explicitly call the dress uncivilized, one can hear the echo of such a claim in his criticism of "tribal" wear. "No style of dress is to be worn, but the style of the real Muslim people and the one that I am offering you. The head piece of traditional and tribal African people who are other than Believers of Islam is also forbidden for you to accept," he said. "God is only after you to make you an example for the world to be guided by. You are being given the tops of Divine Wisdom and He wants to make you the greatest of all people of the earth."[83] A year later, in 1969, the Messenger also reminded male members of his ban on beards, calling them unclean and "non-modern."[84]

In 1969, Sister Kathleen X of Mosque No. 25 in Newark, New Jersey, advised sisters and brothers to "shun the Afro," arguing that the "wearing of bushy hair is uncivilized." This sister challenged the idea that the Afro was a more authentically African style of expression. "Examine pictures of the Original people of contemporary Africa," she wrote. "Of course you do not find plastered-down, greasy coifs. But, you cannot say these hairstyles are towering fly-catchers, either. In civilized countries, the African appears to be intelligent and modest. His hair is neat and becoming. His dress is the costume of his homeland. One can readily match costume with country; because each country has its own particular costume. It is worn in beauty and splendor. It is worn as a lounging outfit or as a work suit." African Americans who choose to wear Afros, she argued, were imitating the "native Bushman," who "would not conform to civilization and is living a savage life." Sister Kathleen concluded her article by reminding fellow members of the fashions and coiffure that the Messenger mandated for African Americans: "He teaches us that we should use only a warm comb in our hair and we should keep our costume neat. We have a costume! Brothers in blue and Sisters bedecked in white (symbol of purity) can be seen in Muhammad's Mosques throughout the country. This is a national uniform which identifies a clean, civilized, and righteous people."[85]

But not all members of the NOI followed these rules. Some women in the NOI, particularly young women, attempted to put aside the white gowns of their older sisters and experimented with African-style *kinte* cloth. These women still covered their hair and their legs, but wore colorfully patterned dresses that looked decidedly different from the normal female dress code in the NOI. Correspondent James L. 4X of the *Muhammad Speaks* New York bureau hailed this style of dress as another victory for modesty, despite the fact that this fashion varied from the black Muslim female norm. In 1969, he wrote a story about two New York University undergraduates Irish Joseph and Darlene Booth, who had been convinced by an NOI missionary to dispose of their miniskirts and to start wearing ankle-length dresses. The two "co-eds," as they are called in the article, reported that while the change of dress had solicited some negative comments at first, they felt like male students and others showed them more respect in their day-to-day interactions and activities on campus. The correspondent mentioned nothing about the style of their garments, but they are pictured wearing dresses made of African-style cloth.[86] The fact that they wore such styles in 1969, well after Elijah Muhammad had published his objections, shows once again that local communities and members of the NOI ignored some directives of Elijah Muhammad while adhering to others.

As Elijah Muhammad's business empire grew, the leaders of the NOI also encouraged or sometimes pressured female members to buy official uniforms manufactured by Elijah Muhammad's clothing factory in Chicago. This policy placed an undue burden on some members of the NOI. Some could not afford to purchase the uniforms, which cost the hefty sum of fifty dollars in the 1970s, according to one member.[87] Some members attempted to help their brothers and sisters meet the new dress code requirements by making clothes for them. Take one sister, whom we will call "Amina." After joining the NOI in the 1950s, she eventually left her job as a domestic worker and became a seamstress. She made clothes for her children and designed her own draperies and slipcovers. But she also sewed for others, sometimes charging them and at other times donating her labor. When her local mosque established an elementary and secondary school, she volunteered to make the school uniforms. "We found a company that would sell us wholesale fabric, and we ordered the fabric," she recalled. "I designed the school uniforms at that time for the girls, and I had a couple sisters to sew, and I found sisters who needed the money, not just sisters who were trying to get rich." They made jumpers, coats, and jackets of different colors, depending on the season. "In the winter time, the colors were gray. Spring of the year, summer, were beige." She would also provide adult females with uniforms that she made herself. "I didn't charge the sister a lot, because we had a lot of sisters embracing al-Islam that actually couldn't afford the garments we were wearing. So, I would sew for them for nothing."[88]

Clothes and other forms of adornment played an important role in the making of the black Muslim body. A clear form of public identification, Muslim styles of dress and adornment became a form of resistance against potential harassment by men and what many female members saw as the temptation to imitate white fashions. NOI members, both male and female, also testified that adherence to these codes of ethical behavior made them feel proud, dignified, civilized, and respectable. By following the guidelines of their Messenger, said the believers, they were also expressing their true identity as God's chosen people. Muslim dress and adornment was a sign of their salvation, and sure protection against the apocalyptic punishment that non-Muslims would face at the end of the times. Finally, Muslim dress and adornment marked the gendered boundaries between men and women, expressing a widely held belief that the modest and moral woman deserved to be protected and cherished by strong black men.

## Protecting the Body and Reproducing the Race

Throughout the 1960s, various images in the NOI represented the black male body as broken and beaten, sometimes literally, other times figuratively. *Muhammad Speaks*, for example, regularly featured images of the abused male body in its coverage of police brutality against members of the movement. Articles chronicled a range of minor annoyances like the New York Police Department's harassment of NOI newspaper salesmen to major incidents like the "cold-blooded killing of one [Ronald Stokes] and shooting of seven unarmed Negroes" at Mosque No. 27 at 56th and Broadway in Los Angeles.[89] These Muslims who opposed integration and supported black self-determination and separatism were depicted as proud and dignified men who were brutally and unjustly victimized by white police officers, government officials, and slavemasters.[90] Many figurative images of the abused male body also appeared in temples and in the pages of *Muhammad Speaks*. In the early 1960s, for example, E. U. Essien-Udom reported that a prominent banner displayed in Chicago's Temple No. 2, which was also shown in other temples across the country, depicted a black man "hanging from a branch." Directly above his head was the flag of the United States. Opposite him was the cross, "another symbol of oppression, shame, suffering, and death." Below the cross was written the word "Christianity."[91] "That flag and the cross," one Muslim told Essien-Udom, "have been symbols of the misfortune and slavery for black people. The sign of the cross represents murder and wickedness since its inception, Christ the Prophet was lynched on that cross and ever since the so-called Negroes started bearing it they have been catching hell on it."[92] In interpreting these symbols of American nationalism and Christian religion, this informant constructed a painful historical narrative that invoked the whipped and broken black male body as the mirror image of a helpless Christ crucified.

Various cartoons and images in *Muhammad Speaks* also represented black men, especially black ministers, who willingly supported the civil rights movement as undignified black bodies. They were pictured on their knees, as small in stature, weak in strength, literally begging the white man to accept them as equals.[93] These African American advocates of racial integration and civil rights were also seen as emasculated figures susceptible to what NOI intellectuals represented as the seductions of loose white women.[94] In one of Eugene Majied's cartoons, for example, an obsequious-looking black man sits on a couch next to a cross-wearing, cigarette-smoking, whiskey-drinking, white female skeleton. The female skeleton is drawn representing the forces of the Christian-led civil rights movement: the word "integration" is tattooed across her chest and the sentence "Christianity tempts her slave" is written across her legs. The solicitous black man who leans toward her smiles and says, "Sure—I love everybody."[95] The loss of black manhood is thus linked not only to a love of white women, but to bodily impurity, integration, and Christianity as well.

In blaming weak black men for the failure of black political and economic self-determination, some NOI leaders also criticized black men for failing to protect black women from white male sexual abuse. Malcolm X, for example, reported in his *Autobiography* that he "would become so choked up" over this issue that he would "walk in the streets until late into the night." Working as an assistant minister at Detroit Temple No. 1 in the 1950s, Malcolm lamented the "rapist slavemaster who emasculated the black man." He cited these painful memories of slavery when confronting his male audience members at the Temple, asking them to "*think* of hearing wives, mothers, daughters, being *raped*! And you were too filled with *fear* of the rapist to do anything about it!" He blamed black men for the slaveholder's abuse, saying that their weakness had produced a black race "polluted" with white blood.[96]

Elijah Muhammad and NOI leaders offered various methods to rid black men of these supposed fears, to strengthen their bodies, and to protect themselves and black women. Among them, said the Messenger, the regulation of sexual desire through the adoption of a strict code of Islamic ethics would be key to the psychological, spiritual, and physical advancement of the black race. Sexuality thus became associated in movement discourse with both biological issues of reproduction and with the destiny of black people more generally. Black men were encouraged to control and regulate their own sexuality and that of women. While criticizing black men for their weaknesses, however, NOI leaders also offered numerous counterexamples of black men who had converted to Islam, and in so doing had become strong and disciplined.

There was no more potent symbol of the strong black Muslim male than Muhammad Ali, the heavyweight boxing champion. On one hand, Ali was seen as another victim of white Christian injustice. In a 1968 edition of *Muhammad Speaks*, for example, a reprinted political cartoon depicted the Christ-like suffering of Ali, who had been stripped of his world title in 1967 for refusing to serve in the U.S. military during the Vietnam War. Ali is seen hung on the cross, arms outstretched, hands covered by boxing gloves. Several pairs of white hands rip off Ali's clothes, which are labeled with the words "World Champion." One pair of white hands throws dice. Below the cartoon the newspaper's editorial

Cartoon by Eugene Majied. *Muhammad Speaks*, 12 November 1965, 6.

caption states, "Christian Cross, which is responsible for so much oppression of Black people, was depicted recently . . . as the instrument by which Muhammad Ali was 'crucified' at hands of white America."[97] On the other hand, Ali was no suffering servant. Picture after picture in *Muhammad Speaks* depicted him as physically strong, pious, and devoted to Elijah Muhammad. There are pictures of the "Muslim champ" training for matches; of the famous "blow heard around the world" when Ali defeated Sonny Liston to win the world heavyweight crown; of Ali performing the *salat*, or Islamic prayer; of the grateful champ studying with his teacher Elijah Muhammad; and of "Minister Muhammad Ali teaching principles of Islam" at a Houston mosque, where he issued a blistering rhetorical blow to the image of a pig.[98] Ali's wife, Sonji, even shared her recipe for roast beef, promising that it was "food high in energy content" necessary to a man's health.[99] Ali himself credited Islam for his physical strength and his victories. "Physical conditioning is a science," he said. "It is a science which the religion of Islam actually has helped me to master. That is why I am able to stay inside the ring—as in my fight with [Ernie] Terrell—for 60 solid minutes and come out without being exhausted." He encouraged others to learn from his example and become a follower of Elijah Muhammad, promising that "what he has done for me, he will do for you, too."[100]

Several women in the NOI enjoyed the protection of strong black male members of the movement, as already mentioned above. Pointing out that many black women faced physical and psychological threats to their person and their property in the 1960s, Cynthia West argues, it is no wonder that female NOI members welcomed their protection.[101] One of her informants stressed how safe she felt as a member of the NOI. "You know, wherever you went, if you had a problem, and you can call the mosque, and tell them, well, you know, there was somebody outside in my yard last night. I heard someone. That next evening maybe two carloads of brothers would be there at your home."[102] Another informant said, "The brothers were so protective of us. They would not allow you to walk at night by yourself. If you came to meeting, you could rest assured that someone would take you home." In fact, being chaperoned from place to place provided another form of protection (and control, depending on one's point of view) against the lies of manipulative and ill-intentioned men who wanted sex. Referring to women who were too quick to give in to the sexual demands of men, one believer said that the women "were lettin' themselves go down this same street again of believing, you know, what the man was sayin' just to get them into the position he wanted them in. . . . Bein' chaperoned was there to benefit them. You know, to eliminate this."[103]

This Victorian attitude toward women and their respectability also translated into a set of ethical principles meant to control and guide sexual reproduction. NOI leaders, following Elijah Muhammad, identified the birth control pill, abortion, and sterilization as threats to the black body and the future of the black race. In many ways, their fears were well founded. From the late nineteenth until the mid-twentieth century, prominent advocates of birth control and eugenics had targeted black women as ideal candidates for coercive and sometimes plainly abusive social and genetic engineering.[104] In the 1960s and 1970s, literally hundreds of thousands of poor black women, like other poor women, were sterilized, at times without their consent.[105] From the beginning of modern family planning in the nineteenth century, African Americans had been split on the question of birth control. "While some community activists promoted birth control as a means of racial betterment," according to Dorothy Roberts, "others denounced abortion and family planning as forms of racial genocide."[106] During the 1960s, arguably no one was more vocal in their opposition than Elijah Muhammad, male and female intellectuals in the NOI, and *Muhammad Speaks*.

In 1962, the front page of *Muhammad Speaks* featured a proclamation from Elijah Muhammad on the "Birth Control Death Plan!" The Messenger warned women to "be aware of the tricks the devils are using to instill the idea of a false birth control in their clinics and hospitals." Citing the example of a clinic in Faquier County, Virginia, Muhammad noted that "poor and helpless black mothers are pressured into accepting sterilization." Sterilization, he informed the reader, "is not 'birth control,' but the end of all possibility to bear children," and all forms of birth control violated the teachings of both the Bible and the Qur'an. He also warned women that no man would want "a non-productive woman."[107] Artist Eugene Majied lent his considerable artistic skills to this campaign to oppose abortion and family planning. His cartoons on the issue, like much of the NOI's discourse, anticipated the presentation of birth control as black genocide by black power and black consciousness advocates in the late 1960s and early 1970s.[108]

In 1962, Majied encouraged his readers to avoid birth control and to have large families as a way to compensate for the loss of black life during slave times. In one of his many cartoons on the subject, an attractive black couple sits together on a bench in a bus or train terminal waiting room. The man wears a fedora and a suit; the woman wears a headscarf. They overhear a white couple complaining about the population explosion. The white man says to his wife, "I'm all for humanity, but most Negroes can't afford kids! It's just so much waste! What do they contribute to society? They need birth control." The black man turns to his wife, speaking loudly enough for the white couple to overhear his response: "And baby, we'll have a boat load of kids! We'll make up for all them boat loads of our people murdered during slavery. Maybe we'll have another Carver, or a Douglass, or a Nat Turner. Even a new Hannibal to help Muhammad!" The black woman turns to face the white folks, who look embarrassed and perhaps even a bit frightened.[109] Majied presented the black couple as proud and dignified, ready to challenge white racism by reproducing the black nation.

Majied also drew much more provocative and morbid cartoons in addressing the issue. In 1965, for example, the front page of *Muhammad Speaks* published a cartoon that pictures a smiling, innocent, and pretty African American woman, dressed in pearls and a low-cut but graceful white evening gown, standing next to a white priest. The priest, who has thinning hair, glasses, an extremely pointed nose, and devil-like ears, holds the arm of the woman. Together, they stare at a large box of birth control pills that sits next to an oversized revolver. The priest smiles and thinks to himself, "Put it to your silly head, and blow your brains out . . . and your nation's brains!" Two black priests in the corner observe the scene. One of them clutches a Bible. The other clasps his hands in prayer, and says, "Amen! Hallelujah! Praise the Lord!"[110] Christianity, white priests, black Uncle Toms, and the birth control movement are all implicated in the campaign to extinguish the black race.

The very next week, the paper published another of Majied's cartoons that pictures the innocent black woman reconsidering her choice to take birth control pills. She holds the pills in her hands, gazing over a cemetery full of the bodies of dead black infants. Their graves are marked with crosses on which are written not the names of the babies, but their aborted careers: Teacher, Scientist, Doctor, Engineer, Lawyer, Inventor, and Artist. The woman bows her head, stares at the pills, and thinks to herself, "Death for my babies and race!" A white gravedigger, slinging a shovel over his shoulders, walks away from the cemetery, declaring, "Birth control (death) . . . now there will be no more Negroes and Indians."[111] It is a disturbing and some would say manipulative scene illustrating Elijah Muhammad's teaching that the black female body is literally the "field" of the nation, and that the fate of the black race will be decided in the wombs of black women.[112] Majied echoed this theme in at least three other cartoons during the latter half of the 1960s.[113]

Women were also told by other females in the movement to control their sexual desires, especially in the female advice columns that regularly appeared in *Muhammad Speaks*. Authored by women generally for other women, these columns tackled a range of issues from romance to family disputes. For example, Los Angelino Harriett Muhammad, a former sociology student at DePaul University in Chicago and a graduate of UCLA, wrote the column, "For You and About You," and encouraged readers to apply the ethical principles of the NOI to their daily lives, especially those related to sexual behavior.[114] In 1966, a "Miss E. L." from South Bend, Indiana, wrote in to ask whether it was likely that her romantic relationship would lead to premarital sex. "I am fifteen and will be sixteen in March," she explained. Very much in love with a certain boy, Miss E. L. explained that she wanted to remain his girlfriend. But, she said, "my mother thinks I am too young." Her mother warned her that having a boyfriend would lead inevitably to premarital sex. "By the time you are seventeen, you will have a baby," her mother told her. Miss E. L. assured her mother that she "would not do such a thing—I don't even see how people who are not married could do it. I think it's a crime before God," she said. But she also expressed sympathy for her mother's point of view, since her mother became pregnant when she was sixteen. The writer concluded her letter by asking whether it is possible to have a boyfriend and abstain from sex.[115]

Columnist Muhammad sided with the girl's mother, explaining that "sex used to not be a problem. . . . Can you imagine—there was a time when most people did not indulge in pre and extra marital sex because it was a religious principle not commonly violated. But that was a long time ago." Taking a socially conservative position that echoed Elijah Muhammad's teachings, Sister Harriett attributed the frequency of premarital sex among teenagers to an increase in "propositions" and the availability of contraceptives. She also criticized parents who only warn their girls about sex, but say nothing to their boys, and cautioned Miss E. L. that boys too often manipulate girls with the words "I love you," in order to satisfy their desires. "This society," Harriett concludes, "has become too weak and relaxed about sex. Sex is powerful, it's wonderful, it's dangerous and destructive. It must be controlled." Marriage, Harriett explains, is the proper institution in which sex can be used for the good of society and the uplift of the race.[116]

In another exchange, Harriett Muhammad also made clear her opposition to homosexuality. A Miss R. K. from San Francisco wrote to say that she had recently discovered that a close friend was a lesbian. This friend made a pass at her, and asked her to be her "woman." "I was shocked," the writer explained, "then felt repulsion mixed with pity and love and anger. Of course I refused, but it was hard for me to accept what had happened—it still is. This girl is such a wonderful person otherwise—very interesting and a good friend." In a state of uncertainty about the future of their friendship, the writer asked Harriett: "Can I as a friend do anything to correct things or is there something basically wrong that makes her situation hopeless?" Harriett responded by explaining that there was hope for her friend if she would seek the "assistance she needs." Homosexuality, she argued, is "learned" behavior; "homosexuals are not born—they are made by their environment." She admitted that many modern psychologists "have suggested that homosexuals have inherited such tendencies," but argued that "this [claim] has no foundation and has never been proven." Echoing a claim made by an older generation of psychiatrists, she classified homosexuality as a "character disorder," one that may be difficult but not impossible to cure.[117] Harriett encouraged the writer to gain the trust of her friend and to suggest that she "seek the professional assistance of a psychotherapist." But she also cautioned that the friend must "want to change her homosexual tendencies."[118]

Finally, Harriett Muhammad also viewed sex as a way to fill a spiritual void. "Confused" wrote to Harriett seeking advice on her problems with "sex and promiscuity." The letter writer discussed her problem in psychodynamic terms, noting that she came from a "broken and very poor home," where her father, a single parent, had been strict and unloving. At the age of fourteen, she become involved with an older man and had a child out of wedlock. Ever since then, she said, she had gone from man to man, looking for someone to suit her "desires and ambitions in life." Harriett responded by complimenting the woman on her self-reflections and encouraging her to take personal responsibility for her actions. Harriett also framed the woman's problems in religious terms. "Your wanting the companionship of a mate is a very natural reaction. Your promiscuity is evidence of a spiritual vacuum. Religious laws weren't given you for the sake of cutting down your 'pleasures.' They are a source of strength to enable you to live a righteous life. Let them be your source of self-discipline." By following religious guidelines on sex, said Harriett, the woman would "stop looking for a man to satisfy your desires," and would "start looking for the qualities in a man that make him the kind of a mate you can respect, obey and enjoy."[119]

Dozens of women and some men testified to how their lives had changed for the better as a result of following such guidelines. One man proudly proclaimed the fact that Islam had helped him to remain faithful and monogamous in his marriage. "Morally," said Hubert X, "Islam stopped me from running around and chasing women."[120] Some women also praised the protection against unwanted sexual advances that the NOI attempted to enforce among its male members. A former child member of the NOI, Sister Elaine no longer participated in movement activities by her late teenage years. Living life outside the NOI, however, she found her interactions with men to be frustrating: "You could not go places with boys without them asking to sleep with you. I went to few parties. I did not like that. I did not go out with boys for this reason. They wanted you to neck with them. . . . When they take you to a show they want you to commit adultery with them. I stopped dating." After rejoining the NOI as an adult, she found comfort in the well-regulated interactions between men and women. "In the Nation you are not afraid of the Brothers. They can take you to places without molesting you and this is why I came back to the Nation. . . . When you go out with Muslim brothers they do not make sex demands upon you."[121]

Not all men and women followed Elijah Muhammad's guidelines on sexuality and reproduction, however. In fact, it is clear that adherence to the strict ban on various modes of birth control depended not only upon the community in which one practiced Islam and the time in which one did so, but also on the life circumstances of individuals. For example, a woman from Syracuse, New York, "Anna," remembered in an oral history interview that many women in the early 1970s complained about the NOI's official policy of birth control. According to Anna, these persons argued that it was irresponsible to have a large number of children when one could not afford to care for them all. In fact, her memory is that "the Nation did not tell women to go out and have as many babies as they can. Procreating is wonderful, but you need to make plans and be prepared to take the responsibility, if you want to do that." In Syracuse, she said, "the sisters tell you not to take the birth control pill, but . . . to find some kind of natural method. We will have to use the natural cycle [officially permitted], or you can use the condom [officially banned]." Sister Anna said that after giving birth to two children, she and her husband decided to use condoms, and she told other women in the NOI that the method worked for them. "I said you can use birth control methods, but you don't want to use the pill or the diaphragm. If you use a condom, it is just latex covering, and it's not going to do any physical harm to anybody." There was little opposition to this technique, she recalled, because the leaders of the local community "were mainly trying to get the women not to have a tubal ligation." But even that prohibition was negotiated within this particular community. Later, Sister Anna decided to have a tubal ligation, because of health reasons. "I had some clots in my blood, so I would bleed a lot when I was giving birth," she said. "The last child I had, I had to have two or three [blood] transfusions." But when she revealed the fact that she had had the tubal ligation to certain members of the community, "one sister went haywire," she continued. Sister Anna then approached a female leader of the community and made her case. "It is better for me," she said, "to . . . take care of the children that I do have, rather than continue having children, lose my life, and leave behind the children I already have." The female leader responded positively, Sister Anna remembered, and supported her decision by saying that it was "rational."[122]

Sister Amina, the seamstress from Washington, sketched a similar portrait of the discussions surrounding reproduction in the D.C. area. Sister Amina noted that women were encouraged to use natural birth control methods, and sometimes monitored their temperatures in an effort to determine when they were ovulating. She said that while contraceptives were not encouraged, "people were still using contraceptives, diaphragms, and things like that, and for various reasons." When childbirth posed a mortal risk to women, she said, her understanding was that the Honorable Elijah Muhammad permitted the use of birth control. "If you were sick," she remembered, "they said, 'use birth control.'" Nevertheless, some women, for one reason or another, continued to have babies. She knew at least two who had died during childbirth. The problem, she said, was not Elijah Muhammad, but the men in her community. In her oral history interview, she summed up her attitude toward men who refused to cooperate with natural methods of birth control by saying simply, "But some of these men," punctuating this comment with a laugh.[123]

In New York, where Sister "Alexandra" first converted to Islam in the early 1970s, a female official at the mosque was quite open in her advocacy of birth control. According to Sister Alexandra, the woman told her class at the temple that women "should not have any more babies than what you alone can take care of. So you don't be sitting here having all these babies to put on welfare for other people to be taking care of, or be a burden to your family, or never be able to make a life for yourself." Sister Alexandra recalled thinking that she did not want to stay home with a "house full of children." She wanted "some enjoyment out of life," so she decided to use birth control. "Sometimes people talked about it, and sometimes people didn't talk about it, but . . . come down to it, you're the one who has to shoulder that responsibility."[124]

In sum, despite the movement's official emphasis on any form of birth control as a form of black genocide, some women in the movement chose to have tubal ligations, take the pill, or use condoms. Other women used natural methods, sometimes successfully, sometimes not. This picture of reproductive diversity shows that the adherence to Elijah Muhammad's directives concerning reproduction varied from woman to woman. It also helps to illuminate that some women did not see a contradiction between their use of birth control and their commitment to Elijah Muhammad's ethics of the body. In fact, at least one woman quoted above understood Elijah Muhammad to be an advocate of family planning when the life of the mother was at risk. Interestingly, there is no textual evidence to support this recollection. Most important, however, is that whatever their feelings about the NOI's policies on birth control, all of the women mentioned above were proud members of the NOI and followers of Elijah Muhammad. Whether their recollections are truly representative of most women in the NOI is difficult to know. But their testimonies suggest that in practice, some members of the NOI may have disagreed over what was considered to be proper Muslim ethical behavior. At the least, their life stories remind us of the potential gap between the rhetoric of NOI leaders and the lived ethics of believers. These stories also provide a helpful reminder of the limitations of any attempt to present an all-encompassing interpretation of body ethics in the NOI, which I essay in the following conclusion, this caution notwithstanding.

## Conclusion: The Politics of the Black Muslim Body

Ironically perhaps, the clean living of many working-class NOI members constituted an achievement of goals long espoused by middle-class African American "uplift" organizations, including the National Baptist Convention, the Women's Club movement, and black fraternal orders.[125] The ethics of the black Muslim body also points to the more general persistence in the United States of what many scholars have identified as dominant and public middle-class Protestant traditions of American culture, including an emphasis on proper diet, proper dress, and the control of sexuality.[126] In fact, it might be tempting to view the NOI and its ethics of the black Muslim body as a capitulation to these American middle-class norms, a view shared by some students of American religion and one famously stated by Sacvan Bercovitch in *The American Jeremiad*.[127] Many of the Muslims quoted above did credit Islam with saving them from drinking, smoking, wearing loose clothing, and more. Was not all this clean living just the guilty reaction of newly religious folks who now regretted their old devotion to a more hedonistic lifestyle?

Like Bercovitch, some students of African American religion and culture have claimed that new religious groups like the NOI, though appearing at first to look like manifestations of dissent, have actually functioned in U.S. history as vehicles of social control, since their teachings have not attacked the root causes of racial, class, and gender oppression. Baer and Singer, for instance, conclude the following about African American messianic-nationalist sects, of which the NOI is a prime example: "Ultimately, in their acceptance of the Protestant work ethic and emphasis on a form of Black Puritanism, messianic-nationalists sects unwittingly serve as hegemonic agencies of the white-dominated status quo."[128] In a similar vein, E. Frances White criticizes the gender hierarchy of the movement as oppressive of women, and dismisses the NOI's program for black empowerment as a "fantasy":

> Searching for easy solutions to our increasingly demoralized state [in the late 1960s], many turned to quasi-religious organizations like the Nation of Islam. The Black Muslims, as they were commonly known, did an admirable job of rescuing alienated drug abusers and imprisoned black men, but . . . the movement's leaders also helped lead the call for greater restrictions on women. The Nation's models of the family had little to do with black reality. Its petty capitalist leaders wanted women rigidly confined to a domestic sphere that was ultimately dominated by men. While I experimented with Afros and cornrows, my female Black Muslim friends in the Nation resurrected their straightening combs. They traded their pants for long skirts, insisted on bras, and asked permission to commute to and from work.[129]

Such arguments too easily dismiss the political implications of a group that both black people and white people of the time considered to be radical. As the FBI itself stated in a May 1965 study of the movement, "One of the FBI's responsibilities is the investigation of 'basic revolutionary organizations or groups' who are dangerous or potentially dangerous to the internal security of the United States. Persons included in this responsibility are leading functionaries and active, militant members of the Nation of Islam, who because of their fanatical antiwhite and anti–United States government teachings and beliefs would be potentially dangerous and likely to seize upon the opportunity presented by a national emergency to endanger the public safety and welfare."[130]

A new model is needed to understand the cultural and religious politics of the NOI during the 1960s and 1970s. Historian Robin Kelley, in his book *Race Rebels*, has offered such an alternative, one that can be used to situate the politics of the NOI inside black working-class resistance more generally. In that work, Kelley analyzes the transition of Malcolm X from a pleasure-seeking, numbers-playing zoot suiter to a pious, clean living member of the NOI. Examining Malcolm X's "participation in the underground subculture of the black working-class youth" during World War II, Kelley argues that Malcolm's time as a zoot suiter "was not a detour on the road to political consciousness but rather an essential element of his radicalization." By becoming a part of this culture, Kelley claims, Malcolm X rejected typical symbols of patriotism, the folkways of rural blacks, and the "class-conscious, integrationist attitudes of middle-class blacks." Malcolm and other black youths developed a language and style all their own: "The zoot suiters and hipsters who sought alternatives to wage work and found pleasure in new music, clothes, and dance styles of the period were race rebels of sorts, challenging middle-class ethics and expectations, carving out a distinct generation and ethnic identity."[131] This kind of resistance revolved around making the body look and act in ways consciously different from what the white mainstream and the black middle-class expected. The collective manipulation of the body, as Kelley suggests, often resulted in a powerful communitarian spirit.[132] Kelley challenges the notion that the only historical forms of resistance in black culture were those that engaged in "mainstream" politics. "Political motivations," he argues, "[do not always] exist separately from issues of economic well-being, safety, pleasure, cultural expression, sexuality, freedom of mobility, and other facets of daily life."[133] Rebellion, he claims, includes cultural acts of resistance that reject the values and expectations of the powerful. His question for further study is: How did various movements or organizations offer this kind of resistance, and why were black working-class folk drawn to them?

In the case of the NOI, working-class African Americans created a religious culture that, like the black working-class youth culture of the postwar era, identified the black body as a locus of social protest. But rather than negating traditional black Christian middle-class ideals, members appropriated them within a new Islamic matrix. Linking the liberation of black people to the purification, strengthening, and protection of the black body, Elijah Muhammad incorporated many middle-class Protestant values into a new Islamic framework. Put in terms of a simple semiotic exercise: the body was a sign. NOI members separated the signifier — the civilizing of the body — from what was normally signified — a capitulation to the values, norms, and beliefs of the middle class. The old signifier now pointed toward a new signified: the Islamized black body.[134] Islam, then, provided an essential element of this ethical complex because it was used to rename old strategies for black uplift and to differentiate them from other behaviors and other movements. Islam played a vital role in providing a new religious framework for the creation of an African American religious protest movement that adopted certain elements and simultaneously rejected the control of the dominant culture in which the movement existed. To change one's life through participating in these activities was yet another way in which one practiced Islam in the NOI.

In adopting old middle-class norms into a new Islamic framework, the NOI can also be seen as a sign of what Amanda Porterfield has described as "the remarkable decline [since the 1960s] in the authority Protestant people and institutions claim in the larger culture . . . [and] the success of many external challenges to their hegemony." Porterfield agrees with scholars who assert that contemporary American religion continues to be marked by the "endurance of Protestant attitudes, ideas, and principles," but insists that Protestant *authority* has waned due to several factors, including the universalizing nature of evangelical religion in the United States, the transformation of American Catholicism, the religious effects of the anti–Vietnam War movement, the influence of Buddhism, greater "gender self-consciousness and body awareness," and the "impact of the academic study of religion."[135] This chapter suggests that the growth of Islam among black Americans should also be added to any list of historical factors that seek to explain the decline of Protestant authority during the latter half of the twentieth century.[136]

Finally, this portrait of ethics within the NOI indicates that while certain Protestant ideals were adopted into a new Islamic framework, the end result was anything but a capitulation to power from the point of view of NOI members themselves. They knew, all too well, the potential threats involved in displaying and performing their Muslimness in public. As Peggy Phelan points out, such identity politics may be in the business of making visible those who feel invisible, but such "visibility . . . summons surveillance and the law; it provokes voyeurism, fetishism, [and] the colonial/imperial appetite for possession."[137] All of that was true in the case of the NOI, as the FBI, the academy, and popular culture attempted to watch, analyze, imitate, and control the NOI. Many Americans felt threatened by the NOI's rhetoric and public performances, which challenged the legitimacy of Christianity during an era of uncertainty for the Protestant establishment and achieved success as a Cold War and Vietnam-era countercultural movement that rejected the notion of any American consensus.[138] Those outside the movement could criticize or dismiss members of the NOI as unpatriotic, angry, misguided, violent, self-oppressing, or illegitimate as much as they liked—as far as the believers knew, in both mind and body they had been made free.

## CHAPTER 5

# Rituals of Control and Liberation

It was a warm, beautiful Savior's Day;
Allah held up the cold and snow
Until we all got away.
Our sweet little Messenger
Was healthy and strong;
After 35 years of teaching,
They can't prove him wrong.
He taught us for $3^1/_2$ hours
And it was going on 4
And we were rejoicing so,
We all wanted more.
The sisters were in unity —
All were in their separate seats,
Dressed in their white uniforms
And they were looking neat.
The Fruit of Islam were there,
Moving swift and looking real good
Like all so-called Negroes would
If they follow the Messenger as they should.
— Muhammad Ali, "An Ode to Savior's Day,"
   *Muhammad Speaks*, 11 March 1966

t is clear that by the early 1970s, many members of the NOI were at least familiar with the ritual requirements of Sunni Islamic religious tradition, even if the practice of these rituals was infrequent.[1] Take the case, for example, of Islam's prescribed prayers, or the *salat*. At first glance, there is ample evidence to suggest that most followers of Elijah Muhammad did not observe *salat*, a tradition that many, if not most Muslims believe to be a requirement of their faith. Malcolm X, for example, said that he did not know the ritual prayers when he arrived in Mecca for his first pilgrimage in 1964. "Imagine, being a Muslim minister, a leader in Elijah Muhammad's Nation of Islam, and not knowing the prayer ritual," he lamented in his autobiography.[2] The evidence that I have collected in oral history interviews confirms that Malcolm's case was typical—many former members have told me that they did not practice *salat* in the NOI. Moreover, some of the movement's official intellectuals, like Pakistani Abdul Basit Naeem, attempted to justify the absence of ritual prayer in the NOI by arguing that the good deeds of NOI members were worth a "thousand heartfelt prayers." Like some other modern critics of religious ritual more generally, Naeem criticized the prescribed Islamic prayers as empty rituals that did not provide a direct link to God, arguing that members of the NOI had more pressing concerns—in his words, "so many suffering souls to be saved from damnation; so many ailing hearts to be healed; so many decaying bodies to be cleansed of filth and foreign matter. . . ; so many eyes to be opened to the reality of the 'devil' and his nature; . . . and so many virtuous black women to be defended from the devil's glances, prances and advances."[3]

At the same time, despite all this evidence that the *salat* was nowhere to be found in the NOI, and not even to be desired, other pieces of information suggest that some members knew portions of the *salat* and did indeed perform them. In 1957, Elijah Muhammad published a prayer manual that described the ritual in detail, although he encouraged believers to say the prayers in English rather than in Arabic, the language in which the prayers are generally recited by most Muslims around the world.[4] The manual described the appropriate times for each of the five daily prayers.[5] It explained the required ablutions, or *wudu*, to be performed before prayer.[6] It instructed believers how to perform the *adhan*, or call to prayer.[7] And it outlined the difference between the obligatory or *fard* elements and the traditional or *sunni* elements of prayer, and teaching believers how to perform a *rak'ah*, a series of "standing, bending, rising, and prostrating" postures that compose the "basic unit" of prayer.[8]

While the existence of this manual does not prove that believers performed the prayers, other evidence does. NOI members recited various portions of the prayers in their temple meetings and their school ceremonies, in other public occasions, and at home. One Muslim prisoner in Massachusetts's Walpole State Prison proudly claimed that he performed the five daily prayers "as taught by the Honorable Elijah Muhammad," and said that "learning the Muslim prayers, the significance of prayers, and the manner of washing before going into prayer is most enjoyable."[9] School children at Chicago's University of Islam, the NOI's primary and secondary school, were taught the prayers, including the proper positioning of the hands during the Islamic *salat*.[10] Perhaps even more surprising is that as early as the 1950s some followers of the NOI learned and practiced the Islamic *salat* in Arabic, as it is performed all over the world—a phenomenon that has escaped the notice or comment of most scholars. According to Spanish Harlem author Piri Thomas, who served a sentence of several years in Comstock State Prison, New York, during the mid-1950s, a group of Elijah Muhammad's followers taught him the prayers while he was in prison. These believers repeated Elijah Muhammad's teachings about the white devil and the need for clean living. But they also read the Qur'an and the *hadith*, the sayings and deeds of the Prophet Muhammad and his companions. These believers instructed Thomas on how to say the *adhan* and insisted that he learn the *wudu*. Thomas eventually converted to Islam and learned the prayers in Arabic, although he did not continue to practice Islam once released from prison in the late 1950s.[11]

Prayer was not the only pillar of Islamic practice that was adapted for use in the religious culture of the NOI. Believers also observed a version of the Ramadan fast, but did so during the month of December rather than during the lunar month of Ramadan. In practice, some observant members of the NOI fasted all year round, following Elijah Muhammad's commandment to eat only one meal a day or his recommendation to fast for a period of three days as needed.[12] In 1969, Elijah Muhammad explained that fasting could be used by believers to relieve them of "some trouble, sickness, or for advancement in the Divine Knowledge of Allah, and to keep away from being tempted to accept evil."[13] In 1970, he also acknowledged the differences between his teaching on Ramadan and that of most other Muslims. "I prescribe for you the month of December to fast in—if you are able to take the fast—instead of the regular month that travels through the year, called Ramadan by the Muslims; the month in which they say Muhammad received the Holy Qur'an." His reason for doing so, he explained, was because "it was in this month [December] that you used to worship a dead prophet by the name of Jesus. And it was in this month that you wasted your money and wealth to worship the 25th day of this month."[14] As he reiterated in *How to Eat to Live*, his book on an Islamic diet, "I set this up for you and me to try to drive out of us the old white slavemaster's way of worship of a false birthday (December 25th) of Jesus." But if other Muslims wanted to fast during the actual month of Ramadan, which he correctly noted was the ninth month of the Islamic year, then they should do so: "Of course, this is the Arab way, in their religious belief, that they should fast."[15] Various NOI officials echoed the Messenger's teachings about Ramadan in a number of venues, and also asked believers to "keep up five prayers a day" during Ramadan and avoid all fighting and immoral behavior.[16]

To what degree individual believers observed Elijah Muhammad's commandment to fast in December and at other times in the year is difficult to know. But there is enough evidence to conclude that, unlike the Islamic *salat*, Ramadan was observed by most NOI communities in some form or another. In 1968, Sister Ivyln X recalled the 1967 celebration of the December Ramadan as a "time of spiritual devotion with much reverence in our hearts," and remarked that during Ramadan, "we all seemed to be more conscious of an atmosphere of total tranquility among the believers."[17] Brother Clifton 3X of Temple No. 27 in Los Angeles said that he had tried to observe the fast in "1969, 1970, 1971, and 1972" but "failed." Then, in 1973, he "tried and really made Ramadan." Brother Clifton summarized the effects of having successfully completed the fast: "Ramadan 1973 really opened my eyes. There is no turning back. . . . This is what Ramadan did for me: It made me strong, it made me happy—happy to know that we have a Saviour."[18] Communities also marked their version of the Ramadan fast with celebrations both before and after the period of fasting.[19] And in several prisons, NOI members successfully demanded the right to practice the fast or even to make supervised visits to their local temple during its observance.[20] In the infamous federal penitentiary in Marion, Illinois, for example, believers received permission to observe Ramadan. They held a Ramadan feast on 4 January 1971 and, throughout the month that preceded it, observed a strict Muslim diet, "a daily menu that wouldn't cause any conflict in the cooking department but yet rendered to us that which we desired to have."[21]

In sum, at least some followers practiced some Sunni Islamic rituals at various times and places in the NOI. But to stop there in analyzing the ritual activities of NOI members is to miss out on the ritual lives of many members who did not practice the five pillars of Islam. Moreover, to analyze Islamic rituals in the NOI by merely measuring the presence of the five pillars imposes a normative view of

Islamic religion that ignores what it meant to be Muslim to many NOI followers and to other Muslim practitioners around the globe. Finally, any comprehensive analysis of ritual in the NOI must pay attention to the question of why these rituals were meaningful and how they functioned within the overall religious culture of the movement.

This chapter considers the ritual activities of the NOI using a different lens. According to Catherine Bell, ritualization—a word she uses to emphasize the process of performing rituals—involves "the differentiation and privileging of particular activities," including the deliberate manipulation of time and space; "restricted codes of communication; distinct and specialized personnel"; special objects, texts, and dress; particular physical or mental states; and the "involvement of a particular constituency."[22] In addition to offering a list of ritual's constitutive elements, however, Bell insists that ritualization is "first and foremost a strategy for the construction of certain types of power relationships effective within particular social organizations."[23] By interrogating ritual as a strategy for the shaping of power relationships, Bell's approach pushes scholars not only to identify a particular activity as a ritual, but also to understand the political and social implications of that activity in its specific context. She suggests that scholars raise four "artificial, but useful" questions about the way that power is construed through ritual activities, including "(1) how ritualization empowers those who more or less control the rite; (2) how their power is also limited and constrained; (3) how ritualization dominates those involved as participants; and (4) how this domination involves a negotiated participation and resistance that also empowers them."[24]

All of these questions help to illuminate the ways in which relationships between leaders and followers operated within the religious culture of the NOI. Without a doubt, the NOI was a religious group headed by a prophetic authority that demanded obedience from its members and that used ritual as a way to construct the power of its leader, the Messenger of Allah. It is for this reason, among others, that some scholars and observers have dubbed the movement a "cult," and sometimes depicted its members as brainless or hapless followers of a charismatic but ultimately misguided and corrupt leader.[25] In my view, that understanding of the movement effectively silences the voices of thousands of African Americans whose lives were changed for the better (according to them) through their devotion to a man whom they considered to be a prophet and savior-figure. At the least, it makes it easier to ignore their voices. Bell's approach suggests an alternative model. While paying attention to the way that ritual activities established the power of the Messenger, her theory of ritualization also suggests that observers should understand the limits of the prophet's power. In a similar way, one should seek to understand how followers are both "dominated" and "empowered" by their participation in ritual activities.

The religious culture of the NOI was highly ritualized. Ritualized elements appeared in members' participation in the all-male Fruit of Islam (FOI) and all-female Muslim Girls Training (MGT), temple meetings and Muslim conventions, and even members' business ventures, especially the selling of *Muhammad Speaks*. Thousands of African American Muslims in the 1960s and 1970s participated in these activities, and left records of what their participation meant to them at the time. Since most of those comments were published in *Muhammad Speaks*, they give an overwhelmingly positive impression of the activities themselves and participants' reactions to them. These records help to reveal how some members understood the performance of rituals as synonymous with practicing Islam. Of course, not all members of the NOI participated in these rituals, and not all members had a positive impression of them. In order to capture some of their voices, I rely on selected oral history interviews, memoirs, and ethnographic accounts of the movement. Thus, in describing ritualization as a process in which many if not most Muslims participated, I also attempt to show how the meaning and function of ritual activities differed for individuals at different times and places. As Tom Driver points out, rituals can have personal meanings, public meanings, and sometimes both. They can entertain and inspire. They can do harm and they can liberate.[26]

But while accounting for the diverse meanings and functions of ritualized activities in the NOI, I also argue that generally speaking, the practice of ritual duties in the NOI served as a primary mode of Islamic identity construction. For some, the ritualized activities of the movement constituted the most important aspect of their involvement with the organization. Though the NOI's ritualized activities inscribed unequal power dynamics between the movement's leaders and followers, NOI rituals also created a powerful sense of communal identity among the believers. This communal identity revolved around a shared commitment to proper social and ethical behaviors. Thus, for those who participated in the ritualized activities of the NOI, Islam became not merely something one believed in — it was also something that one performed and practiced.

## The Fruit of Islam

Trained in military protocol, boxing, judo, and wrestling, the members of the FOI modeled proper male behavior for other members and blacks outside the

Nation. This elite force, a unit of which existed in many NOI temples throughout the country, was "expected to follow all 'Islamic laws' more strictly than other followers," including directives to keep themselves clean and to show "Love of our Leader and Teacher, the Honorable Elijah Muhammad." According to one FOI member, the FOI was also charged with the protection of the temple and, according to one member in Chicago, with the "duty" of defending "the life of a Muslim Sister with his own life."[27] Many of their activities were ritualized, including their dress, forms of salute, and drill routines. While the official uniform of the FOI changed at various points throughout the 1960s and 1970s, members often wore either a dark suit and bow tie or a military-like outfit that included a fez and a three-button coat with small lapels and stripes across the ends of the sleeves. A talented member of the FOI could aspire to become a lieutenant or even captain of his local FOI chapter. In meetings at the temple or mosque, they practiced military drills, where they strove to achieve perfect synchronicity and discipline. They were often pictured in stiff military-like postures, displaying what *Muhammad Speaks* called "absolute fitness and precision."[28]

Members of the Junior FOI, designed for boys and adolescents, were to be trained in the values of the NOI by focusing their attention on the following:

1. Cleanliness: Physically, mentally, and property of the Temple . . .
2. Love and Unity:
   a. Love of our Leader and Teacher, the Honorable Elijah Muhammad.
   b. Love of each other.
   c. Knowledge of unity.
   d. Purpose of uniting with one another.
3. Religious view:
   a. Brotherhood of Islam read at every meeting . . .
   b. A portion of Muhammad's Life as told by Maulana Muhammad Ali [the Ahmadi scholar of Islam]
   c. *The Supreme Wisdom*
4. Physical Training: Hikes, healthy games, exercises and drilling.
5. Military Courtesy:
   a. Giving proper respect.
   b. Saluting an officer by his rank.
   c. Addressing an officer by his rank.
   d. Obeying all orders given by an officer.
6. Educational Trips:
   a. Museums

b. Zoo

c. Planetarium

d. Aquarium

7. Drawing Class . . .

8. Woodcraft Class . . .

9. Self-defense

a. Art of boxing

b. Judo

c. Wrestling forms.[29]

Though this list is taken from the Junior FOI chapter of Temple No. 2 in Chicago during the late 1950s, it effectively captures the spirit of many FOI activities for both children and adults throughout the 1960s and 1970s.

The FOI was a hierarchical organization in which the communal disciplining of individual male bodies was an activity ultimately controlled, through a chain of military command, by the Messenger of Allah. FOI captains often reported directly to the Supreme Captain of the FOI in Chicago, rather than to the local NOI minister.[30] If someone stepped out of line, either literally or figuratively, he was punished, and in some cases, expelled from the NOI. If a brother had sex with an unmarried sister or was caught drinking, he could expect to receive a trial and punishment. For example, one brother who left the NOI to date a non–Muslim woman and later asked to reenter the movement was interrogated for four weeks by the captain of the FOI about his activities. "After these four weeks of questioning," he explained, "I was brought before the entire Muslim congregation at a Wednesday night meeting and court-martialed. The Captain acted as judge and jury. I was denounced in vigorous terms for adultery, fornication, gambling, drinking, smoking, and for breaking nearly all the laws of Islam. . . . After this period of humiliation I was asked how I pleaded to the charges. Guilty was my only plea. The Captain found me guilty and suspended me from the Temple for another year. I was placed also in 'isolation.' This means that no Muslim can speak to me and I cannot attend any meeting, public or private, of the Temple. . . . The Captain said to me: 'Do you think that the Honorable Elijah Muhammad is joking? Do you think that he is playing games? What right have you to go risk disgracing his efforts?'"[31]

But while the FOI served as a mechanism of control that effectively dominated its participants and empowered the leadership of the NOI, it also offered its rank-and-file members a kind of black (male) liberation. The disciplines practiced by members of the FOI were designed to make "men out of boys."[32] One caption of a picture taken of FOI members lined up at the Chicago International Amphitheater explained that "these resolute followers of the Messenger of Allah for[m] a corps of black manhood . . . unequaled in this hemisphere."[33] Sister Beverly 3X of Mosque No. 27 in Los Angeles said that Elijah Muhammad provided an example of manliness that every brother should follow: "The boy-child has a God, a Man, a Father (in every sense of these words) to pattern from, The Lamb of God. My Husband is putting into practice that which Messenger Muhammad teaches (selling *Muhammad Speaks* Newspapers and striving to put into practice the other phases of righteousness.) This enables him to be patterned after, because through my husband, the head of the Family, the children and grandchildren see the works of the Hon. Elijah Muhammad." The teaching of strict gender roles was necessary to the moral health of all black people, according to this believer. "Will our boys be girls? Will our girls be boys? What a sad state of affairs! In the Nation of Islam, our children are guided in the way of Righteous[ness] put into practice; our male children become Men of Men and our female children become Women of Women."[34]

As Sister Beverly mentioned, all members of the FOI in the 1960s and 1970s were expected to sell copies of *Muhammad Speaks*, an admittedly profane activity that became a religious ritual in the minds and bodies of its practitioners. Well-dressed, bow-tied men peddled the paper at major intersections or even door to door throughout many areas in urban black America, including San Francisco, Baltimore, New York, Detroit, Chicago, Atlanta, Washington, and Dorchester, Massachusetts.[35] "Every able brother sold the paper," reported Abdul Shabazz, a member of Temple No. 28 in St. Louis, Missouri. "If you couldn't deal with *Muhammad Speaks* newspaper, you were kind of frowned upon. I think my quota was 150 papers a week. I couldn't tell you how many papers we sold, but when the shipment of papers came in . . . the brothers would go down . . . and unload bundles."[36] In Los Angeles, sales manager Silas A. Baker used a 1965 Falcon Club wagon painted or silk-screened with a *Muhammad Speaks* company logo to distribute the paper to mosques and communities on the West Coast.[37] In 1969, believers in Washington turned out to welcome the arrival of Brother Otis X Perlotte, the driver of an NOI-owned "Emeryville" International Van, a ten-wheeled truck with a "hauling capacity of 45,000 lbs." After its arrival, the truck, which was also used to transport NOI farm produce, was "eagerly emptied by enthusiastic brothers, anxious to break the bundles and begin delivering them [copies of *Muhammad Speaks*] to . . . readers in the district." For Washington minister Lonnie Shabazz, who reportedly directed each FOI member to sell two hundred per week,[38] "this was a historic occasion . . . for all believers and lost-found here as well, to see that we have our own truck, delivering to us our own papers, so that we can get them to our people."[39] In 1969, the NOI also purchased its own printing plant on 26th and Federal in Chicago to produce the paper; it had been printed previously by Lerner's Newspaper Co., a division of Myers Publication. The editors of the paper bragged that their new "modern," "scientifically advanced" plant contained two four-color Goss Urbanite presses "with an average printing speed of more than 50,000 papers per hour."[40]

Throughout the 1960s and 1970s, the NOI regularly rewarded FOI members for meeting or exceeding their quotas, featuring them in the pages of *Muhammad Speaks*. Teenagers Harrell Chancey and Stanley Johnson, for example, were flown from New York to Chicago for an all-expenses-paid vacation in 1964.[41] Johnson, who is pictured smiling as he holds up his trophy, said that before joining the NOI he was "just a hoodlum enslaved to all of the white man's vices." But after visiting his local temple, he explained, he heard of the black man's historical achievements in Mali, Ghana, and Songhay, and then converted to Islam. His only hobby before joining the NOI was having "a good time"; his new hobby was selling the paper. In marketing the paper, Johnson often told potential customers that buying the paper would help uplift all black men. "I say to them that it is no time for shucking. It is no time for ducking. The black man in America must have justice," he explained.[42]

According to the believers, FOI members who sold the paper offered tangible proof to the public that Elijah Muhammad's program of black uplift produced "respectable" and successful human beings. As Brother Clayton X of Baltimore, Maryland, remarked, "Being in the public eye . . . makes a brother a living witness to the greatness of the Honorable Elijah Muhammad."[43] One sign of this success, according to FOI members, was the fact that they often received compliments on their manners and dress. For instance, on 29 August 1970, reported Brother Jeyone X, four members of Mosque No. 4 in Washington, D.C., "were out canvassing with our newspaper, *Muhammad Speaks*, going door-to-door seeking to get customers. We were in an area which one would describe, in this world, as being elite." While doing so, Brother Jeyone encountered three potential customers, including two whites and an elderly black woman, who complimented them on their "mannerism and appearance." The African American woman asked, "When have I seen four young men dressed so neatly?" According to the brother, "she went on by putting emphasis on our haircuts, white shirts, bow ties, conservative style suits, nice shoes and our business-like approach. The sister complimented us from head to toe and the two white people sitting with her backed her statements." The brother then used the opportunity to proselytize, telling her that Elijah Muhammad, "through his teachings and example . . . gives us the inspiration to look and act the way we do." The African American woman said that these brothers were a "credit to our organization" and wished that she could say the same about her eighteen-year-old son. Brother Jeyone invited her and her son to the mosque. And at the end of the exchange, one of the white persons bought a paper from him.[44]

Some FOI members were also proud that their presence in black neighborhoods offered a counterexample to "dope pushers and pimps." For example, Kevin X Burke of Passaic, New Jersey, said that as he sold the paper in Passaic he met many young blacks whose use of drugs had blinded them to the truth. The community's drug pushers, who were willing to make money off of teenage addicts, were "most anxious to get the Muslims out of Passaic." He acknowledged that many in the black community, and not just the drug dealers, had criticized members of the FOI for "pushing" the paper, but countered that the real source of their criticism was the challenge that FOI members posed to dealers and pimps. "To most people who live like a dope addict or prostitute . . . *Muhammad Speaks* newspaper is like a photograph," he argued, "and they are ashamed of what they see." The NOI, he said, offered them a way out.[45]

Not all members of the FOI, however, were this piety-minded. Those who sold Elijah Muhammad's newspaper did not necessarily practice every rule issued by their Messenger. For example, Washington University professor and essayist Gerald Early reports that he "almost joined the Black Muslims" when he was eighteen and living in San Francisco around 1970. Dubbing Muhammad's followers in San Francisco a "wonderful community of saints," Early wrote that NOI members had helped him find a job, given him a suit jacket, and taken him to temple meetings. These same brothers, however, would also "take me to their apartment where, after the Muslim service, they would dump their paid-for copies of *Muhammad Speaks* in a closet, break out some marijuana and play jazz records all night." To be sure, smoking pot was not part of Muhammad's program for the disciplining of the black body. But while these followers may have violated some of Elijah Muhammad's ethics concerning the black Muslim body, they clearly followed other rules—like the commandment to sell the newspaper.[46]

For many in the movement, whether they smoked pot on the side or not, selling the paper also represented an opportunity to conduct missionary work, or, as they put it, to go fishing. "These hawkers of *Muhammad Speaks*," wrote former *Muhammad Speaks* editor and Northwestern professor Leon Forrest, "would indeed get all up in your face, with the good news, concerning their new faith; they were a blast, with the zeal of the old-time religion pitched to a tune loud enough to awaken the dead—or to chase the Negro out of any Blackman, as the saying goes."[47] It was an effective missionary technique, as evidenced by the fact that many men, who would eventually sell the paper themselves, first learned about the movement from these salesman missionaries.[48] In a similar fashion, some women reported that the paper introduced them to Islam.[49] Brother George 11X of Muhammad's Mosque No. 4 in Washington, D.C., reported that on every Wednesday, Friday, and Sunday, "a huge battalion of righteous soldiers" gathered to sell the paper. The junior FOI, a youth group of boys aged six to eleven, joined the senior FOI to invite "our people to hear the life giving teachings of our Beloved Leader, Teacher, and Guide, Messenger Muhammad." Using a loudspeaker, these members of the Fruit spoke "truth . . . to our lost brothers and sisters. . . . When these little brothers approach a lost brother or sister, their righteous beauty captures the hearts of our people. The people know not why they fling open their hearts and doors to these brothers, as well as purchase from the *Muhammad Speaks* Newspaper." After their work was done, they marched in step back to "headquarters," singing the following words again and again: " 'All Praises Are Due to Allah, for the Honorable Elijah Muhammad.' Some people stopped in their tracks; some people stopped cars, and others came out to witness a righteous procession of brothers spiritually elevated from seeking to help in the work of Elijah Muhammad."[50]

On occasion, these spirited marketing and missionizing techniques annoyed various passersby, who attempted to engage or mock the members of the FOI. In 1972, for example, one man began to harass Brother Clarence 6X in Atlanta. According to *Muhammad Speaks*, the incident turned violent when the man prepared to hit the Muslim salesman with his belt. "The tussle which followed carried them into the middle of Broad St." and attracted the attention of patrolman R. L. Jackson. Through a comedy of errors, the police officer became involved in the fight, and both the police officer and the Muslim called for backup. Up to this point, all of those involved had been black. And then white police officers arrived on the scene. Amid "screeching tires and slamming doors, white cops leaped out, swinging slap jacks and night sticks (also popularly called 'nigger sticks') at any available Black body wearing a coat and tie. They asked no questions and sought no answers. . . . The [unarmed] Muslims, under attack, swung into action. Crying 'Allahu Akbar!!!' they fought fearlessly and boldly, wreaking havoc on the attacking ranks of patrolmen." Eventually, according to the Muslim reporting on the incident, the fighting stopped and the Muslims declared victory; as the article's headline exclaimed, "Power of Allah Gave Victory to Muhammad Speaks Salesmen in Fight with Southern Cops."[51]

For our purposes, the actual details of the fight matter less than the religious frames in which Muslim reporters and participants placed this incident and the selling of the newspaper more generally. According to my informant, Abdul Shabazz, and others, men were *expected* to sell the paper in the movement. One might say that they were pressured to sell the paper. But this duty was a sacred one. As Brother Frank 8X Lopez, a New York man whose father had moved to the United States from St. Kitts, put it: "The paper is sacred. When we are holding the paper we must be careful how we react to people, because we are holding the words of Almighty God, who is represented by the Honorable Elijah Muhammad. The clothes we wear, the smile on our faces, consideration, justice are all part of our sales technique."[52] For many, selling the paper meant more than simply filling the coffers of the movement. It represented an opportunity to display one's devotion to the Messenger, to spread the good news of his message, to train younger members, and to prove one's commitment to the NOI on the streets, even if harassed or attacked. Circulation Manager Abraham Pasha praised the bravery and nobility of FOI salesmen, exclaiming that they "will withstand the barrage of jealousy, envy, physical abuse and even the prospect of death to get the life-giving words of Islam to a people in need."[53]

Selling the paper was a rite of passage in which Muslim soldiers performed their religious devotion to the Messenger, and, in return, could feel pride and satisfaction at their accomplishment. George E. X Berry memorialized this sacred task in a poem that casted the selling of *Muhammad Speaks* as an honorable and proud religious vocation:

Hail to the Fruit of Islam!
Fighting for their own
In the army of Allah,
The mighty, the wise, the strong.
With His sword of Truth and Justice,
And His Messenger as their guide,
They walk the streets, with 'Muhammad Speaks,'
To turn the opposing tide.
'Muhammad Speaks' to the wealthy;
'Muhammad Speaks' to the poor.
His 'Message to the Blackman'
Is to live forever more.
No matter what the sacrifice,
His mission must be done.
To the proud Black Brothers of the F.O.I.,
March On! March On! for freedom
'Til the victory is won.[54]

As important as selling the newspaper was to members of the FOI, however, it was not the only activity in which its members displayed their commitment to the NOI and attempted to recruit new members. Some members of the FOI were also charged with fishing for new members in federal and state prisons, from which the NOI recruited hundreds if not thousands of members during the 1960s and 1970s. Though some prison officials expressed concern about the popularity of the NOI among incarcerated males, by the 1970s various court decisions had made it easier for prisoners to observe various rites associated with the religious culture of the NOI.[55] Some prison officials even praised the members of the NOI inside their institutions, noting that followers of Elijah Muhammad were often model prisoners. At the Lorton Reformatory in Virginia, for example, superintendents, clinicians, instructors, and even some guards said that the Muslims under their supervision valued education, treated others with respect, maintained a neat appearance, and took pride in their work. These comments appeared in a pamphlet that brothers had written about their practice of Islam in prison, entitled "Black Muslims on the Move in Prison." According to these Muslims, they were able to leave the prison to attend religious services at Washington's Mosque No. 4.[56]

Nevertheless, many prisoners complained about their treatment. For example, Marvin X Mathis, Thomas X Farrow, and Ralph X Davis, prisoners at the New Jersey State Prison in Trenton, petitioned the United Nations to intervene in the cases of several death row inmates and accused the prison of genocide and human rights abuses.[57] The wife of Clifford 8X, an FOI member involved in the infamous Attica prison uprising, said in 1971 that though members of the FOI showed courtesy and respect toward the guards taken hostage during the riot, they were savagely beaten during the assault on the prison ordered by Governor Nelson Rockefeller, and some of those who lived remained "in dire need of medical help."[58]

Though *Muhammad Speaks* regularly chronicled prisoner abuse, it seems that Elijah Muhammad and leaders of the FOI did not focus their efforts on fighting for prisoners' rights as much as they did on ministering to the needs of the prisoners to which they could gain access. Assistant Minister Charles 19X, for example, visited the Cook County Jail in Chicago from nine to eleven o'clock every Saturday morning, attempting to recruit members through an appeal to the inmates' reason. Rather than "ridiculing" Christianity, Brother Charles asked the prisoners to compare in a logical fashion the benefits of Christianity to the benefits of Islam. He promised prisoners that if they converted to Islam, they would "(1) want for their brothers that which they desire for themselves; (2) enjoy sincere brotherhood; (3) encounter no more grieving, mourning and begging for justice; (4) no longer would they be the last hired and first fired; and (5) no longer would they have to endure petty leadership."[59] In addition to sending missionaries to the prisons, FOI members supplied inmates with copies of movement literature and *Muhammad Speaks*. Thomas X Howard, a Muslim inmate at the Lorton Reformatory in Virginia, even sent a copy of "Black Muslims on the Move in Prison" to his fellow incarcerated brothers at the Florida state prison in Raiford.[60]

In various prisons throughout the country, inmates formed chapters of the FOI and celebrated various NOI rituals inside the walls of the penitentiary. At the Lorton Reformatory in Virginia, acting FOI captain Clarence X Mitchell said that he and fellow inmates held their first Unity Bazaar inside the institution on 20 June 1970, serving pastries from the Shabazz bakery in Washington.[61] At Trenton State prison in New Jersey, members formed an FOI chapter of at least forty members. Dressed in white shirts, bow ties, and FOI hats, they posed for a picture in 1972, proudly displaying a flag of the Islamic star and crescent. The chapter included a captain, lieutenants, squad leaders, a secretary, and ministers.[62] On 26 February 1971, Muslims at the federal prison in Springfield, Missouri, celebrated Saviour's Day in the cafeteria of the prison's health care facility. Several "honored" guests were on hand to observe the event, including the director, Dr. P. J. Ciccone, the associate director, Mrs. C. W. Campbell, and Rev. and Mrs. Harold Washburn. Brother Eugene C. X Diggs, the acting assistant minister, called the proceedings to order and began the service with "customary Opening Prayer," probably the first chapter of the Qur'an, called *al-fatiha*. Acting FOI lieutenant George X Chancy then called on Dr. Ciccone to say a few words as part of the service, but the physician apologized and admitted to being unprepared to do so. Clancy then called on the Christian chaplain to address the crowd. Rev. Washburn "did not say much, but did acknowledge that he was impressed upon seeing how well the group performed." Brother George X then lectured on "The Coming of Allah," and afterward those in attendance enjoyed a "100 per cent pork-free meal" that brothers familiar with the dietary guidelines of the movement had prepared by using recipes from "the Muslim's dietary guide, the book, *How to Eat to Live*."[63]

Elijah Muhammad's program of uplift also attempted to change the culture of the prison life, at least for African Americans. Dilbert X of the Holman Unit Prison in Atmore, Alabama, admitted that "Mr. Muhammad's program has not been able to bring a total abrupt halt to the problems of rape (which has decreased greatly among Blacks), murder (which has slowed down to some degree) and stabbing (which has almost ceased among the Blacks)." But he said that among "civilized men it is known that these things will continue to occur as long as the devil unravels his diabolical scheme against Black Men." In the meantime, he said, the acting minister of the Muslims at the prison "continues relentlessly to speak before these Black Men, trying to put an end to the help that they are giving the devil at being successful in his overall plot of genocide." For Brother Dilbert, black men were simply playing into the hands of a white plot when they raped, murdered, or addicted their black brothers. He pledged to continue the fight against such behavior, framing his vow in millennial terms: "As the war of Armageddon continues we here at Holman Unity Prison, who are on the righteous side of Almighty God Allah shall do all we can to civilize our Black Brothers away from savagery, homosexuality and murder, as Mr. Muhammad has civilized us away from such things."[64]

Brother Dilbert's comments, in addition to the descriptions of prison rituals, show that even in prison, members of the FOI attempted to enforce Elijah Muhammad's code of ethics and to celebrate the major rites of the NOI.[65] For at least some men, this path offered a new set of behaviors that they could practice outside the prison walls by joining their local temple or mosque. If a convict were willing to change, he would be welcomed into full membership in the NOI. In the early 1960s, C. Eric Lincoln noted that the NOI found success in its prison ministries because it did not attach any special stigma to incarceration; prison inmates were precisely the "lost" black persons whom Elijah Muhammad wanted to save from the hells of North America.[66] Once released, former inmates could join the NOI as regular members, and advance through the hierarchy of the organization. The most dramatic example of this social mobility was Malcolm X, a convicted criminal, who eventually became national spokesman for Elijah Muhammad. But Malcolm X was not alone. Large numbers of NOI members were recruited from prisons, where they heard "the teachings of Elijah Muhammad" from NOI missionaries like Isaiah Karriem. According to his comments and those of other NOI ministers in *Muhammad Speaks*, their "progress" was entirely the result of Muhammad's teachings.[67] In speeches, statements, even poems, NOI members testified again and again to the power of Muhammad and the success of his programs in rehabilitating even the most hardened criminal. In so doing, they affirmed the authority of their prophet, while also taking pride in their personal transformation.

## Muslim Girls Training and General Civilization Class

Just as the FOI ritualized proper male behavior within the movement, so did the Muslim Girls Training and General Civilization Class (MGT-GCC) seek to discipline, train, and cleanse the bodies of women. According to Essien-Udom, the MGT was "concerned with the training of good Muslim women" and watched "over the conduct and behavior of female members." Women were taught "how to keep house, how to rear children, how to take care of a husband, sew, cook, and in general, how to act at home and abroad." Hygiene, personal cleanliness, reading, writing, and maintaining the proper body weight were also stressed. In the late 1950s, members of the Chicago chapter of the MGT met each Thursday night to pray, sew, and study art, English, spelling, penmanship, refinement, beauty, hygiene, and cooking.[68] During the 1960s, meetings in Newark, New Jersey, took place on Wednesday and Friday nights.[69] In addition to offering various classes to members, the MGT sometimes provided opportunities to meet other African American women outside the movement who were committed to social reform. In the late 1960s, for example, MGT-GCC hour was held each Tuesday at Chicago's Salaam Restaurant from 1:00–2:30 P.M.[70] In February 1969 Mrs. A. O'Connor, chair of the usher board at Antioch Baptist church, and Mrs. Claudia Ross, president of the general mission of St. Paul Missionary Baptist Church, joined sisters from the MGT to discuss their concerns about "education" and "slum reform."[71]

In Washington, D.C., during the early 1970s, Sonsyrea Tate remembers attending MGT classes on Saturday mornings with her grandmother, a long-time member of the NOI. When they would arrive at the temple around 9:00 A.M., a brother "dressed in his F.O.I. uniform rushed to the taxi and snatched open the door," greeting the women with the words of peace, *as-salam alaykum.* It made Tate feel like "a queen, a little Goddess of the Universe." During these meetings, said Tate, an MGT sister "taught us little girls basic sewing stitches so we could mend our socks and make clothes for our dolls." Eventually, she said, these girls were able to make clothes for themselves. Like other children in the NOI, Tate also learned arts and crafts. A sister captain of the NOI taught the older ladies' classes, and might devote as much as one hour of lecturing on subjects like the navy bean. "What are the qualities of the navy bean?" the sister would ask. Another would respond, "The Honorable Elijah Muhammad teaches us that the navy bean is very rich in protein. . . . It is very high in fiber, and it will prolong our life."[72] In addition, says Tate, the MGT attempted to instruct its members in ladylike behaviors. "We learned not to use profanity and not to raise our voices, and we practiced walking with a book balanced like a crown on our head. If the book fell, it meant that a sister was still walking with her head down." They also studied self-defense. "Some Saturdays we practiced karatelike self-defense exercises, and Sister Captain reminded us, 'The Honorable Elijah Muhammad teaches us that we are never to be the aggressors. But if someone attacks us for our beliefs, then we are to do what?'" Tate answered, along with the rest of the crowd, "Fight like hell to the bitter end!" After class, some women would practice with the MGT drill team, a group "five sisters wide and six sisters deep." Marching in a military-like fashion, one member would cry out,

"Two, four, six, eight, who do we appreciate?"
"Elijah," they responded.
"Once more."
"Muhammad."
"Break it down."
"Elijah." Step. Step. "Muhammad." Step. "M-U-H-A-M-M-A-D!"[73]

Tate also remembers that as a child coming of age in the era of women's liberation, she identified with advocates of the Equal Rights Amendment, and took issue with the MGT's idealized vision of "respectable" and domestic women. The message that one received as a female child of the movement, she said, did not support her aspirations to become a writer and a career woman: "I knew I'd have to marry somebody since that was the only reason I was on this Earth—to become a good wife and mother."[74] But her mother and grandmother, she said, "sided with Elijah Muhammad on this one. Working women were the reason our society was going to hell, they explained to me. . . . And GrandWillie [her grandmother] said the society was better when women stayed home."[75] As we saw in the last chapter, many women in the movement often defended these Islamic codes of behavior and understood them to be liberating, not oppressive.[76]

In her memoir, Sonsyrea Tate is also very critical of the strict controls that a sister captain of the MGT would place on fellow members. "In fact, she could be downright mean," reported Tate. "I felt bad for any woman she sent home because her uniform wasn't clean enough. She'd talk about the woman in front of everybody. And sometimes, instead of sending the woman home, she'd take her in the bathroom and talk to her until she cried, then make her go back to the group with a tear-stained face. . . . Sister Captain didn't miss a beat. If someone pranced into the Temple with her headpiece pulled back halfway off her head, she'd pull her aside and tell her to stop being vain."[77] Tate's feelings are echoed by other former members of the MGT. Though Sister "Nancy" from Durham, North Carolina, expressed her appreciation for what she learned about eating right and liked the emphasis on self-esteem, she was uncompromisingly critical of the MGT and what she regarded to be its corrupt and malevolent leaders. Like Tate, she emphasized the humiliation of being confronted in public about a supposed mistake or fault, and said that some sisters would act as spies for the sister captains, reporting unfavorable comments to the leaders of the group. She also said that despite all of her work for the MGT, "you didn't ever see the result of that money." It went to Elijah Muhammad and his ministers, she said. Finally, she thought that the activities of the MGT monopolized too much of its participants' time. "We would go to MGT and GCC class like on a Tuesday at nine o-clock [in the morning] and we might not get out until nine o'clock that night," she said.[78]

Some women, however, resisted the authority of the sister captains and negotiated their own space within these mechanisms of control. Sister "Amina" joined the NOI in Washington in the late 1950s and has practiced one form of Islam or another since that time. A former teacher at the University of Islam and a long-time participant in the MGT, she remembered an incident in which she was harshly criticized by two sister captains. According to her recollection, the MGT in Washington attempted to enforce strict regulations on the movement of female members, acting as proxies for the male leadership of the movement. "They were rough on you, and they made you feel you can't go this place, you can't go that place [especially on your own without male supervision]. I remember once they told me I couldn't go to Baltimore." When Sister Amina went to Baltimore anyway, they confronted her, "trying to say I was wrong, and I couldn't do such and such for so many days." Like the men of the FOI, the women of the MGT faced several levels of disciplinary action for disobeying orders. The two captains attempted to place restrictions on Sister Amina. "And I said, 'You have to prove it to me, because my Islam told me that . . . I could go to Baltimore. I didn't have to ask you if I could go to Baltimore.'" She was, she remembered, "a little rebel." In another run-in with the MGT authorities, Sister Amina challenged a sister captain who attempted to control where Amina was buying cloth for her sewing projects. The captain criticized the poor quality of Amina's supplies, and even told her to buy clothes from another member of the MGT. Part of the problem, Sister Amina explained, was that the sister captain did not like the style of her creations, especially the long skirts that she made. Her response to the sister captain was firm: "'My husband will think I'm crazy if I have two good sewing machines sitting on my dining room table and I have to go to sister so-and-so to have her make my clothes for me.' I said, 'Economically, I am managing my household and buying my fabric. If I go buy fabric, inexpensive fabric, that is what my budget is telling me to buy.'"[79]

Sister Amina's testimony is important, because it suggests that some women challenged the authority of certain MGT officials and maintained good standing in the movement. As a member of high status in the Washington community—she had been in the movement a long time and was a teacher at the local school—it is not entirely surprising that Sister Amina could do so. But it is also noteworthy that Sister Amina insisted that her activities, whether it was going to Baltimore or making the kinds of clothes she wanted, did not violate the larger principles of the NOI. Sister Amina did not dispute the need for discipline. "As far as the discipline was concerned . . . I didn't have any problems with it." The problem, she said, was that leaders abused their authority at times.[80] By creating her own clothing styles, Sister Amina preserved the idea of modest adornment while also questioning the authority of MGT leaders and the idea that all MGT members must be dressed alike.

Not all female members of the NOI, however, explicitly challenged the ritualized control of the MGT. In fact, some heartily embraced it. A woman whom we will call "Fatima" converted to Islam from Roman Catholicism, due mainly, she said, to the influence of other family members who had become Muslims. As a single mother, she worked in various jobs throughout the 1960s and 1970s, including a stint as the assistant to a clinical supervisor in a Washington-area jail. Often, Fatima said, she would wear one set of clothes to work and another to the temple, an arrangement that was approved by a sister captain of MGT. Sister Fatima's memories of the Washington MGT are the most positive of the three recollections that have been mentioned here:

> MGT classes were wonderful . . . because they really exposed us to things that women really need to know. . . . We learned proper etiquette, how to set a table properly, how to prepare food—nutritional food. . . . And you learn how to care, I mean, fish, there are so many ways to prepare fish! We even had fish soup. And there were things that we didn't eat, like we didn't eat— sweet potatoes, so ate carrots in place of that, and we ate squash, and we learned how to make vegetables. . . . And how to take care of our families, how to take care of ourselves. They were just really wonderful. And I kind of miss it, because you had a chance to share information with people. . . . We really had a close bond. That's one thing the Nation taught me. We had that unity. If something had to be done, all we had to do was ask, and it was taken care of. Even if we weren't going to attend the meeting, we called. It taught responsibility, and how to be accountable for everything. Which was excellent, because it was the discipline that we needed. . . . It was part of what the Nation was all about. It was about discipline, but that discipline was necessary to build a nation. And to give the African American community or the African American race the dignity and respect that we really needed and we really deserved. And it is not given to us. We have to earn it. . . . So that right there let us know that we could accomplish anything we wanted to, but we had to be willing to do what it took to accomplish it, and not think that somebody was going to hand you something. I have an analogy and I use it; I say that God gives us the rain and the sun, and if we don't plant the seed, then we should go hungry.[81]

For Sister Fatima, the MGT was central to the practice of Islam, which, for her, involved learning domestic skills, discipline, and a "can-do" attitude. What others may have found humiliating, Sister Fatima found to be dignifying and liberating.

Sister "Anna," whom we met in the last chapter, has similar memories of the MGT from the early 1970s in Syracuse, New York, where she became a member of the NOI. Her chapter of the MGT, like the chapter in Washington, would meet on Saturdays and sometimes on other days as well. "The class itself taught women a variety of things, like health, personal hygiene, cooking, sewing, and just knowledge in education—reading and writing skills. . . . They had classes on early childhood development, childbirth, and all of that." She would get to the mosque, she remembered, at ten or eleven on a Saturday morning, and stay until six or seven in the evening. Women at her mosque, like other female members of the NOI, performed domestic duties, held fundraisers for the NOI, and ran various businesses from their homes. Sister Anna, for example, made bean pies at home, directly marketing them to other members and African Americans outside the NOI. Some women also worked outside the home, usually as teachers and nurses, she said. These sisters would often share their knowledge with others at MGT meetings. Like other chapters of the MGT, the Syracuse community was strict. "They were serious," said Sister Anna. "They wouldn't let you sit around and have a negative attitude. You have to respect authority. If you are going to be part of this organization, you have to respect leadership, and you have to follow through on what you say you're going to do. . . . They would penalize you, they would ask you to leave. And if you really admired this [organization and its activities], you didn't want to be kicked out, so you did what you were supposed to do."[82]

Like Sister Fatima, however, Sister Anna interpreted both the MGT and its strict controls in a largely positive light. "I would not trade this experience because it gave me inspiration," she said. "We admire what we have, and appreciate every little thing that we had, and if we even just had a recipe and I know how to make bread, we appreciated it and took pride in it, and then other people saw it and appreciated it too." The strict controls of the MGT, she said, "made us responsible, respectable. It just did all of that for us. I just admire the Nation of Islam so much." Sister Anna also likened the discipline of the NOI to the disciplined nature of her upbringing. "I came from a family of ten people, ten children. . . . I came from a family of discipline. You can't eat where you want to eat at, and you can't eat what you want. The portions were counted and measured to a T. Bath time, girls first, boys second. Dinner time, your portion will be placed on your plate, no one touches anybody else's food."

But not all members of the NOI came from this kind of background, and Muslims from "broken homes" without "structure" had difficulty with the discipline of the NOI, she said. For Anna, such discipline was necessary to self-improvement:

There are some that thought it was too strict, it was too hard, but I thought it was necessary and good. Some said they didn't like the way the sisters talked to us: "I don't think she should talk to you like you were a little kid." But I never had a problem with people speaking out against you, or to rectify things that weren't correct, because like I said, they were firm and strict. Some of the people who were placed as directors, they were serious, but that's how they dealt with everybody. You know we came from different families and different backgrounds. Some people came from backgrounds of real poor structure. Some came from families who were broken homes, too. I was lucky enough not to come from a broken home. I thought it was extremely good. I know people who left the NOI, because it was too strict for them. And I know a lot of sisters who said they didn't like it but they stayed. Some people thought they were taking away personal freedoms. It was firm, but I think it was being consistent. . . . And consistency was in the organization at all times. As long as no one was physically doing harm to you, or verbally, but it takes a critic to rectify and make things perfect. Because if you don't criticize, and don't let people know what could have been better, how will you improve on it?

Anna also attributed the need for this strict regime of what she called self-improvement, or what Elijah Muhammad called "civilization," to the history of racism and slavery in the United States. She argued that during slavery, slaveholders did not educate their slaves. Understanding that history, she said, freed African Americans to begin again, and learn essential life skills. "It's just like when you're lost on the highway," Sister Anna analogized. "You need a map to go back. You don't want to go back past where you came. You take the map and say here's where I was supposed to go. Because you know where you came from, you can use the map to find your way back. You need to get the knowledge to get better financially and [to get] healthy."[83]

What is striking in all of these testimonies is just how differently various former members interpret the regime of control implemented by sister captains and other officials of the MGT. What might have been liberating for one member of the MGT was clearly oppressive to others—at least in how the meanings of these controls have been interpreted in retrospect. Looking back, one of Cynthia West's informants in Newark, New Jersey, remembered that her MGT class produced a powerful sense of solidarity among members who sometimes became alienated from their own family members: "We bonded because there was a genuine thrust of sisterhood and love, and the connections we made with one another. And it was like we were family. We were really family. I mean, we depended on each other. Our lives were so intertwined with one another. You know, so it was like the MGT was almost an extension of your family. In fact, it became for many people, unfortunately, and I didn't necessarily agree with that, became their only family."[84] The creation of an MGT community, like the creation of any community, involved the making of boundaries between the in-group and the out-group. A system of controls was the mechanism by which such a community was created, and such controls, inevitably perhaps, had a social cost.

## The University of Islam and Youth Education

While children were trained in the ways of Elijah Muhammad at home and in the mosque, another key site where young brothers and sisters participated in ritualized activities of the NOI was the University of Islam and other programs designed explicitly for children. By the early 1970s, at least a dozen Universities of Islam existed in various Muslim communities throughout the country. *Muhammad Speaks* copyeditor Charles 67X claimed in 1973 that there were forty-two such schools; scholar C. Eric Lincoln said that there were fourteen.[85] The University of Islam began in the 1930s as a primary school with two branches, one in Detroit and the other in Chicago. In 1954, the same year of the famous *Brown v. Board of Education* decision that ordered the racial integration of public schools, the University of Islam in Chicago added a high school.[86] Around 150 students attended the school in the late 1950s in Chicago.[87] By the 1970s, according to C. Eric Lincoln, there were 600 students enrolled in Chicago, and 700 at Harlem's University of Islam.[88] In Washington during this period, there were approximately 200 students.[89]

While most of the school principals in the 1950s were men, this pattern was reversed in the 1960s. Female members of the NOI brought educational experiences as public school teachers to their leadership of the Chicago school during the 1960s; they included Sister Christine Johnson, Effie X Pope, Zella X Prince, and Agnita X.[90] The editors of *Muhammad Speaks* framed their leadership of NOI schools as female success stories, arguing that while other schools limited the career advancement of women in the field of education, the NOI did not: "The University of Islam . . . [has] a woman, Mrs. Christine Johnson, to head its faculty as principal for two years," one article boasted. "The school maintains a system of advancement on merit, rather than by sex."[91] Johnson, a graduate of Loyola University of Chicago, brought fifteen years of experience in the public schools of Chicago to her work at the University of Islam.[92] As other Muslim schools opened across the country, she acted as a consultant.[93]

Like other parochial schools, these institutions offered students a standard curriculum of reading, writing, arithmetic, and science in addition to covering more religiously oriented subjects like the teachings of Elijah Muhammad, elementary Arabic, and black history (the kind of black history that was explored in depth in chapter 3). Students also learned arts and crafts. The nonreligious curriculum in Chicago was modeled after that of public schools in Illinois.[94] Instructors issued grades based not only on student performance on examinations, but also on attendance, conduct, cooperation, effort, and reliability.[95] Some schools had a year-round schedule, though students only attended classes for half of the day.[96] In the early 1960s, when most Muslim temples did not have a full-fledged University of Islam, many mosques offered a similar curriculum on the weekends. For example, the youth program in 1962 in New York held classes from two to five every Saturday afternoon on 102 W. 116th Street in Harlem. The classes included English, in which students were taught parts of speech, pronunciation, grammar, and public speaking; physical and human geography; Arabic, in which students learned Arabic numbers, words, letters, and Arab history; arts and crafts, in which female students studied sewing and jewelry making; math and beginning chemistry; and drilling, in which boys learned "good self control."[97]

Though women in the University of Islam system may have studied home economics and dressmaking,[98] they also studied traditionally male-dominated subjects like science. Teenage girls, in a separate class, studied chemistry and biology.[99] *Muhammad Speaks* covered various aspects of female science education, including a 1968 frog dissection in Chicago by Sister Alberta 4X, a registered nurse, who attempted to "illustrate functions of various frog organs" for tenth-grade female students of anatomy.[100] Girls were also acknowledged frequently for their achievement in science. Valencia Jones, for example, won second place in the 6 July 1965, science fair in Chicago, and is pictured, without a headscarf, proudly displaying a trophy for her project about coal.[101] And Zanabid Sharrieff was pictured in Islamic dress adjusting her microscope in the NOI's science classroom.[102] It is worth speculating that such training recognized the need for African American women to prepare for careers not only as domestics and teachers, but also as nurses—one of the few professions open to black women for much of the twentieth century.[103] Perhaps the most famous nurse in the history of the NOI was Betty Shabazz, the wife of Malcolm X. But she was one of many. Female nurses were frequently pictured in *Muhammad Speaks*.[104] The most popular career tracks for college-bound women who graduated from Chicago's University of Islam from 1962 to 1965 were teaching, home economics, and nursing. College-bound men who attended during the same years declared their intent to major in business, agriculture, or engineering.[105]

But the education that one received at the University of Islam was designed to do more than prepare students for careers. It was also designed to teach obedience to God and his apostle, Elijah Muhammad. Each day began and ended with prayer. In the early 1970s at the University of Islam in Washington, D.C., Sonsyrea Tate remembers peeking to see whether other students had their eyes closed during these prayers. She joined others in reciting the following prayer from memory:

> Surely I have turned myself to Thee, O Allah. To Him who created the heavens and the Earth. I am not of the polytheists. I am of those who submit. Surely my prayers and my sacrifice, my life and my death are all for thee, O Allah. Lord of all the words. No associate has he and this I am commanded. I have been greatly unjust to myself and I confess my faults. Grant me protection against all my faults, for none grants protection against faults but Thou. Oh, Allah, bless Muhammad and the followers of Muhammad. As Thou did bless Abraham and the followers of Abraham. For surely Thou are praised and magnified. Amen.[106]

A University of Islam education was also designed to instill pride in being black. In 1962, school director Christine Johnson explained the importance of an all-black and black-centered education by pointing to the poor self-image that many black children developed in white schools. She blamed textbooks, among other things, for the problem: "In the textbooks used, he [the black student] is taught that Africans and descendants of Africa are inferior and that white Christian missionaries went to Africa to educate the 'poor misguided heathens.' He is taught that America was settled by civilized people from Europe, who came here seeking freedom. . . . Our children are taught America was discovered by whites even though the Indians were here."[107] Up to this point in its history, the University of Islam had used textbooks that maintained such historical narratives. Purchased from the Follett Book Company in Chicago, these texts included a standard American history text.[108] To correct this problem, Johnson wrote a textbook for elementary school children, and dedicated it to Elijah Muhammad. The text covered a number of subjects, including "Muslim religion," the African American community in the United States, phonics, spelling, African art, black businesses in the United States, African heads of state, and African geography. "Through these pages of history," said the author, "our little ones will see faces that are similar to their own and will grow up in a belief that it is great to be born

Black. . . . I hope this book and others to follow will arouse and stimulate young minds to see that there is hope and dignity for the black man."[109]

In trying to instill pride in students, said Principal Agnita X in 1968, the school also taught discipline and dignity. "Upon entering an Islamic school," she explained, "a child will show marked changes in behavior, in physical appearance, and in rate of learning. He will exhibit good manners and respect because by nature he is good and wants to do good. He becomes clean internally and externally, and his clean mind allows him to be at ease in order to grasp instructions. By nature he is the best and upon him rests the fate of our nation."[110] Students were often searched before entering the classroom in the morning, and if anyone misbehaved, they answered to a captain of the FOI charged with enforcing the school rules.[111] In Washington in the early 1970s, discipline started before the student even set foot in the school. Sonsyrea Tate rode the NOI bus to school, and "the rules said that we couldn't talk on the bus. So the boys buckled into their seats and remained silent as Uncle Hussein, junior F.O.I. captain, paced up and down the aisle making sure nobody talked or ate on the bus. Some of the boys had lunch bags full of doughnuts from our bakery bought after school, and they inched off bites because they couldn't wait until they got home. If Uncle Hussein caught anybody, he made him hit the floor right there on the bus and do push-ups."[112]

NOI schools also maintained a dress code. In the late 1950s, the Chicago University of Islam told female students to wear brown, beige, or blue jumper dresses with matching headscarves. Dresses for teenage girls aged thirteen to seventeen could be no higher than eight inches from the floor and blouses were to have three-quarter-length sleeves and high neck bands. Socks were to match dresses and all girls were supposed to wear black slippers. Boys were asked to wear blue, brown, or gray suits, and black or brown shoes. According to Essien-Udom, however, the dress code was "not widely used."[113] This lack of full adherence to the dress code seems to have continued throughout the 1960s. While many students wore headscarves, for example, others did not, including Sister Miriam Saunders at the Chicago school.[114] Sometimes, even the director, Sister Christine Johnson, was pictured at school without a veil.[115] Enforcement of the dress code, however, seemed to have differed depending on the time and place. In Washington, D.C., Sonsyrea Tate remembers, most of the girls observed the code, which in the early 1970s meant that they wore "the same green uniforms, wide-legged pantaloons, long tops that reached almost to our knees like a short dress over our pants, and white headpieces."[116]

Like other institutions in the NOI, the University of Islam and NOI youth programs included a number of highly ritualized activities, activities that involved the regulation of time and space, special personnel and dress, special codes of communication, and other ritualistic elements. For example, children often performed music or drama for adult members of the community that utilized official NOI clothes, images, and narratives. In Chicago, an August 1962 performance of poetry, prose, and music included the "surprise appearance" of a speaking choir, "composed of girls in the fifth and sixth grade English classes." Members of the group, lined up on stage in front of a scrim featuring the image of a traditional Islamic shrine or mosque, wore "attractive floor-length full green skirts, white blouses and white head scarves decorated with green appliquéd leaves." They recited various passages from the works of Elijah Muhammad, the farewell sermon of the Prophet Muhammad of Arabia, one of black abolitionist Frederick Douglass's speeches, quotes from Shakespeare's *Macbeth*, and a selection from poet Langston Hughes.[117] These public performances oftentimes included a visit from a high-ranking NOI official, Muhammad Ali, or a member of Elijah Muhammad's royal family.

The daily activities of these schools also included several ritualized elements, such as the recitation of certain prescribed prayers. During school assemblies in Chicago, like one photographed by Emerson Muhammad in 1973, members of the Junior FOI presented the colors of the NOI, a flag that featured the Islamic star and crescent. Boys ages five to ten would stand in a line, arranged in order from the shortest to the tallest, and give a military salute to the flag. A male honor guard then executed "precision drilling movements after smartly presenting the Holy Flag of the Nation of Islam." Girls held a separate assembly. According to the article, "Kindergarten girls," dressed in pants, loose blouses, and headscarves, "also salute their flag and their Nation" in a "separate assembly from the Muslim boys, allowing both to fully express themselves in a civilized atmosphere." Both assemblies, according to *Muhammad Speaks*, were designed to honor "the hard life and struggle of the founder of the University of Islam, the Honorable Elijah Muhammad."[118]

Students also recited various catechisms that, both in their very repetition and in their substantive claims, helped to construct the authority of Elijah Muhammad and his movement. "Every day," wrote Sonsyrea Tate, "we were drilled on a few of our twenty-five Actual Facts, information about the dimensions of planet East and other celestial bodies. . . . We also had to memorize and recite Student Enrollment Rules of Islam, which were bits of history according to Elijah Muhammad."[119] The *Actual Facts* and *Student Enrollment* had been a part of the NOI at least since the 1950s if not before, and based on Tate's account, remained a part of the NOI's religious curriculum into the 1970s. Essien-Udom reported that all members of the organization in the late 1950s were expected to memorize lessons gleaned from these documents, as well as from Elijah Muhammad's *Supreme Wisdom* and the Qur'an, before being granted full membership in the NOI.[120] The FBI also reported that at some temple meetings during the 1950s, believers were quizzed on these lessons. The *Student Enrollment* consisted of ten questions concerning Elijah Muhammad's teachings about the true nature of the black people, the number of black people in the United States, the number of square miles of "useful land" on the earth, and the origins of Islam, which was seen as the only timeless faith in human history. The first question was "Who is the original Man?" The answer: "The Original Man is the Asiatic Black Man, Owner, Maker, cream of the planet earth, God of the Universe and Father of Civilization." The *Actual Facts* contained arcane information about the weight of the original man's brain, Elijah Muhammad's myth of black origins, the weight of the earth, the meaning of Allah's name, the nature of heaven and hell, the measurements of the planets, and several other numerological observations. According to the FBI, these facts were meant "to impress the members and potential members of the Cult with the supreme wisdom of their teacher, and the great knowledge they can obtain by being members" of the NOI.[121] Indeed, both sets of documents attempt to communicate a set of seemingly secret teachings that evoke the larger tradition in African American and American religions of esotericism, a word used to describe various groups and persons who attempted to combine religion, science, and mystical teachings into one holistic understanding of the universe.[122]

In the NOI's schools, some students became master esotericists, offering their own interpretations of Elijah Muhammad's cryptic teachings, especially on the nature of time. Practically speaking, students were encouraged to use time not for play, but for work. Observing this rule of behavior meant that "in Islam we are taught that we have Tuesday set aside as our day of recreation. The other days we continue to work and learn the infinite wisdom of Islam and Allah." As twelfth-grader Sister Rhea X explained in 1968, sport and play were generally to be avoided by Muslims. "Today," she said, "we are living in a world built on sport and folly which is soon to be destroyed." The reasons for avoiding play were complicated, however, and required explanation. According to Sister Rhea, students should reject a culture of recreation and live instead, she argued, in a world "built on wisdom and knowledge. Time spent in wisdom is endless because wisdom can be passed on and on to further the intellectual pursuits of man and better the world in which we live." Sister Rhea said that time spent in play is fleeting, while time spent in gaining wisdom is eternal. Sister LaVenia 3X, also in twelfth grade, expanded on this Islamic theology of time: "In relation to Islamic teachings the hours of folly are measured by the clock, because

vas preaching to the choir, to men and women who sent their children
 precisely because they wanted them to have a black-centered educa-
e Sister Claretha's speech may not have been an attempt to convert
v-converted to her cause, it was a reaffirmation of the choice made by
nembers to support the school and its goals. The substance of Sister
speech, like other ritualized elements in the movements, testified once
he authority of Elijah Muhammad and his program to support the
f exclusively black institutions in the United States. To implement this
lijah Muhammad relied on others who would teach at those schools,
 children to the schools, fund them, and offer convincing rhetoric on
were valuable. There was perhaps no better place to offer rhetorical
r Muhammad's schools than a ritualized ceremony filled with those
m he relied to make them a success. Sister Claretha spoke from her
ority as an experienced educator, and offered an important endorse-
e Messenger's plan to educate black children.

## etings, Muslim Conventions, and Religious Rallies

g to E. U. Essien-Udom, the only identifiable religious rituals at temple
 on Wednesday and Friday nights were the prayers said at the opening
ng of the service and the verses of the Qur'an and the Bible occasion-
aloud by ministers.[127] In the late 1950s at Chicago's Temple No. 2, he
nister would rise and welcome the congregation with the Arabic words
*alaykum*, peace be unto you. Those audience members in the know
spond in Arabic by saying *wa alaykum as-salam*, unto you be peace.
gregation then stood, faced east, and assumed a traditionally Islamic
sture with their hands outstretched and their palms facing up. They
eir heads, closed their eyes, and recited a prayer, usually in English, but
lly, according to Essien-Udom, in Arabic. This prayer evidenced the
ic or "combinationist" nature of NOI religious themes, a phenomenon
in chapter 2; it incorporated words from the first *sura*, or chapter, of the
words that are recited by observant Muslims around the world as part
scribed daily prayer, into supplications on behalf of Elijah Muhammad
ollowers:

Name of Allah, the Beneficent, the Merciful. All praise is due to Allah,
ord of the Worlds; Master of the Day of Judgment [Qur'an 1:1–4]. I
vitness that there is none other to be worshiped, but Allah, and that
mmad is His servant and Last Messenger. O! Allah, Bless Muhammad

as Black People we cannot continue to foolishly
ignorant beliefs of the Christian World. The time
Islam teaches us to be wise because the time is
Their beliefs, being foolish, are not made to last f
LaVenia, by avoiding frivolous play and devoting
of the NOI were not so much preparing for a comii
ing here and now in Islamic time, a form of time
every moment spent in study was a ritualized mor
a believer's ontological reality.

Another ritualized activity in the schools was tl
graduation ceremony. At Chicago's 1969 graduat
male valedictorians were celebrated, a class gift w
extolled the benefits of their Muslim education ar
the NOI and its schools. Former SNCC activist turne
gave the "stirring main address," and graduates s
sity of Islam / May thy name forever ring. / The
Blessed forever may thy be; / With Muhammad
as our God, / We will ever love and cherish, / '
not unusual for a woman to be the main graduate
included male and female graduates.[125] In 1962,
Shabazz of San Fernando addressed graduates at
ceremonies. According to *Muhammad Speaks*, sh
experience in public schools, and "put over a dyi
enlightenment and inspiration, not only of intere
graduates but to everyone of all ages and occupati

In her address, Sister Claretha also preached
schools. "The Honorable Elijah Muhammad has
that whoever controls your education, controls yo
your education, you control your future," she said
white privilege and black self-loathing perpetuated
tions. Criticizing textbooks and children's reading
of white children, she issued this warning: "Wh
Dick and Jane don't look like him. The fire chief do
master doesn't look like him. The mayor, the go
look like him. Consequently, he has no reason to
these things because nobody that ever did anythin
Black children can never reach the heights that otl
given a thorough knowledge of themselves."[126] Ex
Claretha's address is important to understanding it

---

the s
to a s
tion.
the a
audio
Clare
again
creat
strate
send
why
supp
upon
own
ment

## Temp

Acco
meeti
and c
ally re
said,
*as-sal*
would
The c
prayei
bowed
occasi
syncro
explor
Qur'ai
of the
and h

In t
the
bea
Mu

here in the Wilderness of North America, and bless the followers of Muhammad too, as Thou did bless Abraham, and the followers of Abraham. O! Allah, make Muhammad successful, and the followers of Muhammad successful, here in the Wilderness of North America, as Thou didst make Abraham successful, and the followers of Abraham. For surely Thou are Praised and Magnified in our midst. Amen.[128]

After congregants concluded the prayer, using the Arabic pronunciation of the word "Amen," they passed "their palms over their faces," which is another gesture derived from historically Islamic traditions of prayer.

Though Essien-Udom claimed that religious rituals in temple meetings were limited to such prayers and the occasional recitation of a verse from the Qur'an or the Bible, he also provided a rich description of other activities that many contemporary students of religious studies would view as religious ceremony and ritual.[129] He noted, for example, that "meetings begin promptly. Members must be punctual, and unless they have good excuses for being late, they may be suspended from the Temple for repeated offenses."[130] Once again, then, we see how a ritual in the NOI manipulated time and invested it with a certain meaning. Enforcing punctuality was a form of control that attempted to train the black body to observe Elijah Muhammad's rules of civilized behavior. Another ritualized element of temple meetings was "the search." After arriving at the temple, male visitors were searched by the FOI and females by the MGT. "At first," one visitor told Essien-Udom, "I felt that the search was ridiculous. But when I discovered that it was taken so seriously and done so thoroughly, I was frightened. For the first hour at the temple, I was exceedingly uneasy and afraid. The members looked at visitors with curiosity, if not utter suspicion."[131]

The search was supposed to produce this particular mental state, Essien-Udom argued. An "important aspect of the initiation process, this invasion of the privacy of the individual person humiliates him and makes the visitor feel guilty about his previous way of life. Initiates are thereby readied for submission and obedience to the will of Allah and Muhammad, and to the many exacting demands of personal obedience and loyalty."[132] In conducting the search, FOI and MGT members looked not only for objects like firearms and knives, but also for cosmetics, cigarettes, matches, and nail files—anything associated with the exploitation of the black body. "In the Old World," Minister Lucius, a former Seventh Day Adventist preacher turned Muslim, told Essien-Udom, "the so-called Negroes had been used to carry knives, guns, cigarettes, liquor, etc., with them. In coming to the New World they must leave these things behind." Not all members of the NOI regarded the search with such seriousness, however. As a child, Sonsyrea Tate remembers, she would lift her arms "like an airplane about to take off, and Sister Muriel smiled as she began patting my head to make sure nothing was concealed beneath my headpiece." Sister Muriel was always nice to her, she said, probably because Muriel was fond of one of her uncles.[133]

Once the search was completed, FOI members, who maintained a complex protocol of military-like salutes in executing their duties, then showed visitors to their seats—an important detail since most Muslim mosques around the world do not have seats. In early 1970s Washington, according to Sonsyrea Tate, the members of the FOI "looked sharp in their dark blue suits with a thick white stripe running down the pant legs, a high collar on the jacket, and the matching cap that bore a backward crescent and star." These model Muslim males "moved with swift precision, walking straight lines stiffly, turning corners sharply with a clock of their heels." Members of the MGT, she said, "were equally dazzling in their special uniforms: a long white skirt, a knee-length cape, white gloves, and a white box-hat with flaps tied under the chin."[134]

Essien-Udom reported that in late 1950s Chicago, members were quiet and sober in tone and avoided what Elijah Muhammad had deemed "slave" behaviors—especially the get-happy ecstaticism of the slave religious meeting. "Shouting and wailing," said Essien-Udom, "is considered characteristic of Negro Christian preachers who want to arouse the emotions of the congregations in order to get money 'which is tied up in churches and Cadillacs.'" Most members exercised what Essien-Udom saw as remarkable self-constraint throughout the long temple lectures, given by one of the NOI ministers. Occasionally, he reported, one could hear a subdued form of the call-and-response so famous in African American religious culture, including comments like "preach it, brother Minister." The minister spoke from a simple lectern at the front of the mosque, flanked by two guards of the FOI. He was surrounded by movement symbols like the flag of Islam, which featured an image of the moon and stars and the initials I., F., J., and E., which stood for Islam, Freedom, Justice, and Equality.[135] From Essien-Udom's description, it is fair to conclude that ritualized elements existed not only in the prayers, but also in the objects used during services, the specialized personnel, the specialized dress, and the particular mental states of participants.

These ritual elements were even more in evidence during the annual celebration of Saviour's Day on 26 February, the day on which Muslims in the NOI remembered the founder of the organization, W. D. Fard. Thousands of Muslims boarded buses and created caravans to travel to Chicago each year for a series of events that, like many conventions, included speeches, performances, trade, and informal networking among members from across the country. The official

Saviour's Day schedule in 1965, for example, promised to offer a welcome by Minister James Shabazz of Mosque No. 2 in Chicago, prayers, testimonies from members of the FOI and MGT about "what the birth of the Saviour means" to black men and women, music by jazz artist Osman Karriem, an exhibition by boxer Muhammad Ali, a business meeting, and various addresses by Elijah Muhammad on W. D. Fard, his three-year economic development program, and the coming apocalypse.[136] Members of the FOI and MGT donned their official uniforms and spent hours at a time listening to various speakers. In 1960, members of the FOI were asked to wear a different uniform for each day of the convention: on the first day, a blue suit with white tie; on the second day, a brown suit with brown tie; and on the third day, a gray suit with a black tie. Women were to wear white gowns.[137] In 1964, the convention was held in the Chicago Coliseum. Hundreds of MGT members, dressed in long flowing white gowns and white headscarves, sat in bleachers behind the speaker's platform, from which NOI leaders would address both their followers and the visitors who would attend. A huge banner at least fifty feet long was hung above the MGT members, proclaiming in capital letters that "there is no God but Allah, Muhammad is his Apostle." Hanging on either side of this banner were two large portraits of the Messenger, dressed in a dark suit and bow tie.[138] The choreography of the hall, its participants, their dress, their shouts of approval, and the speeches given—all of this signified the power of the man at the head of the ritual. No wonder boxing promoter Murad Muhammad later explained to journalist and author Stephen Barboza that "people don't understand. The Honorable Elijah Muhammad had an unbelievable power in America—more than any other black man, ever."[139]

Even the visitors in attendance noted the power of Elijah Muhammad's presence. In 1964, *Muhammad Speaks* reporters, including Sister Harriet Muhammad, asked first-time visitors, "What brought you here?" and "What is your opinion?" William L. Rydan, a lift-truck driver, explained that he had been "referred here by Brother McKinley 2X." After seeing Elijah Muhammad in person, he concluded that "he's the greatest man alive—now and in the past, too. I've just started listening to the teachings, and so far what I've heard is the truth." Helen Henderson, a student at Chicago's Wilson Junior College, explained that she had come to hear "Elijah, and also to see him. I think he's marvelous. His teachings have united us. He has to have some truth behind him because he has so many followers." Ulysses A. Ewell, a hotel clerk, said that he had also come to "hear the Messenger, and I think he delivers a very excellent message and makes a very impressive speech."[140]

But not all of the visitors interviewed by *Muhammad Speaks* agreed with Elijah Muhammad's claims, and it speaks to the journalistic quality of the paper that their opinions were included in the reporting of the event. Delores Griffith, a graduate student at the University of New Mexico, came to understand the movement better, and was impressed by the self-respect and dignity of Elijah Muhammad's followers. She also admitted, however, that while she admired the Muslims, "I can't say that I fully understand the religion, Islam; its concepts, its theories." Similarly, Richard Hubbard said that he was "very impressed with some of the teachings . . . on the meats, smoking, and about the so-called white man." But he could not "agree with him [Elijah Muhammad] on there being no spiritual God. I'd have to question this point," he explained.[141] These statements help to show that, as much as Saviour's Day was focused on the "life giving teachings of the Honorable Elijah Muhammad," the ritualized event had multiple meanings for those in attendance.

At least one NOI intellectual, for example, compared the convention to the *hajj*, the annual Muslim pilgrimage to Mecca. Dr. Leo P. X McCallum, the writer and dentist, called Saviour's Day a modern pilgrimage, a "power-packed, wisdom-laden meeting of the minds of men and women bent on a single errand — to achieve for themselves, their families and own kind freedom, justice and equality under one leader . . . one religion, Islam, and one God, Allah." It was not, he said, a "ritualistic display of emotion and worship." McCallum also acknowledged that the *hajj* was a requirement for Muslims, but questioned its relevance for members of the NOI: "For the so-called orthodox Muslim (and we must say here that we consider ourselves just as Muslim as anyone else. We herein use the word orthodox only to distinguish the followers of Messenger Muhammad from the Muslims of the East) a principle of Islam is that he must make a trip to Mecca at least once during his lifetime if he is financially able." During the *hajj*, he said, "many rituals are performed, such as circling the Kaaba seven times and kissing the black stone resting within its walls. But what really is the significance of performing these feats? Does the Muslim do it just because he read it somewhere in his early study of religion?" he asks. Brother Leo offered a critique of ritual performance shared by many modern Muslims and Christians alike. Why, he asked, does one circumambulate the Ka'ba seven times instead of two or fifteen? "There is a science behind all of these things," he admits, but "we know that the signs and rituals in Arabia at the Holy City of Mecca are but signs of the future of Islam and the last Messenger and his people." Whether a Muslim makes a pilgrimage to Mecca or to Chicago, for McCallum the importance of that pilgrimage rests not in the performance of rituals, but in the intellectual and political training that occurs during the occasion. The purpose of a pilgrimage is not to say "Amen," to laugh, or have a good time. It is, rather, to give participants "an opportunity to shake some of the cobwebs from our brain . . . to understand what it means to be free to exercise freedom, justice, and equality in a brother-hood and with a display of unity."[142]

Whether or not other Muslims in the NOI agreed with McCallum's interpreta-tion of Saviour's Day, it is clear that their descriptions of Saviour's Day belied his claim that it was an unemotional and ritual-free event. Numerous contributors to *Muhammad Speaks* spoke of the various ritualized elements that shaped their experiences in Chicago. Bayyinah Sharrieff, for example, claimed that unity displayed during the convention was "beautiful," noting the role of dress in the making of such harmony. "One did not have to speak with another to learn that there was harmony present," she said. "All one had to do was look out over the auditorium and see the Sisters all in white robes sitting together, and the Brothers in their neat and trim, F.O.I. blue uniforms, to see unity. . . . The joy in the eyes of the Believers was apparent to any onlooker as they listened to the Message which would bring happiness and peace of mind," she wrote.[143]

In addition to attending the annual Saviour's Day celebrations in Chicago, NOI members would travel on buses and create caravans to attend Elijah Mu-hammad's religious rallies, held throughout the country. In 1961, for example, at least four busloads of followers traveled from Chicago to New York to hear Muhammad speak on 27 August.[144] On 8 August 1965, hundreds came to see Muhammad in Detroit's Cobo Arena.[145] The preparations for such visits were extraordinary, and Muhammad was treated like a visiting head of state, or the Messenger of Allah. As C. Eric Lincoln reported:

Several days before the Messenger is scheduled to arrive, members of the Fruit of Islam security corps cover every inch of the route he is to travel from the airport to the temple. On the day of his arrival, Muslim guards are posted at strategic points along his route several hours in advance. Each guard is briefed as to precisely what he should do in case of an emergency. . . . The Messenger always travels with a personal security force, composed of three to four members of the FOI from Temple No. 2. This guard is usually headed by Supreme Captain Raymond Sharrieff in person. When Muhammad deplanes, he is always preceded and covered from behind by this personal guard. As soon as he is on the ground, the local security force takes over. The Messen-ger is immediately surrounded by a force of twelve to twenty men, and other Muslims are scattered inconspicuously among the crowds at the airport. An additional force in several automobiles takes over as he leaves the airport, some preceding and others following the car in which the Messenger is riding. The FOI captain of the local temple, riding in one of the lead cars, exchanges signals with individual guards previously stationed along the way. Should the guard not return the proper signal, the entire force is put on "emergency alert" and an alternate route is chosen.[146]

By the time Elijah Muhammad arrived at the auditorium, the crowds had been "searched and seated—men to the right, women to the left." Finally, an FOI honor guard escorted the Messenger into the hall.[147]

In his autobiography, Malcolm X provided a description of the moment when Elijah Muhammad would enter the hall. His testimony illustrates the efficacy of this ritual and evidences how the special dress, body postures, personnel, texts, and speech helped to construct the power of his prophet. As Elijah Muhammad entered, Malcolm remembered,

> The audience would begin a rustling of turning. . . . Mr. Muhammad would be rapidly moving along up a center aisle from the rear—as once he had entered our humble little mosques—this man whom we regarded as Islam's gentle, meek, brown-skinned Lamb. Stalwart, striding, close-cropped hand-picked Fruit of Islam guards were a circle surrounding him. He carried his Holy Bible, his Holy Qur'an. The small, dark pillbox atop his head was gold-embroidered with Islam's flag, the sun, moon, and stars. The Muslims were crying out their adoration and their welcome. "Little Lamb!" "As-Salaikum-Salaam!" [sic] "Praise be to Allah!" Tears would be in more eyes than mine. He had rescued me when I was a convict. . . . I think that my life's peaks of emotion, until recently, at least, were when, suddenly, the Fruit of Islam guards would stop stiffly at attention, and the platform's several steps would be mounted alone by Mr. Muhammad.[148]

The ritualized nature of the event may also help to explain why Elijah Muhammad, known to those outside the movement to be a rambling and dull speaker, was received enthusiastically by those inside the hall. In chapter 2, I mentioned that Sonsyrea Tate, who grew up in the NOI, found that Muhammad's "speech was broken and his grammar was bad compared to the grammar we learned in his schools."[149] Journalist Louis Martin argued that "Elijah Muhammad . . . is one of the few, if not the only, mass leaders in the national Black community who is not regarded as a great orator. He talks softly with almost none of the eloquence one traditionally associates with Black leadership and especially Black religious leadership."[150] But for many who followed Messenger Muhammad, those who credited him with changing their lives, such characterizations of his speaking style did not ring true. As C. Eric Lincoln put it, "The response his presence evokes in the black masses is phenomenal, especially in light of his difficult to follow delivery."[151] Though Sonsyrea Tate may not have been moved by Elijah Muhammad's speeches, she notes that her grandmother certainly was: "Sometimes tears would well up in GrandWillie's eyes when she listened to the Messenger speak."[152] Similarly, Roosevelt 6X of Temple No. 7C in New York reported that after listening to one of Elijah Muhammad's lectures, "I felt so good until I was just happy and filled with joy. The Messenger sounded so clear and bright, so crisp and filled with a deep deep love for His people. He sounded so strong and powerful, yet, His call for us, the Black man in America, was so humble and from a base of Love." The brother could not "hold back the tears." In explaining why, he said that "the one thing that really got to me was the sound of His voice. I could actually hear the deep, beautiful resonance, a sound of love that is born out of long sacrifice and suffering. The sound of a man calling his own flesh and blood out of the path of destruction." As a musician, he said that he was especially sensitive to sound. But he cautioned that "I do not say I am an authority of this, all I know is what I feel when I hear what I hear and when I heard the Messenger's voice it struck something so deep in me that I had to write about it and talk about it."[153] Even the FBI seemed to notice the effects of Muhammad's charisma on believers, although they never offered a penetrating analysis of why the charisma was so effective. A 1965 internally published FBI monograph about the NOI admitted that "this small, frail, seemingly meek and humble man, who has only a fourth-grade education, is a master at creating mood, myth, and mystery. . . . Never appearing before the public without his black pillbox hat generously encrusted with jeweled stars and crescent, Elijah seems to have touch of the patient Oriental in his face."[154]

## Total Ritualization and Its Limits

Though all members of the NOI did not observe all of Elijah Muhammad's rules at all times, there is evidence that some certainly tried to do so. In their life examples, one can see what might be called total ritualization, the attempt to turn every moment of the day into an enactment of Elijah Muhammad's prophetic commandments. Moreover, the ritualized structure of each local Muslim community offered believers the opportunity to do so. If one desired, one could spend nearly every day involved in economic, social, political, and cultural activities that were seen by many believers as Islamic acts. The testimony of one NOI member, as reported by Essien-Udom, illustrates this idea:

> Before I joined the Nation I went out Friday nights and all weekend nightclubbing and drinking. . . . I began having sex life at eleven and my first girl friend was about fifteen. . . . Now, instead of chasing women and nursing

liquor bottles, I spend my spare time at the Temple of Islam. Mondays: 7 to 11 P.M. studying Arabic, English, writing, social science, arithmetic, and *The Supreme Wisdom* at the F.O.I. meetings. After that I go home to bed. On Tuesday nights, I am at the Unity Party. Wednesdays, I attend the regular Temple meeting. Thursdays, I am on M.G.T.'s Guard Duty. This means that I along with the other members of the F.O.I. [go] to guard the doorways to the Temple and to the University of Islam in order to protect the Sisters. . . . Friday nights are regular meeting nights. I work eight hours a day. On Saturdays, I work at my laboratory—a mechanical shop. Sunday afternoon is regular meeting. There is no time for visiting friends except on Saturdays and Sundays.[155]

Such testimony was not unusual. Some members of the NOI in St. Louis also moved into the mosque. As Abdul Shabazz remembered, "We were like a vanguard. I was about fifteen, sixteen years old, and at that time about fifteen to twenty brothers would stay above the mosque. It was like a dormitory."[156] Even those who were not part of the "vanguard" in St. Louis participated in similar processes that helped to build a strong sense of community among members of the NOI. Believers met in each other's homes to create their own sense of community away from what they saw as the temptations of mainstream culture. "We couldn't smoke. We didn't drink," said Abdul Shakir, a former captain of the Fruit of Islam. "We were pretty puritanical in our beliefs. We couldn't go [to] the movies, couldn't go to nightclubs, so we had to socialize at somebody's house. The sisters would cook pastries and dinner; the brothers would listen to tapes and study their lessons. It brought strong cohesiveness among the Muslims."[157]

Some accounts of what I have called total ritualization in the NOI have been far more critical, including Sonsyrea Tate's 1997 memoir, *Little X*. The author notes that "there was always something to do at the Temple or for the Nation. We went to the Temple almost every day of the week for something—school through the week, Fruit of Islam (F.O.I.) meeting on Tuesdays for the boys and men, Muslim Girls' Training and General Civilization Class (M.G.T. and G.C.C.) on Saturday mornings for us girls and our mothers, and the general meetings, which were sort of like church services, on Sundays." Though Tate depicts such ritualization as a rich religious culture, she also critiques its patriarchy, its control, and its cultic nature. She compares Elijah Muhammad to the Wizard of Oz: "I thought Elijah Muhammad was a wizard and that black people needed his power and wisdom to deliver them from all the stuff the bad white people did." Extending the analogy, Tate also observed that some "of the men and women at the Temple were as stiff and uptight as any Tin Man. Some of the officials seemed like the Lion—ready to take charge as soon as some great Wizard gave them permission. But some of the grown-ups at the Temple seemed as brainless as the Scarecrow, acting like they didn't have minds of their own." After listing several mechanisms of control that Elijah Muhammad utilized in his leadership of the NOI, she concludes this chapter with the following line: "Elijah Muhammad had our minds completely."[158]

It is a dramatic conclusion that is undermined by evidence that she presents elsewhere in the book, which shows how women and children in the NOI often subverted, ignored, or questioned the authority of Elijah Muhammad and his commandments. For example, Tate's grandmother and mother had a long-standing feud about the use of non-Muslim media in Tate's childhood home. Tate's mother, a sometimes reluctant member of the NOI, was also a devotee of *One Life to Live*, the popular soap opera. Tate's grandmother frequently objected to the program, warning that this "junk" would brainwash her. "But," writes Tate, "Ma still found a way to do what she wanted to do, so she let the TV run and did her chores during commercials."[159] Tate's strict grandmother even violated NOI prohibitions at times, especially the policy against celebrating the birthday of anyone other than Elijah Muhammad. Reflecting back on the negative impact that this practice had had on her own son, Tate's grandmother decided to ignore the rule; for her grandchildren, she baked cakes and sang "Happy Birthday" every year.[160] Tate herself also questioned the absolute authority of the Messenger, even though she was just a child. "GrandWillie and the other grown-ups believed that Elijah Muhammad was the smartest man in the world," she wrote. But "some of us kids were suspicious."[161] Tate's somewhat contradictory statements, when read and analyzed together, help to illustrate just how complex the religious culture in the NOI actually was. Her family members were not the only Muslims to pick and choose which prophetic commandments to obey. We have already seen how certain members of the NOI, like the pot-smoking sellers of *Muhammad Speaks*, selectively observed the rules of Muslim conduct.

But total ritualization was also limited in another way. Despite the attempts by the leadership to control every aspect of movement life, the sheer size of the organization—dozens of mosques in dozens of communities run by dozens of different people—seemed to have posed a challenge to the centralized control of the NOI's religious culture. In fact, at times, it was unclear exactly what the rules were, as can be seen by examining the place of musical performance and jazz culture inside the movement during the 1960s and 1970s. In various locales throughout the country, the FOI and MGT would host banquets and evening performances for themselves and the general public. For example, at Buffalo's Mosque No. 23's annual "Nite with the FOI," awards were presented, and Dr.

Lonnie Shabazz, the Atlanta University math professor who became the NOI minister in Washington, gave an address criticizing Martin Luther King Jr. Members of the FOI chorale also sang the "New Battle Hymn of Islam" and "Go Down Elijah." A quintet performed "When the Roll Is Called in Heaven," and the mosque's drama group "drew applause with their skit entitled 'Raisin of a Negro.'"[162] In 1966, the FOI brothers in Springfield, Massachusetts, performed a play entitled "The Trial," a standard of NOI drama from the 1950s that put the white man on trial for his various abuses of people of color, including blacks and American Indians.[163] This was the same play that had been featured in Mike Wallace's television documentary, *The Hate That Hate Produced*, in the late 1950s, and it was seen both by media observers and members of the NOI alike to be a powerful recruiting tool.[164]

Throughout the country, local mosques also organized community bazaars where visitors could learn about the movement at various booths, purchase literature and other goods, listen to movement speakers, and enjoy dramatic and musical performances. A 1962 African-Asian bazaar in Harlem, for example, included booths where one could observe a professional glass blower, purchase jewelry, and subscribe to *Muhammad Speaks*. Nigerian drummer Babatundi Olatunji performed, and comedian Dick Gregory stopped in to sign autographs.[165] Similarly, Buffalo's Annual Bazaar in 1966 offered entertainment by the "Fruit of Islam choral group, a short skit, an interpretative dance, a jazz combo and a series of selections by the famous 'Durations.'" In addition to selling the baked goods and clothes made by NOI members, the bazaar also featured non-Muslim merchants, who marketed their "photography, art, jewelry, men's clothing and samples of black journalism."[166] In Washington, at the fall 1969 Unity Bazaar sponsored by Muhammad's Mosque No. 4, more than one hundred "Black businesses exhibited their support through their contributions and participation. Items on display ranged from gold-plated household ornaments to silken robes and oriental tapestry." For example, one could purchase tapestries featuring the image of camels, pictures of the Ka'ba in Mecca, and framed posters of a star and crescent.[167]

These events frequently featured the performance of jazz music. In Washington, the Webster Young Quintet performed, Minister Lonnie Shabazz delivered an address entitled "Muhammad's Way is the Only Way," and Brother Lieutenant John 20X directed a karate demonstration.[168] Miami's MGT chapter hosted a banquet at Mosque No. 27 in which the Noble Watts Jazz Quintet performed with the help of temple members Guy X, Elvin X, and Ernesto X.[169] In 1967, Muhammad's Mosque No. 26 in Denver featured jazz music played by Brothers Harold X on the vibes, Jesse 4X on the bass, Richard X on the piano, John 10X on the sax, and Thaddius X on the trumpet; each member of the ensemble wore the official FOI uniform of the time, which included a type of sport coat with narrow lapels, a bow tie, and a fez with the letters "FOI" embroidered on its front.[170] In 1966, in St. Louis, the Shahid Quartet "provided electrifying entertainment" for students "who completed their first spelling bee at the [temple] school. They received thunderous applause for their original number entitled Grand Avenue," the St. Louis street where the mosque was located.[171] Several months later in 1967, this quartet, whose players included Sonny X Kenner on guitar, Ezekiel X Cleaves on tenor sax, Edward X Skinner on drums, and George X Hudson on bass, also performed at a New York Muslim Unity Bazaar in St. Alban in Queens.[172]

The quartet was formed in 1966 after NOI member Sonny Kenner moved to Kansas City, Missouri. According to Kenner, he was already an accomplished musician before joining the NOI. "At 19," he told *Muhammad Speaks* reporter Darryl Cowherd, "I joined Sonny Thompson and Lula Reed and traveled with them for two and a half years. Then I was drafted into the army. All the time I was in the army, I played—providing music for the officers. . . . I also played in the army production of 'Kiss Me Kate.'" After being discharged from the army, he became a studio musician in Los Angeles, where, from 1959 to 1965, Kenner recorded with Jimmy Witherspoon, the Jazz Crusaders, and others. "I was on the Steve Allen and Jerry Lewis shows and I recorded for most of the top Mercury recording artists." In 1965, he moved to Kansas City, where he opened a bookstore and helped to organize the Shahid Quartet in 1966. One of his collaborators, vocalist Larthey X Cummings, said that the group hoped to "specialize in and utilize clean musical material. Music that has dignity and respect." He said that he had been inspired to do so by Elijah Muhammad, whom he had met personally after entering the NOI. "Through his guidance and teaching, I have learned how to conduct myself musically, and then inner peace that Islam brings has enabled me to fully concentrate on this area of my music." He concluded the interview by thanking National Secretary John Ali, "who always encouraged us."[173] Such support indicated that at least one highly ranked official of the movement publicly condoned the performance of jazz music.

By late 1967, Pakistani columnist Abdul Basit Naeem observed a shift in NOI policy toward musical performance. In the early history of the NOI, he said, "music, as a form of collective or public entertainment had no place in the then-infant Muslim movement's scheme of things." Since the late 1950s, however, "both music and musical entertainment (inclusive of highly interpretive African ethnic dances) have . . . played an increasingly significant role in the presentation of American Muslims' overall social and cultural program." He noted that an upcoming benefit concert would feature "such top-rated artists as the Shirells, Ruby and the Romantics, Joe Tex and his orchestra, [and] Pucho and the Latin Soul Brothers." But Naeem also admitted that Elijah Muhammad had not explained why he supported such a change in policy toward music (if he did). "Exactly why the gracious and noble Muslim leader, Elijah Muhammad, removed or relaxed the erstwhile ban on the use of music, this, of course, I cannot say—though I trust the Messenger will someday, when he deems it proper or necessary, enlighten us all on the matter."[174]

Naeem's comments notwithstanding, severe criticism of jazz artists and jazz music appeared in the newspaper the following two years. In 1968, Elijah Muhammad warned followers to avoid any contact with Max Spears, or Osman Karriem, one of the most prominent black Muslim jazz artists of the 1960s. In 1966, Karriem, a jazz saxophonist, had been the "principal attraction" at a buffet dinner sponsored by the MGT-GCC in Chicago.[175] And in 1967, *Muhammad Speaks* was proud to praise Karriem's trip to Ethiopia, where he was featured on Ethiopian television blowing his horn.[176] But in 1968, when Karriem's drug use came to the public's attention, Elijah Muhammad proclaimed that the NOI "had no association whatever" with a man "now charged with drug addiction." The Messenger said that while Karriem "wants the public to think that he is still one of my followers and still associated with me and my followers," it was the duty of every Muslim to "keep away from him."[177]

Then, in 1969, the newspaper launched a public campaign to limit the types of performers at Muslim bazaars and community events. "The Honorable Elijah Muhammad teaches us not to listen to Jazz music," the unattributed announcement said. It criticized the "Brotherhood Bazaar and Trade Fair," a fundraising event planned for the Boston area in the fall of the year, arguing that any Muslims who would invite African dancers and jazz artists are "indeed very weak believers in Islam. . . . The idea that people who call themselves Muslims would present such an affair to invite others to hear disgraceful music is a discredit to their belief." According to the article, "such a weak follower is trying to hold on to the ways of this filthy American society." It concluded with a call to place moral decency above the almighty dollar and forego such fundraising techniques.[178] In 1971, Minister Louis Farrakhan also criticized the indecency of the La Roc Bey African-style dance troupe, whose performance had preceded his speech at a 1971 Harlem Black Solidarity Rally on October 13. "How foolish it is to strip a Black woman in public before sick Black men who have been made weak, wicked, filthy, and indecent in his outlook toward the Black woman. And, all of this filth you do in the name of Africa," he lamented.[179] During this period in the early 1970s, virtually no reporting on Muslim jazz or popular artists associated officially or loosely with the NOI appeared in *Muhammad Speaks*.

But the music never really stopped. For example, Pucho and the Latin Soul Brothers performed at the Harlem bazaar in 1968.[180] Mosque No. 27 in Los Angeles presented an afternoon of entertainment in January 1969 with the Curtis Amy Quintet, the Natural Five, and the Debonairs.[181] In 1973, the paper reported that the Delphonics performed at a Muslim bazaar.[182] And Kool and the Gang, whose songs "Whiting H & G," "Hereafter," and "Fruitman" referred to various aspects of NOI culture, performed for a Temple No. 57 event at the Scope Exhibition Hall in Norfolk, Virginia, in 1974.[183]

## Conclusion

The diverse musical culture of the NOI shows that there were practical limitations on the power of the Messenger and his cadre of movement leaders, or perhaps that they disagreed over the appropriate role of music in community entertainment. In either case, what is clear from this brief discussion of music in the NOI is that the authority of Elijah Muhammad was never absolute in the movement, certainly not in the 1960s and 1970s. Even though many institutions, including the FOI, the MGT, and the local mosques, were in theory supposed to enforce the ethical commandments of the Messenger, there could be no complete control of movement members. This lack of total authority also suggests that subordination to the Messenger and other NOI leaders involved some degree of choice on the part of the individual believer.

The key to understanding why thousands of African Americans voluntarily submitted to their prophet, I have argued, lies in the ritualized nature of their activities. Of course, not all members felt positively about the ritualized activities of the NOI. As we saw above, some Muslims observed certain aspects of the NOI's ritualized code of behavior, while ignoring others—like the MGT member who refused to follow the orders of her superior. Some NOI members, like Sonsyrea Tate, also disliked the controlling nature of the NOI's religious culture. For them, perhaps, there was more domination than liberation in the NOI. On the whole, however, the ritualized practices of the NOI were efficacious enough for a sufficient number of persons to establish and maintain a national community of human beings committed to their performance. Whether these Muslims were selling newspapers, donning elegant uniforms, attending mass religious rallies, or singing the praises of the Messenger, they felt empowered by submitting to their prophet and his rules.

The ritualized nature of NOI activities permitted believers to find religious meaning in nearly every human act. These activities were a powerful mode of Islamic meaning-making and communal identification. Practicing Islam in the NOI, then, was a multilayered process that involved not only the adoption of certain theological, eschatological, mythological, and ethical beliefs, but also the performance of particular ritualized actions. Through these religious practices, believers came to feel as if they were living *in* Islam, a realm of being that expressed their true nature as black people and as human beings.

# Conclusion
## Becoming Muslim Again

I don't regret it. I do not regret it. And I tell people often
. . . that I really thank God for blessing me to have been
in the Nation of Islam, because without that, I would not
be where I am today. And people say things that are not
kind about Master Elijah Muhammad. I do take issue with
that, because he is the one that God sent to us to bring us
where we are today. And when I say where we are today,
I'm talking about as a community, because we identify with
Muslims all over the world. And if we had not gone through
the Nation of Islam, we would not be able to appreciate
that today. So, I really thank him for that.
— "Sister Fatima," interview by Katherine Currin,
　　Washington, D.C., 2 November 2003

On 25 February 1975, at the age of seventy-seven, Elijah Muhammad, the Messenger of Allah, died of heart failure. News of his death made the front page of the *New York Times*.[1] The next day, during the annual Saviour's Day convention in Chicago, his son Wallace D. Muhammad was declared the new leader of the organization.[2] Born in Detroit, Michigan, in 1933, W. D. Mohammed, as he is now known, had been a frequent critic of his father's interpretations of Islamic religion. In the 1960s and 1970s, he left or was expelled from the movement several times, although he always rejoined. Like his brother, Akbar, Wallace Muhammad became committed to a Sunni interpretation of Islam. After inheriting the mantle of leadership from his father, he initiated a remarkable reformation of the NOI. In a span of less than three years, he aligned the NOI with basic Sunni Islamic doctrines and debunked his father's teachings about the nature of W. D. Fard, the origins of the black race, and evil genes of white people. In 1976, he changed the name of the organization to the World Community of al-Islam in the West, and later to the American Muslim Mission.[3] During this period, Wallace Muhammad also instructed his followers to observe the five pillars of Islamic practice, including the daily prayers, the pilgrimage to Mecca, and the fast during Ramadan.[4] And he told them that the ultimate authority in all religious matters was not his father, but the Qur'an and the Sunna, or the traditions of the prophet. He called these dramatic changes the "Second Resurrection."[5]

In one sense, Wallace Muhammad's reforms ratified a trend already growing before 1975 — namely, the commitment to Sunni Islamic traditions by an increasing number of African American Muslims. As Aminah McCloud has pointed out, there were practicing African American Sunni converts in the United States well before 1960, and some of them had never associated with the NOI.[6] But the number of African American Sunni Muslims increased during the 1960s.[7] The NOI played a vital role as a conduit through which many African Americans in this era passed on their way to practicing Sunni Islamic traditions. Malcolm X is an excellent example of someone who first converted to the NOI and then again to Sunni Islam during this period.

There were many other Sunni Muslim defectors from the NOI as well. For example, one of Sonsyrea Tate's relatives converted to "Orthodox Islam" before 1975. Eventually, her mother began to read the Qur'an on her own, taught the children the *Fatiha*, the first chapter of the Qur'an, in Arabic, and attempted to arabicize the children by requiring them to eat on the floor. There were even rumors that change was coming in the NOI, according to Tate. "A few people in the Nation knew that our leader was preparing the younger people for a new kind of Islam, the universal Islam that's practiced by black and white and yellow and red people all over the world." Her mother began using Arabic words, like *shukran*, or thank you, in her everyday speech, and gave some of her children Arabic names. Sonsyrea resisted these changes, defending the Islam of the NOI. But more and more African Americans in Washington were becoming orthodox Muslims, she said. The extended Tate family was split between NOI and orthodox Muslims, and Tate changed her dress according to which group she was visiting at the time. Some members prayed the words taught by Elijah Muhammad; others performed the Sunni prayers.[8]

Despite the defections, thousands of African American Muslims stayed in the movement until the death of Elijah Muhammad and then followed Wallace Muhammad through the Second Resurrection. Some of these persons, like Sister Fatima quoted above, explained these changes as the result of a divine plan meant to bring African Americans to Sunni Islam. Sister Alexandra, who became a member of the NOI in New York during the early 1970s, echoed this thought, and also argued that the NOI deserved some credit for bringing African Americans to the "real" Islam:

Overall my experience with the Nation of Islam was a positive one. And I always said, only a few of us came in that way, but Allah is into every plan and nothing happens without his permission. And if that's the way I came into Islam, then that's the introduction that He wanted me to have. . . . And I see a lot of the Muslims today in America, and especially the immigrant Muslims benefit greatly on the sacrifices that were made by those of us who were in that first movement, who were bold enough to say, "We are Muslims," even though we weren't practicing as the world community of Muslims practice. And maybe we were offbeat, but . . . everything was in God's plan. But it opens the door for Islam to be widely accepted in this country. Now, because if it had not been for that little voice of Elijah Muhammad and that pioneering group—because there were Muslims in America, but you didn't hear from them or you didn't see them. It was that bold statement out there of your Muhammad Ali or Malcolm X, and . . . we may have been off-key, [but] we were still making music and we were still drawing attention to the religion, and paving the way for the religion. Now, it must have just been in Allah's plan, because nothing without his permission is what we believe.[9]

Sister Alexandra's testimony makes an important argument about the role of the NOI in the history of African American Islam. She argues that while members of the NOI may have been "offbeat" and "off-key," they still proudly proclaimed a Muslim identity. That was, according to her, a bold form of self-identification — one that, as we have seen throughout this book, was a powerful cultural and political statement in the context of the 1960s and 1970s. Looking back, one might say of African American Muslims in the NOI what Devin DeWeese has said about converts in Inner Asia: "To adopt a name is to change one's reality, and in this sense there is hardly a *deeper* 'conversion' than a *nominal* one."[10] Before the dramatic changes of 1975, African American members of the NOI already thought of themselves as Muslims. And after 1975, if they remained in the movement, they became Muslims again.

Even more, Sister Alexandra's testimony suggests that there was a historical *connection* between the practice of Islam in the NOI and the practice of Islam under the leadership of Wallace Muhammad. I would go even further and argue that in order to understand the religious practice of African American Sunni Muslims once associated with Elijah Muhammad's NOI, one must scrutinize the extent to which those practices represented forms of cultural continuity. By showing the various ways in which the NOI oriented the imaginations and practices of its members toward the Afro-Eurasian Islamic world and its religious traditions, my study suggests that members of the NOI underwent a transition to Sunni Islam rather than a wholesale change in religious practice.

Scholar Carolyn Rouse has made a similar argument, claiming that there was both change and continuity in the transition from the leadership of Elijah Muhammad to that of his son Wallace Muhammad in the middle 1970s. Criticizing the arguments of scholars who have claimed that the NOI was not a truly religious movement, Rouse asserts, as I have done in this book, that Elijah Muhammad's NOI was both religious and political. In her words, the NOI's "dialogic critique of Christianity was tied to a politically informed spiritual reawakening."[11] In attempting to understand the change of religious orientation of some members in the mid-1970s, Rouse argues that as Wallace Muhammad eschewed more and more of his father's separatist visions of Islamic religion, his followers simultaneously preserved much of the "intent and social impulse behind them."[12] Examining the attraction of various informants to the discipline of dietary guidelines and other forms of religious purification both before and after the change in 1975, she claims that "though the Nation of Islam and Sunni Islam differ in ideology, they share a holistic and ritualized approach to life."[13]

My work, especially in chapters 4 and 5, confirms this assertion that discipline, ritual, and purification were essential elements of practicing Islam for many believers associated with the NOI in the 1970s. In fact, for some Muslims, the focus on a disciplined religious practice even preceded their conversion to Islam. For instance, Sister Alexandra of New York noted that she was religiously disciplined as a young Christian and remained so as a Muslim. Growing up in what she called a strict Missionary Baptist home, she later converted to the NOI. But she came to feel, like other members of the NOI, that the NOI was too military-like. Describing the kinds of hierarchical controls discussed in chapter 5, she said that the discipline of the NOI "was more or less a forced thing, because people kind of watching over you and telling you what to do and what have you." After 1975, however, the surveillance of the NOI was replaced, she said, with the authoritative guidance of the Qur'an and the Sunna, or the traditions of the Prophet Muhammad. "Now [under Wallace Muhammad] . . . everything was based [on] and the reference was with Qur'an, and you start studying to see what God said. . . . I wasn't doing things because someone told me I needed to do this, a human being told me to do this, [but] because God said, in Qur'an, this is the way of the prophet." As a result, she said, her family began to observe the prayers and study the Qur'an together:

> We have always been serious about our religion, our family has, my husband and I. We always start the morning out early with *fajr* [the first of the five daily prayers], and after *fajr*, we would always read the Qur'an for anywhere from fifteen minutes to half an hour. And the children did the same thing when they became of age to do that, and so they knew very well what the book said. And if they didn't, I'd tell them, take it, turn to a *sura* [a chapter of the Qur'an] and you read it. I couldn't always tell them which *aya* [verse]. Or either I would sit down, and I would show it to them. And I'd say, and you read it. We're responsible to God, what you do when you're grown up, when you're grown, and with your children is one thing. But since we know we have to answer to Allah, we raised them to the book.[14]

Sister Alexandra had traveled along a changing religious path from Missionary Baptist to member of the NOI to Sunni Muslim. Along the way, however, she was always disciplined in her religious practice. Better, she associated the practice of religion itself, in whatever form, with ritualized discipline.

The attraction to religious discipline, however, represents only one form of continuity between the practices of the NOI and those of Wallace Muhammad's community of followers. It might also be claimed, following the line of argument found in chapter 3 about black Muslim history narratives, that throughout the 1960s and 1970s, African American Muslim members of the NOI had internalized a dramatic shift in their communal consciousness, a reorientation of themselves in space and time that fused black and Islamic identities. During this period, narratives that linked the history of black people to the world of Islam proliferated in the movement. That genre of religious expression did not disappear after 1975. In fact, the black Islamic history narrative continued to be a main referent in movement discourse and was invested with new vision and strength.

Perhaps the best and most ubiquitous examples of the black history narrative in the post-1975 NOI were stories surrounding Bilal ibn Rabah, the black African companion of the Prophet Muhammad of Arabia and first prayer-caller in Islamic history. On 1 November 1975, Wallace Muhammad said that he would call himself "Bilalian," a new religio-ethnic label that he recommended to other persons of African descent. He also changed the name of the *Muhammad Speaks* newspaper to the *Bilalian News*. He explained that Bilal was "a Black Ethiopian slave who was an outstanding man in the history of Islam. He was the first *muezzin* (Minister) of Prophet Muhammad (may peace be upon Him). He was so sincere and his heart was so pure that the Prophet Muhammad and the other leaders of Islam under him addressed him as 'Master Bilal.'"[15] With this new focus on Bilal, the talk of black ancestors in the movement did not disappear. But instead of disseminating narratives about the mythical tribe of Shabazz, as did his father, Wallace Muhammad created stories about the historical figure of Bilal. Unlike Elijah Muhammad, he did not use this historical narrative to emphasize the genetic foundation of black greatness, but instead utilized the vocabulary of black ethnicity, culture, and history to frame historical black achievement. This emphasis on black ethnicity paralleled in an uncanny way the themes of Alex Haley's wildly popular *Roots*, a story that traced his family's ethnic heritage to an African ancestor named Kunta Kinte.[16]

During this period, various published sources about Bilal, written by Muslims and non-Muslims alike, circulated in the movement.[17] The newspaper marketed Bilalian styles of dress, including the "Bilalian" fez, and the children's page of the *Bilalian News* offered a word puzzle about the historic figure. Placed next to an illustration of a man performing the call to prayer, the puzzle read: "I was once a slave / Who was very brave / I was a man without fear / who gave the first prayer / in a land where Arabia lay / And though there were great odds / I was not afraid / to proclaim the religion of God. Who am I?"[18] All these creative activities focused on the figure of Bilal can be fruitfully understood as practices whereby members of the movement engaged the story of their ancestor to construct, or in some cases to deconstruct, their Muslim identities. Bilal was an example of a Muslim who became great through his devotion to Islam and his refusal to accept the social stigma of being a former slave.

My oral history interviews with followers of Wallace Muhammad in the 1990s confirm that many believers saw parallels between their own life circumstances and those of Bilal, but also indicate that they interpreted the figure of Bilal in several different ways, alternately emphasizing the social, political, cultural, and religious importance of calling themselves "Bilalian." For instance, Imam Samuel Ansari, the leader of St. Louis's Masjid al-Mu'minun, the former NOI Temple No. 28 now aligned with Wallace Muhammad, explained that he decided to call himself Bilalian because

African Americans suffer from an identity crisis. Our circumstances are very parallel to what his was, and he came to a station of dignity through accepting Islam and became a very close companion of the Prophet. . . . And it's synonymous, I think that's the proper term, it's synonymous with us trying to gain our dignity and our station of dignity in America—that if we would come to right guidance, come to a call, whether you become Muslim or not is not important, but it means coming to the call that is calling you to dignity, to integrity, to live to employ principles in your life. . . . I heard the Imam [Wallace Muhammad] talk about it once. He said that Bilal wasn't just a slave; Bilal was an obedient slave. You know, he was a good slave. . . . He obeyed his master up until he heard the call to Islam and the message of what Islam offered, and then, after that, he could no longer accept it. See, and that's the way most of the people, the African Americans who truly convert or revert back to Islam. . . . They can no longer be willing subjects of the Caucasians or people who want to employ or put them in subjected situations, you know. And now you have to treat me with the same respect that you treat anybody and everybody else, and I will not accept anything short of that. . . . So, I still feel that Bilalian is a better term to identify as ethnic group than even African American.[19]

Ansari's rich explanation of the term "Bilalian" shows that for him the figure of Bilal modeled the connections between proper ethical behavior, self-determination, black liberation, submission to God, and self-respect. Imam Ansari emphasized the historical parallels between Bilal and African Americans by juxtaposing Bilal's circumstances in Arabia with the challenges faced by African Americans in the United States. Like Bilal, he said, African Americans can "gain our dignity and our station of dignity in America," if we come "to the call that is calling you to dignity, to integrity."

Ahmed Ghani, another of my informants in St. Louis, echoed some of Ansari's claims, and also stressed that this Ethiopian's contributions to Islam could be seen as a source of ethnic pride and identity for blacks; as an ethical example for all persons, regardless of racial or religious orientation; and finally, as proof for the strength of multicultural societies. "When you get a lot of ethnic groups of people together," he claimed, "they can advance the human society to a greater plateau." Lorene Ghani, his wife, added during this interview that the use of the term Bilalian was part of a larger trend of Muslim naming: "Most of the African American people in this country today do have slave names. And he [Wallace Muhammad] wanted us to feel good by taking on a name of our culture at that time. . . . And from then on we had a book of Muslim names, and we chose names based on the kind we thought was suitable for us with a good meaning."[20]

Khadijah Mahdi, who, during the 1990s, served as principal of the Clara Muhammad School attached to the Masjid al-Mu'minun, emphasized the importance of Bilal in a slightly different manner. For her, Bilal's accomplishments not only evidenced the strength of multicultural societies, but also established the importance of black African contributions to the history of Islam. Mahdi, who converted to Islam in the 1970s in New York, said that she, too, had called herself Bilalian. She explained, like Ansari, that the use of this label provided a sense of identity and celebrated a moral exemplar. But she also argued that anti-black racism, especially among Muslims, helped to create the need for a term like "Bilalian":

> [No one wants to] be said to be black . . . even when you have some [Asian] Indians who are blacker than I am. . . . It just seems as though the Arabs or the Muslims from other countries — immigrants — they want to make this [Islam] seem as though it's more of an immigrant religion or religion for the Arabs. And so that means that all of the darker people that were in it are not given the same credit basically. You have Abu Bakr [the first caliph of Islam], you have the companions, and mostly, well, Bilal was not a companion, but why wasn't he? Why wasn't he thought of being a companion? Why was he just written as though all of his function was to do the *adhan* [call to prayer]?[21]

Of course, one could take issue with Mahdi's claims. Muslim scholars have for centuries considered Bilal to be a companion of the Prophet.[22] And immigrant Muslims have acknowledged the contributions of Bilal, a black African, to the history of Islam.[23] Moreover, many Muslim missionaries have stressed the non-racial character of Islam as one of the religion's central tenets.[24]

But what should not be missed is Mahdi's feeling that Bilal had been excluded in Islamic history because he was black and her view that the recognition of Bilal was an important step not only in telling a more racially inclusive history of Islam, but also in showing how race itself is an unimportant category in God's eyes. By recognizing the existence of skin color, cultural difference, and racial prejudice, she said, one could ultimately transcend the bonds of race and ethnicity. When I asked Mahdi whether she was proud of being black, she responded by saying that "I'm proud of who I am and basically, you know, to say you don't see skin color, you can't say that . . . in America . . . [but] my skin is not going to do anything for me. It's just my exterior. It's what's inside that's going to get me to paradise or take me to hell."[25]

Abdul Shakir, however, offered a different interpretation of Bilal's meaning to African American Muslims. Shakir, a former captain in St. Louis's chapter of the Fruit of Islam, claimed that Bilal symbolized the special and particular role that African Americans should take in leading the *umma*, or worldwide community of Muslims, toward proper Islamic practice and Muslim unity:

> We liken the role, we could relate to the role we was playing, being ex-slaves and having embraced al-Islam, wanting to be right, and we could see a lot of fallacies in the Saudis and the Egyptians, you know, in the difference between the Shi'ites and the Sunnis. . . . So you need someone, someone summons them all together that they all respected and they would . . . get behind when the summons [was issued]. . . . The Imam [Muhammad] say we want to set a good example, we want to follow the exact dictates of Prophet Muhammad, we want to follow the command to the letter. We say that Islamic states have accepted too much of European cultures. . . . And then this racism, you know, most of them, the foreign believers at the Islamic Center [in St. Louis] and cross country, too, because of what had been said about the African Americans, the uncouth: "When you go to America, don't associate with them. They so corrupted and they drink wine and they commit adultery and they are dope fiends." . . . But we, knowing that this was what was being said about us, Imam Muhammad said, we want, now that we in mainstream Islam, we want to inherit this Qur'an one hundred percent, so be it. We step on whoever's feet we step on. If the Saudis are not adherent to this book one hundred percent and to its ideas, we'll be free and we can feel free to make them aware that where they have gone and strayed from the Qur'an. And, if we adhere to these teachings and to the Qur'an, a lot will bless us undergoing what we have went through and come out of slavery and through what Elijah taught. And now we're on the right path. We want to set good examples.[26]

According to Shakir, African American Muslims could offer moral leadership to immigrant and foreign Muslims, who had become too divided, who had adopted too much European culture, and who had become too racist. Because of the African American Muslim journey from slavery and Elijah Muhammad's incorrect Islamic teachings to the "exact dictates" of the Qur'an and the Prophet Muhammad, he argued, African American Muslims could be moral examples for all. To Shakir, Bilal was a poetic symbol calling African Americans to lead and unite the *umma*.

But not all followers of Wallace Muhammad enthusiastically embraced the title of Bilalian. Abdul Shabazz, a carpenter who originally converted to Islam under Elijah Muhammad's leadership and remained in the movement through Wallace Muhammad's reforms, asserted that skin color and ethnic identity were ultimately unimportant. Saying that he "agreed" with the term, he also cautioned that the search for identity was a "waste of time." He said, "In order for me to really say where my ancestry lies at or—all I know is that my ancestors were kidnapped, right? To go into Africa or a city to find out definitely my roots or my origin would be like a non-stop challenge." Instead, Shabazz argued, "Islam solves the identity crisis. Be a Muslim, and secondly, I am of African descent and I am in America." When I followed up by asking him whether the term Bilalian was important to him personally, he responded: "No, not really, you know, because I figure, you know, in the end all of us return to our Creator."[27] Shabazz's mental map was not focused on Africa, but on the primordial origins of all human beings as sons and daughters of God. The historical narrative that mattered to him was the supralocative story that began with God's will. These comments are significant, for they remind us that Muslim identity in the NOI after 1975 cannot be defined in any monolithic way, no matter how important the story of Bilal was to many.

Nevertheless, I would argue, the continued salience of the black Islamic history narrative as a religious genre in the NOI helps us understand how it was that Wallace Muhammad succeeded in altering the religious ideology of the movement without losing all of his followers. In a few years, he convinced thousands of African Americans to change the way that they thought about and practiced aspects of Islam. In so doing, it must be recognized, he was working with persons who already thought of themselves as Muslims. For years before 1975, NOI members had imagined their Muslim identities as being linked to the greater history of Islam, and that style of being Muslim endured after the break with Elijah Muhammad's unique mythologies. While the creation and dissemination of black Islamic history narratives was only one form of religious expression in the NOI, it is a phenomenon that provides a helpful language for understanding the other forms of religious experience in the NOI both before and after 1975. Black Islamic history narratives, like black Islamic rituals and ethics, constituted a discourse that oriented members of the NOI in a universe of religious meanings that were, in one way or another, Islamic.

After Elijah Muhammad died, some Muslims in the NOI may have changed their theological perspective, but they did not necessarily change every other element of their identity as Muslims. Their "Sunnification" did not suddenly begin on 26 February 1975. It had started years before as they adopted various elements of Afro-Eurasian Islamic traditions and incorporated them into their religious narratives, ethics, and ritualized activities. The NOI's increased use of Qur'anic texts in the 1960s, its adaptation of the Ramadan fast and the five daily prayers, its prohibition of both alcohol and pork, and its patterns of veiling for females and gender segregation, among other factors, normalized various traditions of Sunni Islamic religious life and thus paved the way for their adoption by African American followers of Wallace D. Muhammad. Wallace Muhammad's Sunni reformation may have been a dramatic break with the past, but it was also a remarkable perpetuation of already-established African American Islamic traditions.

## The Legacy of the NOI

The history of the NOI should never be read as a story about all African American Muslims, especially today. The African American Muslim community is even more diverse than it was in the 1960s and 1970s. Contemporary African American Muslim communities include black American members of immigrant-led mosques, African American devotees of Salafi and Wahhabi versions of Islam, African American Shi'is, African American Sufis, Five Percenters, Sunni followers of Wallace D. Muhammad, members of the Moorish Science Temple, members of local Muslim Student Associations, and followers of Minister Louis Farrakhan, who reconstituted a version of the NOI in 1978. Many black Muslims are not associated with any organized group. They are part of a growing American Muslim community that may represent anywhere from two to eight million persons.[28] Today, while Louis Farrakhan's NOI may make an occasional headline and still matters deeply to the thousands of African Americans who follow his version of Islam, most Americans have directed their fears of the Muslim other toward the perceived threat represented by transnational Islamic groups. Perhaps it can be said that today's NOI, like the NOI of the 1930s and 1940s, operates largely outside of the consciousness of many Americans.

But despite all these changes in the landscape of American and African American Islam, the history of the NOI continues to present a set of questions and challenges central to American Muslim life. More specifically, in my view, the history of the NOI invites American Muslims of all sorts to confront and debate the issue of diversity in Islam and the extent to which Islamic practice should respond to the local circumstances and exigencies in which Muslims find themselves. While Jim Crow segregation may be gone, racial prejudice and institutionalized racism continue to affect nearly every aspect of American life and the relationship of Americans to the rest of the world. American racism is also part of the American Muslim community, which, like nearly every other religious community in the United States, is divided by race.[29] While some interracial American Muslim movements have arisen to confront racism and other issues of social justice in contemporary society, most American organizations and local mosques are either predominately black American or non-black American, especially when it comes to leadership and power structure.[30] Many African American Muslims also feel that they are the victims of discrimination at the hands of nonblack Muslims.

For those African American Muslims who imagine Islam to be a vehicle of racial equality and human solidarity, the presence of racism is particularly painful. The history of the NOI acts as a touchstone for discussions about these important issues. In fact, it is difficult for many American Muslims to discuss race and religion in the United States without bringing up the NOI. While most American Muslims, including black Americans, would never defend Elijah Muhammad's doctrinal teachings about the nature of God or his myth of black origins, there are large disagreements over other aspects of his legacy. Some, like Sisters Alexandra and Fatima, admire Elijah Muhammad and speak appreciatively of his remarkable accomplishments. Many also continue to be committed to what they see as the NOI's mission of black liberation—social, cultural, political, and economic. As shown in Sister Fatima's and Sister Alexandra's testimonies, they often separate the "good" parts of Elijah Muhammad—his focus on black uplift and empowerment—from the "bad"—his theological heresies. But other Muslims, including some African American Muslims, see Elijah Muhammad only as a heretic, and refuse to acknowledge any good at all in the NOI's accomplishments. In so doing, these critics too easily dismiss the stories of the people described in this book—people for whom Elijah Muhammad's Islam was liberating at the time. If nothing else, I hope that in giving voice to these persons, this book has invited all those not part of the NOI to listen more carefully and compassionately to them.

Finally, the legacy of the NOI also raises important questions for non-Muslim Americans. During the NOI's heyday in the 1960s, its activities prompted a great deal of fear and fascination among governmental agencies, the press, academics, and the American public at large. In retrospect, it seems clear that the radical rhetoric of the NOI, especially when viewed only as a form of political activity, was wrongly assumed to constitute a powerful, violent threat to the American nation-state. Non-Muslim Americans in the 1960s were correct in identifying the ideological challenge that the NOI posed to American nationalism, Christian institutional hegemony, and other forms of American consensus making. But the FBI and the press exaggerated the revolutionary potential of any organized and direct threat to public safety and security. For the most part, members of the NOI were law-abiding persons of faith who may have hoped for a radical change in the social and political fabric of the United States, but engaged in few violent actions to bring about a revolution.

Today, transnational Islamic groups, like the NOI in the 1960s, are assumed to present a challenge to Western civilization, peace, and security, and Muslims who participate in them are often suspected of being potential terrorists. The legacy of the NOI provides a cautionary tale in the all-too-easy conflation of "Muslim" and "terrorist." While it is true that Islamism, a label used to portray the diverse groups and individuals who advocate the politicization of Islam, offers a critique of American and European power, neocolonial dictatorships, and globalization, it is untrue that most Islamists are busily organizing terrorist activities against innocent Americans in the United States. As Americans continue to reel from the tragedy of 9/11 and a difficult war in Iraq, it is all too easy for politicians and fear-mongers to cite the growth of Islamism as a threat to freedom and our way of life.[31] Such comments may provide impetus for an expanded war on terror, but they also help to silence legitimate voices of protest against social inequality, political corruption, and American interventionism. The legacy of the NOI suggests that, rather than assuming an inevitable and cataclysmic clash between Muslim groups and the United States, all of us should search for other ways of framing the current tensions between the goals of Islamism and those of U.S. foreign and domestic policy. The legacy of the NOI also indicates that in so doing, participants in the dialogues of civilizations must take seriously the simultaneously religious and political nature of our activities. To posit that human beings are blindly guided by only one set of religious or political concerns surely underestimates the complexity of the human condition.

# Notes

## Introduction

1. See Mattias Gardell, *In the Name of Elijah Muhammad: Louis Farrakhan and the Nation of Islam* (Durham, N.C.: Duke University Press, 1996), 50–54; Claude Andrew Clegg III, *An Original Man: The Life and Times of Elijah Muhammad* (New York: St. Martin's Press, 1997), 20–21; Richard B. Turner, *Islam in the African-American Experience* (Bloomington: Indiana University Press, 1997), 160–66; and Edward E. Curtis IV, *Islam in Black America: Identity, Liberation, and Difference in African-American Islamic Thought* (Albany: State University of New York Press, 2002), 68–71.

2. See the seminal account of Erdmann D. Beynon, "The Voodoo Cult among Negro Migrants in Detroit," *American Journal of Sociology* 40, no. 3 (May 1938): 894–907; and compare C. Eric Lincoln, *The Black Muslims in America*, 3rd ed. (Grand Rapids, Mich.: William B. Eerdmans, 1994), 11–16, and E. U. Essien-Udom, *Black Nationalism: A Search for an Identity in America* (Chicago: University of Chicago Press, 1962), 43–46.

3. See Clegg, *Original Man*, 21–40, 77–97.

4. Muhammad's criminal record is reproduced in SAC Chicago to FBI Director, 26 May 1969, 7–8, in Reel 3 of the *FBI File on Elijah Muhammad* (Wilmington, Del.: Scholarly Resources Inc., 1996). For accounts of the NOI's rise in the late 1940s and the 1950s, see Essien-Udom, *Black Nationalism*, 63–82, and Clegg, *An Original Man*, 97–118.

5. *Muhammad Speaks*, 29 June 1973, 31. From this point on, I abbreviate *Muhammad Speaks* as *MS*.

6. See further Malcolm X and Alex Haley, *The Autobiography of Malcolm X* (New York: Ballantine Books, 1973).

7. One popular collection of Malcolm X's speeches is *Malcolm X Speaks*, ed. George Breitman (New York: Grove Weidenfeld, 1990).

8. These were official positions of the NOI, printed toward the back of *Muhammad Speaks* newspapers throughout the 1960s and 1970s in a section entitled "What the Muslims Want." The NOI also demanded freedom, justice, equality, an amnesty for black prisoners, a tax amnesty for black citizens, and an end to police brutality.

9. George M. Fredrickson, *Black Liberation: A Comparative History of Black Ideologies in the United States and South Africa* (New York: Oxford University Press, 1995), 286–91.

10. See *Autobiography of Malcolm X*, 288–342.

11. See Abass Rassoull, "Clarifies Muslim Accomplishments," *MS*, 29 March 1974, 3.

12. Claude Clegg has catalogued the various estimates of membership numbers in the 1960s. He notes that the movement itself said that it had over 100,000 members, and journalists like Mike Wallace and Louis Lomax repeated these claims. Clegg's educated guess, however, is that there were 20,000 members at the height of the movement's popularity, while many more people sympathized with the movement. See Clegg, *Original Man*, 114–15. In 1965, the FBI estimated that there were only 5,000 full-fledged members. See "Nation of Islam: Cult of the Black Muslims," May 1965, pt. 2, p. iv, of an internal report declassified under the Freedom of Information Act available through the FBI's Electronic Reading Room: ‹http://foia.fbi.gov/foiaindex/nation_of_islam.htm›.

13. See further "Recruitment and Membership Procedures," in the FBI's "Nation of Islam: Cult of the Black Muslims," May 1965, pt. 3, pp. 57–59. Johnny Percy X Moore, for example, converted to Islam, stopped attending his local mosque, committed a crime, was sentenced to San Quentin prison, and then renewed his commitment to Islam. See "San Quentin Inmate Thanks Allah for Spread of Truth," *MS*, 6 September 1968, 25, and compare Brother Ralph 4X Brown, "Advice to the Lost," *MS*, 28 March 1969, 32. For an example of a believer who went from being a Christian to a Muslim and later repeated the same cycle, see Sharon 2X, "Islam Gives Happiness," *MS*, 7 April 1972, 18.

14. Most African American religionists were, as they are now, Christians of one sort or another. See further C. Eric Lincoln and Lawrence H. Mamiya, *The Black Church in the African-American Experience* (Durham, N.C.: Duke University Press, 1990).

15. For an account of how marginal religious groups have helped to shape mainstream American culture, see R. Laurence Moore, *Religious Outsiders and the Making of Americans* (New York: Oxford University Press, 1986).

16. The best-known academic article on the NOI was the sensationalistic account of Beynon, "The Voodoo Cult among Negro Migrants in Detroit." For an introduction to the FBI's investigation of the NOI and other groups that the FBI's COINTELPRO program classified as "Black Nationalist," see Frank J. Donner, *The Age of Surveillance: The Aims and Methods of America's Political Intelligence System* (New York: Random House, 1980).

17. Louis E. Lomax et al., "The Hate that Hate Produced," on "Newsbeat," WNTA-TV, 23 July 1959, a transcript of which is available in a declassified FBI report. See SAC, New York, Office Memorandum to Director, FBI, 16 July 1959, available through ‹http://wonderwheel.net/work/foia/1959/071659hthp-transcript.pdf›.

18. Essien-Udom, *Black Nationalism*, 73–74.

19. The similarity between C. Eric Lincoln's analysis of the NOI, which was written in the second half of the 1950s, and that of Wilkins was not coincidental; both views were influenced by black middle-class hopes for progress on civil rights. The more these leaders could point to phenomena like the NOI, the better they could argue for a stronger civil rights bill. See further Harold Dean Trulear, "Sociology of Afro-American Religion: An Appraisal of C. Eric Lincoln's Contributions," *Journal of Religious Thought* 42, no. 2 (Fall 1985/Winter 1986): 44–55.

20. Excerpted from "Summary and Conclusions," page iii of a monograph produced by the national headquarters of the FBI for local field offices, available through the

Electronic Reading Room of the FBI Website that publishes previously classified documents. See pt. 1 of ‹http://foia.fbi.gov/foiaindex/nation_of_islam.htm›.

21. Essien-Udom, *Black Nationalism*, 317–19.

22. Louis A. DeCaro Jr., *On the Side of My People: A Religious Life of Malcolm X* (New York: New York University Press, 1996), 146.

23. Essien-Udom, *Black Nationalism*, 313–17.

24. See, for example, Robert Dannin, *Black Pilgrimage to Islam* (New York: Oxford University Press, 2002), 33, 61, 142–44, 170, and 184–87.

25. Constance Wheeler, "A Rebuttal to Charges by So-Called Muslims," *MS*, 1 December 1972, 15.

26. See Shirley Hazziez, "All Blacks Are Muslim, Believe It or Not," *MS*, 2 February 1973, 15, and Minister George 4X, "Scriptures Foretold Charges," *MS*, 9 February 1973.

27. Merv Block, "Elijah Muhammad — Black Paradox," *Chicago Sun-Times*, 26 March 1972, sect. 2, 3–4.

28. His claims that Elijah Muhammad was a fraud prompted a number of responses from NOI intellectuals. Minister Edwin X of Peoria, Illinois, and Minister Yusuf Shah of Temple No. 2 made theological and scriptural arguments on behalf of their leader. See Edwin X, "They Reject the Prophet," *MS*, 14 April 1972, 15, and "Minister Yusuf Shah answers Mr. Hussain," *MS*, 28 April 1972, 15.

29. Due to the nature of historical sources available, attempting to narrate the religious culture of the NOI during the 1960s and 1970s poses a challenge. Most of the historical documents on which this work is based come from the weekly newspaper of the movement, *Muhammad Speaks*. During the period from 1961 to 1975, *Muhammad Speaks* became a major newspaper in black America. The movement claimed a circulation of 500,000, although one editor, Leon Forrest, later said that its real circulation was around 70,000. Though owned and distributed by Elijah Muhammad and the NOI, *Muhammad Speaks* employed a non-Muslim staff in the 1960s that included the award-winning journalist, Richard Durham, who served as its managing editor. According to Leon Forrest, Durham convinced Elijah Muhammad that the paper should not only spread the message of the NOI but also focus on hard news related to the contemporary United States and the "rising tide of color" in the second and third worlds. If the amount of space allotted to movement activities were too large, Durham argued, the integrity of the weekly would be compromised. For more on this, see Leon Forrest, *Relocations of the Spirit* (Wakefield, R.I.: Asphodel Press, 1994), 86–94.

Throughout the 1960s and early 1970s, the layout of the newspaper reflected the formula advocated by Durham. The twenty- to thirty-page paper included news articles about activities both inside the NOI and in the world beyond the small movement.

Even so, *Muhammad Speaks* also functioned as a public sphere for the expression and development of African American Muslim identity. The pages devoted solely to the NOI contained a wealth of information, including the teachings of Elijah Muhammad, a "Women in Islam" column, black Muslim poetry, advertisements from businesses associated with the movement, a "Prayer in Islam" column, coverage of NOI events, advice columns, pictures of NOI members, quotations from the Qur'an, didactic comic strips, letters from believers, and an ongoing feature called "What Islam Has Done for

Me," in which nonpaid contributors gave their personal views on what it meant to be a Muslim and how Islam had changed their lives. In these pages, NOI members and other persons more loosely affiliated with the movement developed their own responses to the message of Elijah Muhammad. Because the paper contains thousands of pages on the movement and its members, it is the richest and most detailed source for the period under consideration, and offers accounts of movement activities not only in Chicago, but also in New York, Washington, Philadelphia, Atlanta, Los Angeles, St. Louis, Boston, Detroit, and many other locales.

Using this source in a critical manner, however, requires some reflection on its status as the official newspaper of the movement. After all, its editors and Elijah Muhammad controlled what appeared in the paper. In selecting and editing items for publication, they helped to shape and construct images of the NOI meant for consumption by the membership of the NOI, the predominately black consumers of the paper, and various governmental authorities, especially the FBI, that ran surveillance of the movement. My reliance on *Muhammad Speaks* presents both limits and opportunities. In using the newspaper, I am careful to note that some of its discourse reveals a conversation between the producers of the newspapers and its various audiences. But even then, the story is a valuable one that depicts how the leadership of the NOI wanted to be perceived as a legitimately religious and Islamic movement that offered a form of black liberation and challenged the boundaries of social and political power in the United States.

There are also good reasons to believe, moreover, that the newspaper presented much more than the viewpoints of NOI leaders. First, the non-Muslim editors of the paper in the 1960s acted as intermediaries between Elijah Muhammad and his followers. On a day-to-day basis, it was Richard Durham, Leon Forrest, and other editors who were deciding what went in the paper. It speaks to the journalistic excellence of the paper that it not only covered hard news unrelated to the internal workings of the NOI, but also included the comments of readers and figures who disagreed with Elijah Muhammad's teachings and opposed the NOI. While the editors followed the general guidelines of Elijah Muhammad, according to Forrest, they still had an important role in shaping the paper's content. Second, it is clear that Elijah Muhammad did not vet many articles in the paper, especially in the 1970s, when editors John Woodford and Charles 67X had to make public apologies for content that, after its publication, met with the disapproval either of Elijah Muhammad or his chief lieutenants in Chicago. See further John Woodford, "Regret Error," *MS*, 10 March 1972, and Charles 67X, "Correction," *MS*, 29 November 1974, 2. And these men were not the only writers who issued public apologies for their "errors." Other leading figures distanced themselves from the statements of regular columnist Margary Hassain, who issued a *mea culpa* filled with shame and regret for writing improper observations in the newspaper. See Sister Margary Hassain, "My Apology," *MS*, 7 April 1972, 18, and S. Hazziez, V. Najieb, A. Ali, A. Karriem, J. Ali, G. Muhammad, J. Allah, D. Wedad, "The Article," *MS*, 10 March 1972, 18.

What these apologies indicate is that the authority of NOI leaders over the paper was not, on a practical basis, absolute. Such public humiliation surely worked to encourage writers to self-censor, but the fact that these "corrections" were needed in the first place also suggests that writers were sometimes genuinely confused about the boundaries of proper speech. Finally, what is most convincing for the purpose of using the newspaper to create a portrait of religious culture in the NOI during this period is the diverse nature of the religious discourse itself. In their words, poems, and artwork, believers offered differing interpretations of their faith and the significance of the NOI's activities to their lives. If the paper was supposed to present a monolithic view of religion in the NOI, it certainly failed.

In addition to relying on *Muhammad Speaks*, I use mainstream newspapers, FBI files, black newspapers, audiovisual evidence, and African American literature to create my portrait of religion in the NOI. While none of these sources provides adequate contemporaneous information on the *meaning* of NOI religion to ordinary believers, they help to situate and interpret the data gleaned from various items in *Muhammad Speaks*. For the most part, mainstream newspapers, the FBI, and even most black newspapers were mainly interested in tracking the activities of NOI leaders, exploring potential ties to the Communists or other subversive groups, constructing the NOI as an un-American hate group that offered a poor solution to the problems of race relations, criticizing the movement as a cult, understanding the role of the movement (and/or the federal government) in the assassination of Malcolm X, and, finally, exposing criminal activity either directly or indirectly related to the NOI. See, for example, Paul Delany, "Internal Struggle Shakes Black Muslims," *New York Times*, 21 January 1972, 1, and Paul Delany, "Black Muslim Group in Trouble from Financial Problems and Some Crime," *New York Times*, 6 December 1973, 37, and compare the critique of such coverage in Sean McCloud, *Making the American Religious Fringe: Exotics, Subversives, and Journalists, 1955–1993* (Chapel Hill: University of North Carolina Press, 2004), 55–94. These topics are not explored in this book because I want to explain what it meant to be Muslim for ordinary believers in the NOI, and most of them were not involved in such intrigues. For more on the sensationalist aspects of the NOI, see instead Vibert L. White, *Inside the Nation of Islam: A Historical and Personal Testimony of a Black Muslim* (Gainesville: University of Florida Press, 2001); Karl Evanzz, *The Messenger: The Rise and Fall of Elijah Muhammad* (New York: Pantheon Books, 1999); and *The Judas Factor: The Plot to Kill Malcolm X* (New York: Thunder's Mouth Press, 1992).

I also draw on African American memoirs, contemporaneous ethnographic accounts of the movement, and, especially, oral histories to present a fuller picture of religion in the NOI, though these sources are also limited in revealing the religious meaning of the NOI. Many former members of the NOI have reinterpreted the meaning of their old religious views. Many of those who became Sunni Muslims after 1975 do not think of their activities in the NOI as religious anymore. This is the nature of oral history, which sometimes tells us more about the construction of memory than about the events of the times. See, for example, John Bodnar, "Power and Memory in Oral History: Workers and Managers at Studebaker," *Journal of American History* 75 (March 1989): 1201–21. When human beings look back on the past, they naturally forget details, reorder sequences, and insert new memories. Although I do use oral historical evidence in this work, I attempt, as much as possible, to verify or delimit it by referring to written documents that describe the same events or themes. The best place to find such documents is in the pages of *Muhammad Speaks*.

30. It is this work's insistent focus on religious ritual, ethics, doctrine, and narrative and its systematic use of the tools of religious studies that sets it apart from the other

major studies on the movement and its figures. At the same time, my work relies on and complements the corpus of scholarship on African American Islam, which includes Lincoln, *Black Muslims*; Essien-Udom, *Black Nationalism*; Sherman A. Jackson, *Islam and the Blackamerican: Looking Toward the Third Resurrection* (New York: Oxford University Press, 2005); Michael A. Gomez, *Black Crescent: The Experience and Legacy of African Muslims in the Americas* (Cambridge: Cambridge University Press, 2005); Aminah McCloud, *African American Islam* (New York: Routledge, 1995); Dannin, *Black Pilgrimage to Islam*; Allan D. Austin, *African Muslims in Antebellum America: Transatlantic Stories and Spiritual Struggles* (New York: Routledge, 1997); Sylviane A. Diouf, *Servants of Allah: African Muslims Enslaved in the Americas* (New York: New York University Press, 1998); Turner, *Islam in the African-American Experience*; Carolyn Moxley Rouse, *Engaged Surrender: African American Women and Islam* (Berkeley: University of California Press, 2004); DeCaro, *On the Side of My People*; Gardell, *In the Name of Elijah Muhammad*; Clegg, *An Original Man*; Martha F. Lee, *The Nation of Islam: An American Millenarian Movement* (Syracuse, N.Y.: Syracuse University Press, 1996); and Clifton E. Marsh, *From Black Muslims to Muslims: The Resurrection, Transformation, and Change of the Lost-Found Nation of Islam in America, 1930–1995*, 2nd ed. (Lanham, Md.: Scarecrow Press, 1996).

31. Jonathon Z. Smith, ed., *The HarperCollins Dictionary of Religion* (New York: HarperSanFrancisco, 1995), 893. As one might expect, debates over the definition of the word "religion" and how scholars should study religious phenomena are eternal questions in the academic discipline of religious studies. Two recent attempts to tackle the problem are Thomas A. Tweed, *Crossing and Dwelling: A Theory of Religion* (Cambridge, Mass.: Harvard University Press, 2005), and Robert A. Orsi, *Between Heaven and Earth: The Religious Worlds People Make and the Scholars Who Study Them* (Princeton, N.J.: Princeton University Press, 2004). See also Carl Olson, ed., *Theory and Method in the Study of Religion: A Selection of Critical Readings* (Belmont, Calif.: Thomson/Wadsworth, 2003), and Daniel L. Pals, *Seven Theories of Religion* (New York: Oxford University Press, 1996).

32. This language is borrowed from John R. Bowen, *Muslims through Discourse: Religion and Ritual in Gayo Society* (Princeton, N.J.: Princeton University Press, 1993), 9.

33. Thomas A. Tweed, *Our Lady of the Exile: Diasporic Religion at a Cuban Catholic Shrine in Miami* (New York: Oxford University Press, 1997), 164n3.

34. This language is from Tweed, *Our Lady of the Exile*, 91, although he credits Jonathan Z. Smith, *Map Is Not Territory: Studies in the History of Religion* (Chicago: University of Chicago Press, 1978), 291, and Charles H. Long, *Significations: Signs, Symbols, and Images in the Interpretation of Religion* (Philadelphia: Fortress, 1986), 7.

35. See further Diana L. Eck, *A New Religious America: How a "Christian Country" Has Now Become the World's Most Religiously Diverse Nation* (San Francisco: HarperSanFrancisco, 2001).

36. See, for example, William L. Van Deburg, *A New Day in Babylon: The Black Power Movement and American Culture, 1965–1975* (Chicago: University of Chicago Press, 1992).

37. See further Scot Brown, *Fighting For Us: Maulana Karenga, The US Organization, and Black Cultural Nationalism* (New York: New York University Press, 2003).

38. See further Stephen Howe, *Afrocentrism: Mythical Pasts and Imagined Homes* (London: Verso, 1998), and Yaacov Shavit, *History in Black: African-Americans in Search of an Ancient Past* (London: Frank Cass, 2001).

39. See, for example, Amanda Porterfield, *The Transformation of American Religion: The Story of a Late-Twentieth-Century Awakening* (New York: Oxford University Press, 2001).

40. See, for example, Robert S. Ellwood, *The Sixties Spiritual Awakening: American Religion Moving from Modern to Postmodern* (New Brunswick, N.J.: Rutgers University Press, 1994); Wade Clark Roof, *Spiritual Marketplace: Baby Boomers and the Remaking of American Religion* (Princeton, N.J.: Princeton University Press, 1999); Sarah M. Pike, *New Age and Neopagan Religions in America* (New York: Columbia University Press, 2004); Joel A. Carpenter, *Revive Us Again: The Reawakening of American Fundamentalism* (New York: Oxford University Press, 1997); and George Marsden, *Reforming Fundamentalism: Fuller Seminary and the New Evangelicalism* (Grand Rapids, Mich.: W. B. Eerdmans, 1987).

41. See further Robert Wuthnow, *The Restructuring of American Religion: Society and Faith since World War II* (Princeton, N.J.: Princeton University Press, 1988).

42. Quoted in Manning Marable, ed., *Dispatches from the Ebony Tower: Intellectuals Confront the African American Experience* (New York: Columbia University Press, 2000), 227.

43. Compare Curtis, *Islam in Black America*, 2–7.

44. Muhammad also referred to Fard as the Messiah and the *mahdi*, a figure who, according to Islamic tradition, will appear at the end of times to establish justice and true religious belief among humankind. See Elijah Muhammad, *The Supreme Wisdom: Solution to the So-Called Negroes' Problem* (1957; repr., Newport News, Va.: National Newport News and Commentator, n.d.), 11, 15, 42, and 48, and Elijah Muhammad, *Message to the Blackman in America* (1965; repr., Newport News, Va.: United Brothers Communications Systems, 1992), 1–11.

45. See D. Gimaret, "Shirk," in *Encyclopaedia of Islam*, WebCD ed. (Leiden: Brill, 2003), 9:484b.

46. Carl W. Ernst, *Following Muhammad: Rethinking Islam in the Contemporary World* (Chapel Hill: University of North Carolina Press, 2003), 204. Some other modern Muslims, notably members of the Ahmadiyya, have disputed the meaning of Qur'an 33:40, which proclaims Muhammad to be the seal of the prophets. Just because Muhammad is the seal, it is argued, does not mean he is the last. For an introduction to this movement, see Yohanan Friedmann, *Prophecy Continuous: Aspects of Ahmadi Religious Thought and Its Medieval Background* (Berkeley: University of California Press, 1989). This dispute over Muhammad as the seal of the prophets is only a small part of larger debates in Islamic history about the nature of prophecy and the authority of the Prophet Muhammad. For an introduction, see further Ernst, *Following Muhammad*, esp. 71–92, and John L. Renard, *Seven Doors to Islam: Spirituality and the Religious Life of Muslims* (Berkeley: University of California Press, 1996).

47. See Muhammad, *Supreme Wisdom*, 11, 15, 29, 31, 33, 36, and 38, and Muhammad, *Message to the Blackman*, 31, 82–84, 110–22, and 230–32.

48. In offering a narrative of black decline and locating the roots of potential renewal,

Elijah Muhammad was participating in a venerable African American intellectual tradition, a famous example of which can be found in David Walker's 1829 *Appeal to the Coloured Citizens of the World*, ed. Peter P. Hinks (University Park: Pennsylvania State University Press, 2000). See also Wilson Jeremiah Moses, *Afrotopia: The Roots of African American Popular History* (Cambridge: Cambridge University Press, 1998).

49. See Muhammad, *Supreme Wisdom*, 13–14, 18–19, 25–26, 31, 33, 34, 37–38, 41, and 42, and Muhammad, *Message to the Blackman*, 15–22 and 46–48. For New Thought's general reverberations in American culture and particularly its impact on American bodily praxis, see R. Marie Griffith, *Born Again Bodies: Flesh and Spirit in American Christianity* (Berkeley: University of California Press, 2004), esp. 155–59.

50. See Muhammad, *Supreme Wisdom*, 22–23, 27, 42, 45–47, 50; Muhammad, *Message to the Blackman*, 56–58, and 135–202; and Elijah Muhammad, *How to Eat to Live, Book No. 2* (1972; repr., Newport News, Va.: National Newport News and Commentator, n.d.).

51. See *MS*, 11 February 1972, 4. "Now, I must tell you the truth," Muhammad said in an interview. "There will be no such thing as elimination of all white people from the Earth. . . . No, because there are some white people today who have faith in Allah and Islam though they are white, and their faith is given credit."

52. For Muhammad's political views, see *Message to the Blackman*, 161–71. For his eschatology, see *Message to the Blackman*, 265–305, and Elijah Muhammad, *The Fall of America* (1973; repr., Newport News, Va.: National Newport News and Commentator, n.d.).

53. The beginning of this trend can be dated perhaps to a 1979 volume edited by Nehemia Levtzion, who questioned popular Euro-American notions that Islam had spread primarily by the sword. Levtzion's many contributors emphasized, instead, the multilayered nature of conversion, examining the role of Muslim traders, legal schools, Sufi (or mystical) Islam, Muslim literatures, and popular culture in the dissemination of Islamic religion. See further Nehemia Levtzion, *Conversion to Islam* (New York: Holmes and Meier, 1979).

54. Richard M. Eaton, *Essays on Islam and Indian History* (New York: Oxford University Press, 2000), 35.

55. Ibid., 2.

56. Emphasis added. See William Cummings, "Scripting Islamization: Arabic Texts in Early Modern Makassar," *Ethnohistory* 48/4 (2001): 559.

57. See, for example, Dannin, *Black Pilgrimage to Islam*, 4; DeCaro, *On the Side of My People*, 84, 88, 183, 193–95; and Michael Wolfe, ed., *One Thousand Roads to Mecca* (New York: Grove Press, 1997), 486.

## Chapter 1

1. In addition to the numerous testimonies examined in this chapter, see Sister Lynice Shabazz, "Countless Blessings Have Been Given Me by Allah," *MS*, 3 January 1969, 29; Sister Beverly 4X, "Black Women are 'Real' Mothers of Civilization," *MS*, 17 January 1969, 35. For the unusual testimony of one brother who refused to call Islam a religion, see Johnny Percy X Moore, "Brother Finds Himself Barraged with Questions

about Islam and Religion," *MS*, 7 November 1969, 15. According to Moore, religion was a mere label of convenience meant to attract the attention of the public. In truth, he wrote, "Islam is not a religion, but is the very nature in which we were created. Thus, it cannot be referred to as a religion, because religion is not created by nature."

2. Compare William L. Andrews, ed., *Sisters of the Spirit: Three Black Women's Autobiographies of the Nineteenth Century* (Bloomington: Indiana University Press, 1986); Clifton H. Johnson, ed., *God Struck Me Dead: Religious Conversion Experiences and Autobiographies of Ex-Slaves* (Cleveland: Pilgrim Press, 1993); and Albert J. Raboteau, *A Fire in the Bones: Reflections on African American Religious History* (Boston: Beacon Press, 1985).

3. The overwhelming majority of personal narratives in *Muhammad Speaks* indicate that, if members had a religious affiliation before joining the NOI, it was Christian. However, I did find one reference to a black Jew turned black Muslim. See Sister Priscilla X Alston, "Pens Poetic Testament of What Islam Means to Her," *MS*, 24 November 1969, 15.

4. Dr. Leo X, "On the Scientific Significance of Teachings of the Messenger of Allah," *MS*, 28 May 1965, 20. For other scientific explanations of Islam, see further Brother Warren X Payne, "Awareness of Self, Allah Are Islam's Gift to Black Race," *MS*, 11 April 1969, 29; Dr. Leo P. X McCallum, "God, Science, Culture, and Knowledge of Self—A Formula for Islam," *MS*, 27 October 1970, 18; and Walter 3X Epps, "The Atom and Islam: The Messenger Is Our Nucleus," *MS*, 5 November 1971, 15.

5. Marie Atterbury, "Inspiration of the Messenger Reaches Woman Deep in the Heart of Dixie," *MS*, 28 January 1966, 25. For the accounts of other believers who found Islam offered "better answers" to life's questions than Christianity, see Violet X; "Learns Islam Is Greatest Religion," *MS*, 10 March 1967, 25; Sister Lucille X, "Understanding Is to Be Found in Messenger," *MS*, 4 August 1967, 25; Brother Alonzo X, "The Evil of the Cross Sent Him to Righteous of Islam," *MS*, 8 September 1967, 25; "Messenger Muhammad's Word Brought Light to Knowledge of Almighty God," *MS*, 2 February 1968, 25; Sister Kathryn 4X Rowe, "How Messenger's Beacon of Truth Lighted Path of Happiness for Distressed Woman," *MS*, 9 February 1968, 25; Sister Alease X, "How Can the Corrupt Teach about an Honest God," *MS*, 9 February 1968, 25; Emma X Robinson, "Message Awakens Once-Fearful Woman," *MS*, 18 August 1972, 18.

6. John X Lawler, "Sees New Day Rise in Islam," *MS*, 27 September 1963, 5.

7. *MS*, 19 June 1964, 7. Other members of the NOI were at least familiar with some Masonic teaching, and had experimented with Masonry before coming to the NOI. See, for example, Sister Vanecia X, "Devil's Mistake Sent Her To Islam," *MS*, 8 September 1967, 25. It is worth remembering that the NOI and other early African American Islamic groups like the Moorish Science Temple had roots partly in black Masonic groups during the 1920s and 1930s. See further Ernest Allen Jr., "Identity and Destiny: The Formative Views of the Moorish Science Temple and the Nation of Islam," in *Muslims on the Americanization Path?*, ed. Yvonne Yazbeck Haddad and John L. Esposito (New York: Oxford University Press, 2000), 180–82, and compare Robert Dannin, *Black Migration to Islam* (New York: Oxford University Press, 2002), 15–34. How much black Masonry was practiced within the NOI by the 1960s and 1970s is difficult to determine.

8. Sister Georgia X Thomas, "Lost and Betrayed, Young Girl Saw Light of Islam," *MS*, 20 August 1965, 24. See also Brother Herbert X, "Declares Devil Seeks to Rise Against, Make War on Almighty Allah," *MS*, 4 August 1967, 25, and 25 August 1967, 25; and Brother Angelo 3X, "How to Have Heaven Here, and Not Pie in the Sky," *MS*, 17 November 1967, 25.

9. See, for example, Brother Robert X, "Islam's Teachings Served as Key to Knowledge Door," *MS*, 6 October 1967, 25; Ronald 4X, "Where Would Black Men Be Without Divine Guidance of the Messenger?," *MS*, 7 June 1968, 25.

10. Theodore F. X Peyton, "Thanks Allah for Sending His Messenger the Honorable Elijah Muhammad," *MS*, 28 January 1966, 25.

11. Warner X Berry, "War Vet Credits Messenger Muhammad for Restoring His Peace of Mind," *MS*, 8 April 1966, 25.

12. George X Tucker, "Black Honduran Finds New Life in Messenger's Teachings," *MS*, 19 August 1966, 25. For the narrative of another believer who focused on the numerological aspects of Islam, see Minister Edwin X, "The Meaning of the Number '10,'" *MS*, 19 January 1973, 15.

13. *Student Enrollment* and *Actual Facts* are reproduced in pt. 1, pp. 72–87, of an FBI report on the NOI available through the agency's Web-based Electronic Reading Room; see ‹http://foia.fbi.gov/foiaindex/nation_of_islam.htm ›.

14. Marvin Omar, "Pastor Tells Why He Chose Islam," *MS*, 14 May 1965, 18.

15. Brother Hiram X, "Former Black Student Union Chairman Tells Why He Joined Nation of Islam," *MS*, 1 August 1969, 22, 26.

16. Charlene M. Whitcomb, "68-Yr. Old Woman Laments Years Wasted before Embracing Messenger's Teachings," *MS*, 3 December 1965, 25.

17. Elder L. Hinis, "Teachings of Muhammad Change Preacher's Outlook," *MS*, 21 May 1965, 8.

18. See Brother Ray 2X, "He Grew Tired of Christian Hypocrisy," *MS*, 6 October 1967, 25.

19. John 11X, "Islam Teaches the Correct Way to Find Dignity," *MS*, 5 April 1968, 27.

20. Sister Ann 3X, "Islam Satisfies Material and Spritual Needs," *MS*, 2 June 1972, 15.

21. Sister Beatrice X, "I Lived in Fear Near Lynch Tree—Until Islam," *MS*, 5 June 1964, 7.

22. See further Joe William Trotter Jr., ed., *The Great Migration in Historical Perspective: New Dimensions of Race, Class, and Gender* (Bloomington: Indiana University Press, 1991), and Eric Arnesen, *Black Protest and the Great Migration: A Brief History with Documents* (Boston: St. Martin's Press, 2003).

23. Albert J. Raboteau, *Canaan Land: A Religious History of African Americans* (New York: Oxford University Press, 2001), 85–87. See also Milton C. Sernett, *Bound for the Promised Land: African American Religion and the Great Migration* (Durham, N.C.: Duke University Press, 1997).

24. The theme of abandonment by one's religious community and African Americans more generally appears in other conversion narratives as well. See, for example, Altoine X Crocette, "Beacon of Messenger's Teachings Enlightens San Quentin Prisoner," *MS*, 25 February 1966, 25.

25. Jerry Wilson, "Once 'Lost' in Miss. until Found by the Messenger," *MS*, 6 No-

vember 1964, 7. For other tales of leaving the South to find one's self and one's true religion, see Minister Clyde Rahaman, "Minister Who Survived the Hell-Holes of Mississippi Thankful for Muhammad," *MS*, 10 June 1966, 25–26; Sister Edna Mae 2X, "I Traveled the Road That Led to the Door of the Messenger," *MS*, 17 March 1967, 25, and 24 March 1967, 25; Paul 5X, "South Carolinian's Journey through Hell," *MS*, 16 April 1967, 25–26.

26. Ronnie X Shorter, "Islam is Natural Religion of Enlightened Black Man," *MS*, 9 May 1969, 22.

27. Marlene Karriem, "Religion of Dynamic Truth," *MS*, 16 February 1963, 5.

28. James 3X, "Minister Testifies to New Dignity," *MS*, 2 August 1963, 5.

29. James D. X, "Islam Opened New Horizon," *MS*, 18 December 1964, 15.

30. See, for example, Ernest 3X, "Out of the Ghettos of Detroit to Life of Dignity, Love," *MS*, 11 November 1966, 25.

31. See Malcolm X and Alex Haley, *The Autobiography of Malcolm X* (New York: Ballantine Books, 1973).

32. Robert 24X, "Learns Power, Salvation of Islam While in Reformatory," *MS*, 22 November 1963, 4. For other narratives of how former convicts credited Elijah Muhammad and Islam for their salvation, see Haynes X McPherson, "Islam's Gift of Freedom to Man Lost in Jail Life," *MS*, 9 October 1964, 6; Brother Oscar, "Why Muhammad Is the Last Messenger of Allah," *MS*, 7 May 1965, 7; Arthur X Coleman, "Former Drug Addict Thanks Messenger for a New Life," *MS*, 30 September 1966, 25; Minister Isaiah Karriem, "Minister Isaiah: With Muhammad's Teachings I Win over My Foes," *MS*, 18 November 1966, 25, 27; and Joseph X Barnes, "Islam Gave Him True Life, Manhood in D.C. Jail," *MS*, 18 August 1967, 25.

33. See Edward 4X, as told to Sylvester Leaks, "Tottering on Brink of Doom Rescued by Muhammad," *MS*, 8 May 1964, 7, and 22 May 1964, 7. For other stories of how Islam helped other drug addicts to recover, see James 2X, "Muhammad's Words Release Addict from Enslavement," *MS*, 8 November 1963, 2; Capt. Clarence W. X Gill, "Islam's Gift to Him: Useful Life," *MS*, 25 September 1964, 9; Quincy Fork, "Islam Opened Doors of the New World for Our People," *MS*, 19 August 1965, 25–26; Brother G. D. X, "Islam Can Give New Hope," *MS*, 9 February 1968, 25; and Brother Monroe 3X, "The Divine Teachings Conquered Fear and All Evil, Self-Destructive Habits," *MS*, 16 February 1968, 25.

34. Cynthia S'thembile West, "Nation Builders: Female Activism in the Nation of Islam, 1960–1970" (Ph.D. diss., Temple University, 1994), 105–6. For an account of a middle-class supporter of Elijah Muhammad, see Leontyne Montague, "Messenger's Truth versus Oppression," *MS*, 3 July 1964, 7.

35. For accounts of middle-class black professional members of the NOI, see Dr. Leo P. X McCallum, "Why Some Professionals Are Blind to Message," *MS*, 23 April 1965, 3, and Dr. Ananian Troup, "Doctor Says Messenger's Teachings More Important Than Schools and Universities," *MS*, 16 September 1966, 25.

36. Brother Theodore 4X, "Believer Finds Self-Acceptance, Dignity in Islam as Taught by the Messenger," *MS*, 27 May 1966, 25. See also Audrey X Lewis, "Muhammad the Master Psychiatrist," *MS*, 7 September 1973, 11.

37. See, for example, Eddie X Gates, "Messenger Teaches True Brotherhood," *MS*,

18 November 1966, 25; Brother Thomas X McBride, "Islam Brought Peace, Unity to Now Grateful Coloradan," *MS*, 21 October 1966, 25; Brother Angelo 3X, "Islam Taught Me to Reach Far Beyond Limitations Set by Mankind," *MS*, 27 January 1967, 25; Brother Samuel X, "Islam Has Plan for Progress," *MS*, 24 May 1968, 25.

38. Some members of the NOI did indeed struggle to find employment before coming into the NOI, and credited Islam and Elijah Muhammad with giving them the knowledge, attitudes, or confidence necessary to identify and maintain any job at all. See, for example, Lt. Luchrie X Jordan, "Found New Freedom with the Messenger," *MS*, 28 August 1964, 10.

39. See, for example, Sister Betty X, "Sister Tells How Muhammad's Teachings Helped Her in Business World," *MS*, 3 March 1967, 25.

40. See James 2X, "Muslim Life Gives Black Businessman Inspiration to Help His Brothers Succeed," *MS*, 16 February 1968, 25.

41. Clyde X Smith, "Track Star Grasped Messenger's Great Truths," *MS*, 13 September 1963, 7.

42. Sister Hattie C. 3X, "Finds New Outlook on Life thru Islam," *MS*, 5 November 1965, 24. For another narrative of how Islam led to greater financial success, see Brother Jacob X, "Businessman Says He's Had 'Nothing but Success' since He Accepted Islam," *MS*, 28 October 1966, 25.

43. Mrs. Grace X Peoples, "Housewife Finds More Rewarding Life in Islam," *MS*, 8 November 1963, 2.

44. Sister Anne 3X, "Girl Counts Her Blessings since Joining With Islam," *MS*, 20 December 1963, 7. For another tale of physical and mental healing, see Sister Mary Tessie 2X, "Signs of Divine Power and Guidance," *MS*, 14 October 1966, 25.

45. Louis X Carr, "Boxer's Greatest Prize Came Not in Ring Wars, but from the Messenger," *MS*, 19 March 1965, 21.

46. Don X Slaughter, "Boston Businessman Made Greatest Gains with Islam," *MS*, 2 April 1965, 15. Other allusions to the clean living of NOI members can be found in Minister Edward, "Cambridge Minister Points Up Failure of Christianity, Blessings of Islam," *MS*, 30 April 1965, 21, and Tom X Polk, "How Islam Brought Family Prosperity and Unity Unlike Any Hitherto Known," *MS*, 13 August 1965, 24.

47. Sister Gwendolyn X Warren, "How Muhammad's Dietary Laws Helped Cancer Victim," *MS*, 2 December 1966, 25. See also the comment of Sister Mable X, who suffered from stomach problems until following the Messenger's dietary guidelines in "Years in Islam Brought Peace," *MS*, 14 July 1967, 25.

48. For historical treatments of the idea of respectability among African American women, see Evelyn Brooks Higginbotham, *Righteous Discontent: The Women's Movement in the Black Baptist Church, 1880–1920* (Cambridge: Harvard University Press, 1993), esp. 185–229, and Victoria W. Wolcott, *Remaking Respectability: African American Women in Interwar Detroit* (Chapel Hill: University of North Carolina Press, 2001).

49. Sister Marilyn A. X, "Messenger's Demonstration of Love and Unity Brought Lost Soul to Islam," *MS*, 16 April 1965, 21. For similar accounts, see Sister Marilyn A. X, "Islam Has Given Me Life and a Purpose for Living," *MS*, 11 February 1966, 25; Sister Mildred 3X, "Islam Awakened Me to New Pride," *MS*, 13 May 1966, 25; Sister Ruth X, "Islam Lifted Her from Degredation [*sic*]," *MS*, 30 December 1966, 25; Sister

Fatima X, "Denver Sister Outlines Life of Muslims," 13 January 1967, 25; and Melva J. X Walker [a former Miss Black Oklahoma], "Muslim Sister Finds Real Meaning of Black Beauty," *MS*, 16 July 1971, 18.

50. Margaret J. X Mayes, "Michigan Mother Tells How Messenger's Teachings Led to Dignity, Self-Respect," *MS*, 23 September 1966, 22.

51. Gretta Hightower, "My Husband Led Us from Darkness to Islam and to Messenger Muhammad," *MS*, 4 February 1966, 25. See also Sister Novella X, "Husband and Wife Found Islam's Blessings Together," *MS*, 16 February 1966, 25.

52. Brother Donald X Thompson, for example, reunited with his wife and children, whom he had abandoned, after converting. See "Life Bears Witness to the Messenger's Teachings," *MS*, 9 December 1966, 25.

53. See, for example, Jessie X Newman, "Once Paid $3 Per Week for Furnace Work, Georgia Man Joins Islam, Buys Own Home," *MS*, 16 April 1965, 21, and Warren X Polk, "The Blessings of Islam Plentiful," *MS*, 25 June 1965, 11.

54. Sister Hilda X, "Like Lightning and Thunder, Messenger Calls His People," *MS*, 7 October 1966, 25.

55. See further Elijah Muhammad, *The Fall of America* (1973; repr., Newport News, Va.: National Newport News and Commentator, n.d.).

56. See further Martha F. Lee, *The Nation of Islam: An American Millenarian Movement* (Syracuse: Syracuse University Press, 1996), and for a helpful introduction to millennialism in American religions, see Catherine L. Albanese, *American Religion and Religions*, 3rd ed. (Belmont, Calif.: Wadsworth Publishing, 1998), 432–500.

57. Sister Pamela X, "Relates Her Deliverance from the Devil," *MS*, 29 December 1967, 25.

58. Ruby X Thompson, "Islam Solution to Family's Problems," *MS*, 31 January 1964, 10.

59. Sister Arnetta X, "How Muhammad Reached into Jungle Regions of the South to Light Her Path," *MS*, 7 May 1965, 21. For another comparison of Islam versus the civil rights movement, see Minister James 3X, "Messenger's Teachings Bring out Best in Man," *MS*, 28 May 1965, 3.

60. Sister Josephine X, "May Allah Bless Messenger Muhammad with Eternal Strength to Carry On," *MS*, 26 January 1968, 25. See also Bernard 4X Jackson, "Embracing Islam's Truth Called Spiritual Awakening," *MS*, 5 September 1969, 17.

61. Henry 15X, "A Word of Life and Beauty," *MS*, 10 March 1972, 18.

62. Clara E. 4X Bell, "Cleveland Sister Finds New Life in Islam," *MS*, 2 September 1966, 25.

63. Gail Green, "Newcomer to Islam Discovers All Blacks are Born Muslims," *MS*, 9 June 1967, 25.

64. "Go, Hear Muhammad—You Have Everything to Gain," *MS*, 12 November 1965, 26.

65. Jean X Reynolds, "Messenger Leads Woman to Truth and Happiness," *MS*, 1 October 1965, 25.

66. For other narratives that define and discuss Islam as a total way of life or cite multiple benefits in practicing Islam, see Sister Marilyn A. X, "Messenger's Teachings Lead the World to Greater Spiritual, Material Rewards," *MS*, 10 December 1965, 25;

Sister Helen 4X Clark, "The Messenger of Allah in Our Midst Has Meant Happiness and a New Life," *MS*, 13 May 1966, 25; Sister Flora Majied, "How Messenger's Teachings Gave Her New Life of Morality, Love, Wisdom," *MS*, 1 November 1966, 25, 27; Sister Hilda X, "Put Christianity Out of Your Mind," *MS*, 29 July 1966, 25; Chester A. X Rhodes, "He Joyously Finds Islam Is Everything and All Things," *MS*, 9 December 1966, 25; Sandra J. X, "Black Woman Finds Peace, Freedom in Folds of Islam," *MS*, 26 May 1967, 25; Brother Charley J. X, "His Family Grows Amid the Many Blessings of Islam," *MS*, 21 July 1967, 25; Brother Sam T. Weathers, "Gives 20 Reasons Why He Prefers to Follow Islam," *MS*, 4 April 1969, 29; Brother Charles W. X Randle, "Islam Is My Soul Food; Made My Mind, Body Clean," *MS*, 11 July 1969, 23; Mathew X Bumphus, "Islam: Peace, Dignity, Clean Mind, and More," *MS*, 14 May 1971, 18; John X Sanford, "Islam Our 'Natural State,'" *MS*, 2 July 1971, 18; Sister Geneva Ragin, "It's So Wonderful to Be Alive," *MS*, 28 July 1972, 18; and Abdul Salaam, "Nation of Islam: Progress Certain," *MS*, 1 September 1972, 18.

67. See further Robin D. G. Kelley, "Looking for the 'Real' Nigga: Social Scientists Construct the Ghetto," in *Yo' Mama's Disfunktional! Fighting the Culture Wars in Urban America* (Boston: Beacon Press, 1997), 15–42.

## Chapter 2

1. Martin Luther King Jr., "Letter from the Birmingham Jail," in *Black Writers in America*, ed. Richard Barksdale and Keneth Kinnamon (Englewood Cliffs, N.J.: Prentice-Hall, 1972), 867–68.

2. For an account of how the mainstream press, scholars, and the U.S. government constructed the NOI as a threat to national interests, see Sean McCloud, *Making the American Religious Fringe: Exotics, Subversives, and Journalists, 1955–1993* (Chapel Hill: University of North Carolina Press, 2004), 55–94.

3. James R. Lewis, following Max Weber, calls this type of legitimation strategy a "traditional appeal." It is worth noting the movement also used appeals to rationality and the prophetic charisma of Elijah Muhammad, other hallmarks of new religious movements, to argue for the authenticity of its religion. See further James R. Lewis, *Legitimating New Religions* (New Brunswick, N.J.: Rutgers University Press, 2003), esp. 13–14.

4. For various treatments of the links between the liberation struggles of African Americans and persons of color in Africa and Asia, see Penny M. Von Eschen, *Race against Empire: Black Americans and Anticolonialism, 1937–1957* (Ithaca, N.Y.: Cornell University Press, 1997); Thomas Borstelmann, *The Cold War and the Color Line: American Race Relations in the Global Arena* (Cambridge, Mass.: Harvard University Press, 2001); George M. Fredrickson, *Black Liberation: A Comparative History of Black Ideologies in the United States and South Africa* (New York: Oxford University Press, 1995); Robin D. G. Kelley, "Stormy Weather: Reconstructing Black (Inter)Nationalism in the Cold War Era," in *Is It Nation Time?*, ed. Eddie S. Glaude Jr. (Chicago: University of Chicago Press, 2002), 67–90; and Brenda Gayle Plummer, ed., *Window on Freedom: Race, Civil Rights, and Foreign Affairs, 1945–1988* (Chapel Hill: University of North Carolina Press, 2003).

5. Cf. C. Eric Lincoln, *The Black Muslims in America*, 3rd ed. (Grand Rapids, Mich.: William B. Eerdmans, 1994), 43, 210.

6. On black messianism, see further Wilson Jeremiah Moses, *Black Messiahs and Uncle Toms: Social and Literary Manipulations of a Religious Myth*, rev. ed. (University Park: Pennsylvania State University Press, 1993).

7. See further Brenda Gayle Plummer, *Rising Wind: Black Americans and U.S. Foreign Affairs, 1935–1960* (Chapel Hill: University of North Carolina Press, 1996), 247–56.

8. Malcolm X often mentioned Bandung in his speeches, including "Message to the Grassroots," given in Detroit on 10 November 1963. See *Malcolm X Speaks*, ed. George Breitman (New York: Grove Weidenfeld, 1965), 5.

9. One "handbook" of this movement was Frantz Fanon, *The Wretched of the Earth* (New York: Grove Press, 1963).

10. "World Muslim Publication Praises American Muslims," *MS*, 15 October 1962, 3; see also *Muslimnews International* 1, no. 4 (September 1962): 25.

11. Sylvester Leaks, "The Messenger of Allah as Seen by an Islamic Leader from Pakistan," *MS*, 8 May 1964, 3.

12. "Black Man's Salvation Lies in Islam, Not in 'White' Christianity or Politics," *MS*, 9 September 1966, 10.

13. Abdul Basit Naeem, "Tells How Study of Languages Can Be Helpful to Messenger, Nation of Islam," *MS*, 24 February 1967, 10.

14. Abdul Basit Naeem, "Gives Views of Overseas Muslims' 'Recognition' of U.S. Islam Nation," *MS*, 31 October 1969, 15.

15. Ibid.

16. "Arabian Sees Messenger as Divine Leader," *MS*, 24 June 1966, 25.

17. Personal correspondence with John J. W. Plampin, Assistant Registrar for Convocation, Office of the University Registrar, University of Chicago, 2 November 2004.

18. Zahid Aziz Al-Ghareeb, "Lauds Leader: Eastern Muslim Calls Nation of Islam 'Great,'" *MS*, 2 July 1971, 15.

19. *MS*, 1 December 1972, 15. For an introduction to the Islamic Party of North America, see Aminah Beverly McCloud, *African American Islam* (New York: Routledge, 1995), 65–69. Its founder, Yusuf Muzaffaruddin, was reportedly influenced by the Salafiyya movement, a modern reformist movement that advocated the restoration of the Islamic practices of the Prophet Muhammad and the first generation of Muslims.

20. *MS*, 9 September 1966, 8.

21. Essien-Udom, *Black Nationalism*, 238.

22. Wallace D. Muhammad, interview with the author, 8 October 1996, and see Zafar Ishaq Ansari, "W. D. Muhammad: The Making of a 'Black Muslim' Leader (1933–1961)," *American Journal of Islamic Social Sciences* 2, no. 2 (1985): 248–62.

23. "MS Set for Meet in Africa," *MS*, 15 April 1963, 10. See also "Director, FBI to SAC, New York," 17 August 1964, in *FBI File on Elijah Muhammad* (Wilmington, Del.: Scholarly Resources, 1996), Reel Two.

24. See the photographs reproduced after page 176 of Essien-Udom, *Black Nationalism*.

25. Ibid., 241.

26. "New York Forges Ahead with Muhammad's Educational Program," *MS*, 30 August 1968, 29.

27. "Open Letter from Trenton State Pen," *MS*, 7 August 1970, 14.

28. Sonsyrea Tate, *Little X: Growing up in the Nation of Islam* (New York: Harper-SanFrancisco, 1997), 39.

29. Ali Baghdadi, "Students Mastering Arabic," *MS*, 28 April 1972, 2.

30. Alonzo 4X, "Native Palestinian Arabic Teacher a 'Blessing,'" 6 September 1972, 4.

31. See Elijah Muhammad, *The Supreme Wisdom: Solution to the So-Called Negroes' Problem* (1957; repr., Newport News, Va.: National Newport News and Commentator, n.d.), 51; Elijah Muhammad, *Message to the Blackman in America* (1965; repr., Newport News, Va.: United Brothers Communications Systems, 1992), 93; and "Revelation Guides Aright," *MS*, 25 December 1970, 8.

32. Tate, *Little X*, 63.

33. In addition to the articles discussed extensively in this chapter, see Sister Margary Hassain, "Muhammad the Last Messenger of Allah (God)," *MS*, 21 February 1969, 2, in which Hassain quotes from Muhammad Ali's translation of Qur'an 29:31–32, 35–40; Minister James Shabazz, "Support Muhammad if You Would Be Recognized," 28 February 1969, 27; Bro. Johnnie Muhammad, "This Is the Time to Run to Allah and His Messenger, If You Would Live," 24 April 1970, 18; James X Glover, "The Divine Mission," 6 November 1970, 18; "This Is the One," *MS*, 5 March 1971, 19; Minister Edwin X Taylor, "The Original People: Soul of Blackness," 11 February 1972, 18. On 25 June 1971, *Muhammad Speaks* included a special pull-out section with depictions of Elijah Muhammad, verses from the Qur'an, and the final verses of the Book of Malachi that predict the coming of the prophet Elijah. Each page is framed by Arabic calligraphy and the star and crescent.

34. See Abdul Basit Naeem, "Inspirational Voice of Messenger Muhammad," *MS*, 10 October 1969, 18, 33.

35. For a history of the African American Ahmadi community, see Richard Brent Turner, *Islam in the African-American Experience* (Bloomington: Indiana University Press, 1997), 109–46.

36. Turner, *Islam in the African-American Experience*, 114.

37. See further Jacob Landau, *The Politics of Pan-Islam: Ideology and Organization* (New York: Oxford University Press, 1990), and Larry Poston, *Islamic Da'wah in the West: Muslim Missionary Activity and the Dynamics of Conversion to Islam* (New York: Oxford University Press, 1992).

38. See, for example, "The Holy Qur-an," *MS*, 12 February 1965, 8, and compare Muhammad Ali, *The Holy Qur'an: Arabic Text, Translation, and Commentary*, 2nd ed. (Columbus, Ohio: Ahmadiyyah Anjuman Isha'at Islam, Lahore, 1951).

39. See Muhammad, *Supreme Wisdom*, 51; Muhammad, *Message to the Blackman*, 23, 254; and Herbert Berg, "Elijah Muhammad: An African American Muslim *Mufassir*?," *Arabica* 45 (1998): 329–30n36.

40. Ahmadi influences on the NOI can be seen perhaps in the fact that, according to Elijah Muhammad, W. D. Fard, the founder of the NOI, apparently claimed to be both Messiah and Mahdi. See Muhammad, *Message to the Blackman*, 10–11. Of course,

Elijah Muhammad also said that Fard was Allah Incarnate, God in Person, an idea that American Ahmadis, like most American Muslims, found completely unacceptable.

41. For a short introduction to the Ahmadiyya, see Yohanan Friedman, "Ahmadi-yah," in *The Oxford Encyclopedia of the Modern Islamic World*, ed. John L. Esposito (New York: Oxford University Press, 1995) 1:54–57. For a fuller treatment, see Yo-hanan Friedman, *Prophecy Continuous: Aspects of Ahmadi Religious Thought and Its Medieval Background* (Berkeley: University of California Press, 1989).

42. Attributed to Abu Hurayra in Abu Dawud 36:1. This *hadith* is reproduced in a number of places, including the Online Library of Young Muslims of Canada. See ‹http://www.youngmuslims.ca/online_library/books/towards_a_sound_awakening/ch1p1.htm›, 7 December 2004.

43. This commentary, originally written by Muhammad Ali, can be found on the official Lahori Ahmadi website: "A person thus raised by God is called a *mujaddid* (*one who revives*) in the terminology of Islam. The mujaddid is a *muhaddath* (*one to whom God speaks though he is not a prophet*), and he is raised up by God to remove errors that have crept in among Muslims and to shed new light on the great religious truths of Islam in the new circumstances which Muslims may have to face in every new age." See also Maulana Muhammad Ali, chap. 19, "Jihad (Hadith)," in *A Manual of Hadith* (Lahore: Ahmadiyyah Movement for the Propagation of Islam, n.d.), 256n3. It is repro-duced at ‹http://aaiil.org/text/had/manhad/ch19had.shtml›, 8 December 2005.

44. *MS*, 9 September 1963, 9.

45. Berg, "Elijah Muhammad: An African American Muslim *Mufassir*?," 344.

46. Herbert Berg, "Elijah Muhammad and the Qur'an: The Evolution of His *Tafsir*," *Muslim World* 89, no. 1 (January 1999): 54.

47. "12,000 Cheer Muhammad's History of Black Man's Role in Islam," *MS*, 31 Oc-tober 1962, 3.

48. See Qur'an 32:29 in *The Qur'an*, trans. M. A. S. Abdel Haleem (New York: Ox-ford University Press, 2004), 265.

49. *MS*, 17 October 1969, 20.

50. Elijah Muhammad, "What Is Islam?: Part II," *MS*, 31 July 1970, 16–17.

51. Elijah Muhammad, "What Is Islam?: Part III," *MS*, 7 August 1970, 6.

52. "Mr. Muhammad Answers Critics: Authority from Allah, None Other," *MS*, 2 August 1962, 2, 4.

53. "First Printing of Holy Qur'an in U.S.," *MS*, 17 August 1973, 23. In this article, Salaam advises the believers how to approach the Muhammad Ali translation of the Qur'an offered to NOI members by Specialty Promotions in New York City.

54. "Muslim Minister Urges All Black People: Read Divine Truths in Messenger's Book," *MS*, 7 April 1967, 25.

55. *MS*, June 1962, 14. Translation is by Muhammad Ali.

56. See E. Geoffrey, "Ummi," in *Encyclopaedia of Islam*, WebCD ed. (Leiden: Brill, 2003), 10:863.

57. *MS*, 19 June 1964, 9.

58. See further Louis A. DeCaro Jr., *On the Side of My People: A Religious Life of Malcolm X* (New York: New York University Press, 1996), 195–98.

59. "Beware of False Prophets," *MS*, 31 July 1964, 1, 3.

60. Tate, *Little X*, 51.

61. *MS*, 2 June 1972, 4.

62. For an introduction to the historical importance of the Exodus narrative to African American religions, see Albert J. Raboteau, *A Fire in the Bones: Reflections on African-American Religious History* (Boston: Beacon Press, 1995).

63. *MS*, 17 July 1964, 9.

64. For more on the Civil Rights Act of 1964 and the African American movements that led to its passage, see Hugh Davis Graham, *The Civil Rights Era: Origins and Development of National Policy, 1960–1972* (New York: Oxford University Press, 1990), and Taylor Branch, *Parting the Waters: America in the King Years, 1954–1963* (New York: Simon and Schuster, 1988).

65. *MS*, 6 November 1964, 17.

66. "As It Was Said of Us, So Shall It Be Said of You," *MS*, 14 August 1964, 13.

67. Claude Andrew Clegg III, *An Original Man: The Life and Times of Elijah Muhammad* (New York: St. Martin's Press, 1997), 194.

68. Isaiah Karriem, "Cites 20-Year Association with Messenger of Allah," *MS*, 11 September 1964, 4.

69. See also "Director, FBI to SAC, New York," 17 August 1964, in *FBI File on Elijah Muhammad*, Reel Two.

70. *MS*, 1 January 1965, 9.

71. See Zafar Ishaq Ansari, "W. D. Muhammad: The Making of a 'Black Muslim' Leader (1933–1961)," *American Journal of Islamic Social Sciences* 2, no. 2 (1985): 248–62; Clegg, *Original Man*, 245, 333n15; and see further Edward E. Curtis IV, "Wallace D. Muhammad (b. 1933): Sunni Islamic Reform and the Continuing Problem of Particularism," in *Islam in Black America: Identity, Liberation, and Difference in African-American Islamic Thought* (Albany: State University of New York Press, 2002), 107–27. It is difficult to determine exactly when Wallace Muhammad was in or out of the movement. In 1971, he is pictured in *Muhammad Speaks* embracing his mother at a graduation ceremony of Temple No. 2's University of Islam. See *MS*, 12 March 1971, 2.

72. See DeCaro, *On the Side of My People*, 4–8, 159–70; Curtis, *Islam in Black America*, 88–96, 99–105; and cf. Malcolm X and Alex Haley, *Autobiography of Malcolm X*, 288–342.

73. *New York Times*, 9 November 1964, 48.

74. *MS*, 4 December 1964, 14.

75. Louis X, "Boston Minister Tells of Malcolm—Muhammad's Biggest Hypocrite," *MS*, 4 December 1964, 11, 12.

76. See Washington Irving, *Mahomet and His Successors* (New York: George P. Putnam, 1850).

77. Ibid., 11–12.

78. Malcolm's assassins were associated with the NOI, but there is no evidence directly linking Minister Farrakhan to the death. See Clegg, *Original Man*, 229.

79. For an introduction that considers the many ways that Muslims approached the figure of Muhammad in their religious practice, see John Renard, *Seven Doors to Islam:*

*Spirituality and the Religious Life of Muslims* (Berkeley: University of California Press, 1996).

80. See further Carl W. Ernst, *Following Muhammad: Rethinking Islam in the Contemporary World* (Chapel Hill: University of North Carolina Press, 2003), esp. 73–92.

81. See Susan Nance, "Mystery of the Moorish Science Temple: Southern Blacks and American Alternative Spirituality in 1920 Chicago," *Religion and American Culture* 12, no. 2 (Summer 2002): 123–66.

82. "Allah and His Messenger," *MS*, 1 January 1965, 1.

83. "Where Others Fail, Our Messenger Succeeds," *MS*, 14 May 1965, 3.

84. "Muslim Minister Reveals: Importance of Knowledge of Self and Kind," *MS*, 26 April 1968, 25.

85. Ibid., 30.

86. For an account of millennialism in American religious traditions, see Paul Boyer, *When Time Shall Be No More: Prophecy Belief in Modern American Culture* (Cambridge, Mass.: Harvard University Press, 1992).

87. Deanar's use of "New Age" vocabularies echoes that of other American religionists. For a scholarly introduction to New Age traditions in the modern West, see Wouter J. Hanegraaff, *New Age Religion and Western Culture: Esotericism in the Mirror of Secular Thought* (Leiden: E. J. Brill, 1996), esp. 386–489.

88. "Women in Islam: Is the Honorable Elijah Muhammad the Last Messenger of Allah," *MS*, 16 September 1965, 18.

89. "Women in Islam: Part II," *MS*, 24 September 1965, 19.

90. "Women in Islam: Part III," *MS*, 8 October 1965, 18.

91. Bart Ehrman also writes that the text "was included in one of our most ancient manuscripts, this time the famous *Codex Sinaiticus*. The epistle came to be attributed to Barnabas, the traveling companion of the apostle Paul, even though it is written anonymously." See Bart D. Ehrman, *Lost Christianities: The Battles for Scripture and the Faiths We Never Knew* (New York: Oxford University Press, 2003), 145.

92. See Jeremiah Jones et al., *The Lost Books of the Bible* (New York: Alpha Publishing, 1926). Notwithstanding Deanar's claims that the book did not appear until the 1920s, it had been copyrighted previously by Gebbie & Co. in 1890 and David McKay in 1901.

93. These are exactly the same words reproduced in the 1926 edition of *The Lost Books of the Bible*, 160–61. 2 Peter 3:8, alluding to Psalm 90:4, also refers to the idea that one day in divine time equals one thousand earthly years.

94. "Muhammad," *MS*, 29 August 1969, 37.

## Chapter 3

1. See further Benedict Anderson, *Imagined Communities: Reflections on the Origin and Spread of Nationalism*, rev. ed. (London: Verso, 1992).

2. Akhil Gupta and James Ferguson, "Beyond 'Culture': Space, Identity, and the Politics of Difference," *Cultural Anthropology* 7, no. 1 (1992): 11.

3. Anderson, *Imagined Communities*, 6.

4. Ibid., 187–206.

5. I argue elsewhere that the production and dissemination of modern religio-racial histories have been central to the construction of African American Muslim identities from the 1920s until the present day. See Edward E. Curtis IV, "African American Islamization Reconsidered: Black History Narratives and Muslim Identity," *Journal of the American Academy of Religion* 73, no. 2 (June 2005): 659–84.

6. Laurie Maffly-Kipp, draft manuscript for "African American Communal Narratives: Religion, Race, and Memory in Nineteenth-Century America."

7. Melani McAlister, *Epic Encounters: Culture, Media, and U.S. Interests in the Middle East, 1945–2000* (Berkeley: University of California Press, 2001), 86.

8. I borrow the term "moving across" from Thomas Tweed, who has influenced my understanding of how religionists use narratives to map their collective identities. See Thomas A. Tweed, *Our Lady of the Exile: Diasporic Religion at a Cuban Catholic Shrine in Miami* (New York: Oxford University Press, 1997), 83–98, and Thomas A. Tweed, "On Moving Across: Translocative Religion and the Interpreter's Position," *Journal of the American Academy of Religion* 70, no. 2 (June 2002): 253–77. And cf. Jonathan Z. Smith, *Map Is Not Territory: Studies in the History of Religions* (Chicago: University of Chicago Press, 1978).

9. Jacqueline Goggin, "Black History Month/Negro History Week," in *Encyclopedia of African-American Culture and History*, ed. Jack Salzman, David Lionel Smith, and Cornel West (New York: Macmillan, 1996), 1:352–53.

10. For an examination of Carter G. Woodson's pan-African views of black history, see Robin D. G. Kelley, "Black History's Global Vision," *Journal of American History* 86, no. 3 (December 1999): 1045–92.

11. "Truth about 'Negro' History," *MS*, March 1962, 18.

12. Priscilla 2X, "Queen of the Universe," *MS*, 12 March 1971, 18. One might argue with the claim that slave women could not express authentic love for themselves or others, and with the notion that "slave mentalities" still defined African American women's emotional abilities in the 1960s, but the sister was surely right that painful and imagined memories of slavery, fueled by ongoing racism, could impact the human psyche and one's ability to have loving relationships with other human beings. See further bell hooks, *Salvation: Black People and Love* (New York: William Morrow, 2001).

13. For a helpful critique of ghetto sociology, see Robin D. G. Kelley, *Yo' Mama's Disfunktional! Fighting the Culture Wars in Urban America* (Boston: Beacon Press, 1997), 15–42.

14. Priscilla 2X, "Queen of the Universe," 18.

15. Sister Edna Mae 2X, "Black Woman Come to Islam," *MS*, 2 February 1973, 18.

16. Eugene Majied, "Lazz," 30 December 1962, 23.

17. "Negro History Emerging as Product Highly Salable," *MS*, 29 July 1966, 21.

18. *MS*, 17 February 1967, 17.

19. On the relationship between Elijah Muhammad and editor Richard Durham, see further Leon Forrest, *Relocations of the Spirit* (Wakefield, R.I.: Asphodel Press), 86–93.

20. Tynnetta Deanar, "Women in Islam," *MS*, 3 May 1968, 20.

21. Minister Angelo 3X, "Muhammad's Call for Unity of Blacks in America Is the Only Path to Salvation," *MS*, 12 July 1968, 21.

22. Anna Karriem, "Why the Messenger Must Lead Black People to True Freedom and Salvation," *MS*, 25 October 1968, 23.

23. Anna Karriem, "Islam in Tuskegee," *MS*, 13 September 1968, 24.

24. Sister Ann 3X, "University of Islam Teaches True Black history," *MS*, 6 November 1970, 18.

25. I use this term differently than does Tweed in *Our Lady of the Exile*, where he defines it more narrowly in reference to the characteristics of diasporic religion. According to Tweed, *supralocative* "names the inclination in later generations of some diasporic peoples to diminish or deny the significance of both the homeland and the adopted land in their religious life" (94–95).

26. Sister Kris X, "The Holy City," *MS*, 27 March 1964, 11.

27. See Elijah Muhammad, *The Supreme Wisdom: Solution to the So-Called Negroes' Problem* (1957; repr., Newport News, Va.: Newport News and Commentator, n.d.), 26; and Elijah Muhammad, *Message to the Blackman in America* (1965; Newport News, Va.: United Brothers Communications Systems, 1992), 161–64, and 230.

28. Leo P. X McCallum, "Why Mr. Muhammad Emphasizes Value of History to Black People in America," *MS*, 24 October 1969, 22, 25.

29. See *MS*, 14 February 1969, 24, and *MS*, 25 April 1969, 36.

30. *MS*, 14 February 1969, 24.

31. Forrest, *Relocations of the Spirit*, 67.

32. Cf. Tweed's use of these terms in *Our Lady of the Exile*, 94–95.

33. *MS*, May 1962, 1, 23. Another article on the same topic, entitled "After the Africans . . . Came the Cave Dwellers," included a reprint of an interview with Louis Leakey. See *MS*, 8 May 1964, 11–12.

34. See also "Blackman's Origins Verified," *MS*, April 1962, 25; "Cave Savage . . . Modern Savage [cartoon]," 31 December 1965, 15; "Muhammad's Message [cartoon]," 4 March 1966, 27; "True History of Black Man in Africa and America Featured by New Detroit Museum," 20 January 1967, 16; "Scholar Says Truth of African History," 8 September 1967, 22; "Christian West Searching for Origin of 'White Man' in India and Pakistan," 1 March 1968, 4; and "Early South Arabian and East African Cultural Ties," 29 March 1968, 28. Leakey's discoveries were avidly followed by other important African American newspapers, as well. See "Man's Origins in Africa Shown By TV Program," *Chicago Daily Defender*, 19–25 November 1966, 13.

35. Tynnetta Deanar, "Black Beauty," *MS*, May 1962, 6.

36. See Fazal Ahmad, *Omar: The Second Caliph of Islam* (Lahore: Sh. Muhammad Ashraf, 1961), 13–16. This book was later offered for sale in *Muhammad Speaks* by Books and Things, a Muslim bookstore on Lenox Avenue in New York City. See *MS*, 14 February 1969, 26, and 23 January 1970, 13. The story of Umar's conversion was canonized by Ibn Ishaq (d. circa 768 C.E.) in *Sirat Rasul Allah*, which was translated into English by Alfred Guillaume in *The Life of Muhammad* (New York: Oxford University Press, 1955), 155–59. For a contemporary and widely available rendering of the story, see Frederick Mathewson Denny, *An Introduction to Islam* (New York: Macmillan, 1985), 71.

37. *MS*, 24 September 1965, 27.

38. *MS*, 1 October 1965, 27.

39. *MS*, 8 October 1965, 27.

40. *MS*, 22 October 1965, 27.

41. Muhammad, *Supreme Wisdom*, 26.

42. *MS*, 29 October 1965, 27.

43. *MS*, 12 November 1965, 27.

44. *MS*, 19 November 1965, 27.

45. *MS*, 3 December 1965, 27.

46. "Milwaukeean Finds New Life in Islam's Teachings," *MS*, 22 April 1966, n.p.

47. *MS*, 2 December 1966, 24.

48. "Muhammad Brings Film on Life of 1st Black Islamic Convert to Chicago," *MS*, 18 November 1966, 17.

49. See David Robinson, *Muslim Societies in African History* (Cambridge: Cambridge University Press, 2004), 54–55, and D. T. Niane, *Sundiata: An Epic of Old Mali*, trans. G. D. Pickett (London: Longmans, 1965), 2.

50. See W. Arafat, "Bilal ibn Rabah," in *Encyclopaedia of Islam*, WebCD ed. (Leiden: Brill, 2003), 1:1215; Muhammad Abdul-Rauf, *Bilal ibn Rabah: A Leading Companion of the Prophet Muhammad* (Indianapolis: American Trust Publications, 1977); M. A. Qazi, *Bilal, the First Muadhdhin of the Prophet of Islam* (Chicago: Kazi Publications, 1976); and H. A. L. Craig, *Bilal* (New York: Quartet Books, 1977).

51. See *MS*, 14 February 1969, 26.

52. See Allama Syed Sulaiman Nadwi, *Heroic Deeds of Muslim Women*, trans. Syed Sabahuddin Abdur Rahman (Lahore: Sh. Muhammad Ashraf, 1964), 19–22.

53. According to Robert Coolidge, Nadwi was the rector of Darul Uloom Nadwatal Ulama in Lucknow, India. Robert Coolidge, Personal Correspondence, 22 December 2004. Ashraf Dockrat also identifies him as a khalifah of Mawlana Ahraf Ali Thanwi, who opposed the Qadiani Ahmadi interpretation of Islam. Ahraf Dockrat, Personal Correspondence, 21 December 2004.

54. *MS*, 17 December 1965, 27.

55. "Muhammad's Message," *MS*, 24 December 1995, 27. Many Damascenes were monophysite and disliked the Byzantine rulers, who were Greek Orthodox. In fact, one account has Mansur b. Sarjun, father of St. John's Cathedral, negotiating with the Muslim conquerors to avoid unnecessary bloodshed among the indigenous population. See "Dimashk," in *Encyclopaedia of Islam*, 2:277.

56. *MS*, 28 January 1966, 27.

57. *MS*, 4 February 1966, 27.

58. *MS*, 18 February 1966, 27.

59. See Elijah Muhammad, *Message to the Blackman*, 58–59.

60. E. U. Essien-Udom, *Black Nationalism: A Search for an Identity in America* (Chicago: University of Chicago Press, 1962), 157–58.

61. See Dorothy Van Ess, *Fatima and Her Sisters* (New York: John Day Co., 1961).

62. See "Zubayda bt. Dja'far," in the *Encyclopaedia of Islam*, 11:547.

63. Tynnetta Deanar, "Muslim Women in History," *MS*, July 1962, 26.

64. Zaheer Ali, "'Black Mecca': The Nation of Islam's Mosque No. 7, Harlem, and

Islam in New York City," paper presented at a meeting of the American Academy of Religion, San Antonio, Texas, 21 November 2004.

65. Diogenes X Grassal, "How White Conquerors fought Islam among Indians and Latins," *MS*, 9 July 1971, 3.

66. For a classic account of black power and black consciousness, see William L. Van Deburg, *A New Day in Babylon: The Black Power Movement and American Culture, 1965 – 1975* (Chicago: University of Chicago Press, 1992).

67. See, for example, Robert Weisbrot, *Freedom Bound: A History of America's Civil Rights Movement* (New York: Penguin, 1991), 154 – 261.

68. Robin D. G. Kelley also locates the beginning of black American solidarity with the third world in earlier movements of the 1950s and 1960s, offering an account of the Revolutionary Action Movement (RAM). See "Stormy Weather: Reconstructing Black (Inter)Nationalism in the Cold War Era," in *Is It Nation Time? Contemporary Essays on Black Power and Black Nationalism*, ed. Eddie S. Glaude Jr. (Chicago: University of Chicago Press, 2002), 67 – 90.

69. For a comparative analysis of various black liberation ideologies during this period and before, see George M. Fredrickson, *Black Liberation: A Comparative History of Black Ideologies in the United States and South Africa* (New York: Oxford University Press, 1995), esp. 277 – 318.

70. Karenga inspired some of the intellectuals whom scholars would come to call "wild Afrocentrists." For accounts that help to situate Karenga's contributions within the larger context of various Afrocentric movements, see Stephen Howe, *Afrocentrism: Mythical Pasts and Imagined Homes* (London: Verso, 1998); and Manning Marable, ed., *Dispatches from the Ebony Tower: Intellectuals Confront the African American Experience* (New York: Columbia University Press, 2000). For a reconsideration of the term "Afrocentrism" and its relationship to "Egyptocentrism," see Wilson Jeremiah Moses, *Afrotopia: The Roots of African American Popular History* (Cambridge: Cambridge University Press, 1998).

71. Van DeBurg, *New Day in Babylon*, 171 – 74.

72. In another comic strip, not discussed here, Majied also refers to Muhammad Askia and Mansa Musa. See *MS*, 21 March 1968, 24.

73. *MS*, 4 March 1966, 27.

74. *MS*, 11 March 1966, 27.

75. Ira M. Lapidus, *A History of Islamic Societies*, 2nd ed. (Cambridge: Cambridge University Press, 2002), 404.

76. *MS*, 11 March 1966, 27.

77. "Separation Remains Only Answer for the Black Man," *MS*, 31 March 1967, 25.

78. *MS*, 1 January 1965, 16.

79. *MS*, 22 September 1967, 26.

80. McAlister, *Epic Encounters*, 104 – 10.

81. For an account of Baraka's evolving views on black identity and politics, see Komozi Woodard, *A Nation Within a Nation: Amiri Baraka (LeRoi Jones) and Black Power Politics* (Chapel Hill: University of North Carolina Press, 1999).

82. McAlister, *Epic Encounters*, 116 – 18.

83. Howe, *Afrocentrism*, 282, and see further Chancellor Williams, *The Destruction of*

*Black Civilization: Great Issues of a Race, 4500 BC to 2000 AD* (Dubuque, Iowa: Kendall/Hunt Co., 1971).

84. Carmichael repeats the claim that Arabs invaded Africa in a 1971 compilation of his public speeches, although he does not explicitly mention Islam. See Stokely Carmichael, *Stokely Speaks: Black Power Back to Pan-Africanism* (New York: Random House, 1971), 222.

85. *MS*, 4 June 1971, 29–30.

86. Brother Robert 7X, "Is Carmichael Right in Saying Islam not African Religion?," *MS*, 4 June 1971, 29–30.

87. Edward L. X Truitt, "Islam: The Original Way of Life," *MS*, 1 October 1971, 21–22.

88. For an introduction to Swahili history and culture, see Robinson, *Muslim Societies in African History*, 32–38; Randall Lee Pouwels, *Horn and Crescent: Cultural Change and Traditional Islam on the East African Coast, 800–1900* (Cambridge: Cambridge University Press, 1987); and Ali Mazrui and Ibrahim Noor Shariff, *The Swahili: Idiom and Identity of an African People* (Trenton, N.J.: Africa World Press, 1994).

89. Diogenes X Grassal, "How White Conquerors Fought Islam among Indians and Latins, Part Two," *MS*, 16 July 1971, 21–22.

90. Edward W. Blyden, one of the first English-speaking blacks to depict Islam in a positive light, hailed the civilizing influences of Islam on African natives. See further Edward E. Curtis IV, "Edward Wilmot Blyden (1832–1912) and the Paradox of Islam," in *Islam in Black America: Identity, Liberation, and Difference in African-American Islamic Thought* (Albany: State University of New York Press, 2002), 21–43. For more on the salience of civilizationism in African American literary traditions, see Wilson Jeremiah Moses, *The Golden Age of Black Nationalism, 1850–1925* (New York: Oxford, 1988).

91. Charles 67X, "Muhammad: Black Studies I," *MS*, 6 September 1974, 6.

92. To cite but one glaring example, E. U. Essien's 1962 ethnographic treatment of the NOI was titled *Black Nationalism*.

## Chapter 4

1. For various scholarly treatments of this issue, see, for example, Robert F. Reid-Farr, *Conjugal Union: The Body, The House, and the Black American* (New York: Oxford University Press, 1999); Shane White, *Stylin': African American Expressive Culture from Its Beginnings to the Zoot Suit* (Ithaca, N.Y.: Cornell University Press, 1998); and Katherine Fishburn, *The Problem of Embodiment in Early African American Literature* (Westport, Conn.: Greenwood Press, 1997).

2. Arguably, bodily abuse was as prevalent after slavery as before. For examples, see Sarah E. Chinn, *Technology and the Logic of American Racism: A Cultural History of the Body as Evidence* (London: Continuum, 2000); Dorothy E. Roberts, *Killing the Black Body: Race, Reproduction, and the Meaning of Liberty* (New York: Pantheon, 1997); and James H. Jones, *Bad Blood: The Tuskegee Syphilis Experiment* (New York: Free Press, 1993).

3. As Patricia Turner shows, much of contemporary urban African American rumor

and folklore is dominated by "metaphors linking the fate of the black race to the fates of black bodies." See Patricia Turner, *I Heard It Through the Grapevine: Rumor in African-American Culture* (Berkeley: University of California Press, 1993).

4. See Paula Giddings, *When and Where I Enter: The Impact of Black Women on Race and Sex in America* (New York: Bantam, 1984), 17–30.

5. Michael Bennett, "Frances Ellen Watkins Sings the Body Electric," in *Recovering the Black Female Body: Self-Representations by African American Women*, ed. Michael Bennett and Vanessa D. Dickerson (New Brunswick, N.J.: Rutgers University Press, 2001), 19–40.

6. Ibid., 35.

7. Wilson J. Moses, *The Golden Age of Black Nationalism, 1850–1925* (New York: Oxford University Press, 1978), 61. Another of Moses' works situates the NOI, Elijah Muhammad, and Malcolm X within the literary and philosophic tradition of black messianism. See Wilson J. Moses, *Black Messiahs and Uncle Toms* (University Park: Pennsylvania State University Press, 1993), 183–95 and 207–25.

8. Cf. Roberts, *Killing the Black Body*, 8–21.

9. Elijah Muhammad, *The Supreme Wisdom* (1957; repr., Newport News, Va.: National Newport News and Commentator, n.d.), 34.

10. See Arthur Huff Fauset, *Black Gods of the Metropolis* (New York: Octagon, 1974), 73–75.

11. Albert Raboteau, *Canaan Land: A Religious History of African Americans* (New York: Oxford University Press, 2001), 97.

12. Joseph R. Washington Jr., *Black Sects and Cults* (Garden City, N.Y.: Anchor, 1973), 134.

13. See, for example, Hans A. Baer and Merrill Singer, *African-American Religion in the Twentieth Century: Varieties of Protest and Accommodation* (Knoxville: University of Tennessee Press, 1992), 143.

14. E. U. Essien-Udom, *Black Nationalism: The Search for an Identity in America* (Chicago: University of Chicago Press, 1962), 205–6.

15. Elijah Muhammad, *How to Eat to Live, Book No. 2* (1972; repr., Newport News, Va.: National Newport News and Commentator, n.d.), 78.

16. Muhammad, *How to Eat to Live*, 87–93, 141.

17. Excerpted from a list given to Essien-Udom, *Black Nationalism*, 205–6.

18. Muhammad, *How to Eat to Live*, 108, 113.

19. For an illustrated guide, see "The Devil's Diet for the Righteous," *MS*, 26 May 1967, 14. And compare Muhammad, *How to Eat to Live*, 65–66.

20. Muhammad, *How to Eat to Live*, 105.

21. Ibid., 101–24.

22. *MS*, 12 February 1971, 15.

23. Muhammad, *How to Eat to Live*, 7, 13, 23, 151, 191.

24. Samuel 25X, "Recent Scientific Research Confirms Messenger's 40-year Dietary Teachings," *MS*, 7 May 1971, 22. See further C. M. McKay, "Effect of Restricted Feeding and Chronic Diseases in Rats and Dogs," *American Journal of Public Health* 37, no. 5 (1947): 521–28.

25. Muhammad, *How to Eat to Live*, 49.

26. Ibid., 151.

27. Jamillah Muhammad, "The Dog Worshippers, Part II," *MS*, 13 October 1972, 15.

28. Jamillah Muhammad, "The Dog Worshippers, Part III," *MS*, 20 October 1972, 15.

29. Charles 67X, "The Enemy at the Door," *MS*, 22 November 1974, 2.

30. Sylvester Leaks, "The Messenger Was My Savior," *MS*, 4 December 1964, 5.

31. See, for example, "Tobacco Death List Shows Bladder Cancer," *MS*, 27 August 1965, 12.

32. *MS*, 31 December 1965, 14.

33. *MS*, 9 July 1965, 3.

34. See further Norrece T. Jones Jr., *Born a Child of Freedom, Yet a Slave: Mechanisms of Control and Strategies of Resistance in Antebellum South Carolina* (Hanover, N.H.: Wesleyan University Press, 1990), 69–71.

35. *MS*, 9 July 1965, 3. For another cartoon libeling the hog, see *MS*, 2 May 1969, 2.

36. "Gordon's Meat Market Newest Pride of Boston's Muslim Businessmen," *MS*, December 1961, 22.

37. *MS*, 4 March 1963, 18.

38. *MS*, 23 October 1964, 23.

39. Other examples of Shabazz businesses include the Shabazz Restaurant and Bakery in Newark, New Jersey, on 257 S. Orange Avenue; the Shabazz Grocery and Meat Market in Milwaukee; the Shabazz Restaurant in the Roxbury neighborhood of Boston; and the Shabazz Bakery of 414 R Street NW in Washington, D.C. See *MS*, 22 May 1964; 5 June 1964; 29 July 1966, 22; 13 January 1967, 22.

40. Sonsyrea Tate, *Little X: Growing Up in the Nation of Islam* (New York: HarperSanFrancisco, 1997), 66–67.

41. "A Dream Comes True: Muhammad's Plans Move On with Opening of Salaam Restaurant," *MS*, 15 March 1968.

42. *MS*, 10 May 1968, 21.

43. "Notables at Salaam," *MS*, 21 August 1970, 15.

44. Margary Hassain, "New Salaam Restaurant: A Palace of Paradise," *MS*, 7 June 1968, 27. See also Portia Pasha, "Magnificent Salaam," *MS*, 2 August 1968, 24.

45. Bayyinah Sharrieff, "The Miracle of Muhammad: Development of Cattle Industry," *MS*, 13 November 1970, 18.

46. *MS*, 2 August 1968, 19.

47. Larry 14X, "An Oasis in an Economic Desert: Muhammad's Fish Program, A Blessing for Many," *MS*, 18 October 1974, 9.

48. "Historic First: Muslims Charter Entire Ship for Huge Fish Cargo," *MS*, 1 March 1974, 10.

49. "Hundreds Employed in New York Alone: Muhammad's Fish Sales Take Black Man's Mouth out of White Man's Kitchen," *MS*, 1 March 1974, 11.

50. "Muslim Fish in Okla.," *MS*, 15 March 1974, 3.

51. Larry 14X, "Oasis in an Economic Desert," 9.

52. Bayyinah Sharrieff, "The Great Hinderance [*sic*]," *MS*, 17 December 1971, 18.

53. Brother Rachi X, "Dangers of Eating Scavenger Fish," *MS*, 23 November 1973, 11.

54. *MS*, 17 January 1969, 2.

55. "How to Eat to Live," *MS*, 21 August 1970, 18.

56. *MS*, 26 February 1965, 15. See also *MS*, 10 January 1965, 32.

57. *MS*, 7 November 1969, S6.

58. Jamillah Karim to author, 19 and 20 January 2005.

59. Ibid.

60. Sister Josephine X, "Islam Has Started Life Anew for Me," *MS*, 10 January 1969, 31.

61. *MS*, 19 June 1964, 7.

62. *MS*, 13 September 1963, 7.

63. Bayyinah Sharrieff, "Good Health with Muhammad's Program," 23 April 1971, 15.

64. My thanks go to medical historian Margaret Humphreys, M.D., Ph.D., for preventing me from reading too much into this case history.

65. Allen 3X, "How Messenger Muhammad's Dietary Rules Saved My Life," *MS*, 9 April 1971, 28.

66. Ermine X Love, "Blessing of Islam Include Dignity and Self-Respect," *MS*, 14 May 1965, 8.

67. "Islam Helps Brother Set Up a Jewelry Business," *MS*, 26 February 1965, 10. And compare Tate, *Little X*, 100–101.

68. "Women in Islam," *MS*, 18 February 1963, 16.

69. *Muhammad Speaks*, 16 April 1965, 8. See also Eugene Majied, "Whom Shall You Serve?," *MS*, 11 September 1964, 5.

70. Tynnetta Deanar, "Dress Should Identify Black Woman," *MS*, July 1962, 27.

71. Tynnetta Deanar, "Why No Makeup?," *MS*, June 1962, 24.

72. Sister Wilma, "Black Woman Sets Clothes Pattern," *MS*, March 1962, 15.

73. Sister Claudine X, "A Cherishable Debt," *MS*, 11 February 1972, 18.

74. Sister Geraldine, "How to Avoid Divine Chastisement of Modern Babylon," *MS*, 1 September 1967, 25. See also Margary Hassain, "The Woman in Islam," *MS*, 27 March 1970, 18.

75. Dorothy Wedad, "The Black Woman," *MS*, 18 August 1972, 15.

76. Quoted in Cynthia S'thembile West, "Nation Builders: Female Activism in the Nation of Islam, 1960–1970" (Ph.D. diss., Temple University, 1994), 139.

77. Tate, *Little X*, 44.

78. Gertie M. Kirk, "Islam Brings Happiness, Security to Housewife," *MS*, 20 December 1963, 14.

79. Sister Shirley Moton, "What the Teachings of the Messenger Mean to Women," *MS*, 3 June 1966, 25.

80. Sister Edna Mae 2X, "I Traveled a Road that Led Straight to the Door of the Messenger," *MS*, 14 April 1967, 25.

81. Sister Beverly 3X, "Modesty," *MS*, 3 May 1968, 24.

82. William L. Van DeBurg, *New Day in Babylon: The Black Power Movement and American Culture, 1965–1975* (Chicago: University of Chicago Press, 1992), 192–98.

83. Elijah Muhammad, "Warning to the M.G.T. and G.C.C," *MS*, 28 June 1968, 4. And compare Tate, *Little X*, 105.

84. Elijah Muhammad, "Beards," *MS*, 4 July 1969, 5. Some readers will note that this prophetic commandment contradicts the tradition of another prophet—namely, the Prophet Muhammad of Arabia's reported practice of wearing a beard.

85. Sister Kathleen X, "Shun the Afro!," *MS*, 12 September 1969, 21.

86. James L. 4X, "New York Black Co-Eds Quit Mini-Skirts; Discover New Dignity in Modest Attire," *MS*, 27 June 1969, 35.

87. Tate, *Little X*, 104.

88. "Amina," interview with Katherine Currin, Washington, D.C., 2 November 2003.

89. See, for example, "Muslim Drive for Justice Stirs Nation," MS, July 1962, 4; Joseph Walker, "Justice Mocked at Muslim Trial in New York City," *MS*, 4 February 1963, 4–5; "The Shocking Facts about Los Angeles Police Brutality," *MS*, 24 May 1963, 23; *MS*, 22 September 1963, 3; and "Cave Savage, Modern Savage," *MS*, 31 December 1965, 15.

90. See *MS*, December 1961, 32; July 1962, 36; June 1963, 2; 24 May 1963, 23; 31 December 1965, 15.

91. Essien-Udom, *Black Nationalism*, 217.

92. Ibid., 221.

93. *MS*, 17 May 1968, 1.

94. *MS*, 25 February 1966, 12.

95. *MS*, 12 November 1965, 6.

96. Malcolm X and Alex Haley, *The Autobiography of Malcolm X* (New York: Ballantine, 1987), 201–2.

97. *MS*, 5 April 1968, 4.

98. See, respectively, *MS*, 2 April 1965, 6; 15 October 1965, 9; 4 June 1965, 6; 10 April 1964, 5; and 17 February 1967, 12.

99. "Wife Tells Secret of Champion's Energy," *MS*, 11 September 1964, 21.

100. "World Champion Moves Step Closer to Full-Time Task as Muhammad's Minister," *MS*, 3 March 1967, 7.

101. West, "Nation Builders," 146–51.

102. Ibid., 149.

103. Ibid., 150.

104. Roberts, *Killing the Black Body*, 58–91.

105. Ibid., 90–95.

106. Ibid., 56.

107. "Birth Control Death Plan!," *MS*, 15 December 1962, 1.

108. See further Roberts, *Killing the Black Body*, 98–100.

109. *MS*, 15 December 1962, 23.

110. *MS*, 9 July 1965, 1.

111. *MS*, 16 July 1965, 1.

112. Elijah Muhammad, *Message to the Blackman in America* (1965; repr. Newport News, Va.: United Brothers Communications Systems, 1992), 58.

113. See *MS*, 30 July 1965, 10, 12 and *MS*, 21 July 1967, 14.

114. *MS*, 22 November 1963, 17 and *MS*, 25 February 1966, 16.

115. Harriett Muhammad, "For You and About You," *MS*, 14 January 1966, 18.

116. Ibid., 18–19.

117. For the story of how the American Psychiatric Association stopped classifying homosexuality as a disease, see Ronald Bayer, *Homosexuality and American Psychiatry: The Politics of Diagnosis* (Princeton, N.J.: Princeton University Press, 1987). See also C. A. Tripp, *The Homosexual Matrix*, 2nd ed. (New York: New American Library, 1987).

118. Harriett Muhammad, "For You and About You," *MS*, 21 January 1966, 18.

119. Harriett Muhammad, "For You and About You," *MS*, 28 February 1964, 16.

120. Hubert X, "Marcus Garvey Said: 'A Messenger Will Follow Me,'" *MS*, 5 June 1964, 7.

121. Essien-Udom, *Black Nationalism*, 87.

122. "Anna," interview with Katherine Currin, 29 October 2003.

123. "Amina," interview with Katherine Currin, Washington, D.C., 2 November 2003.

124. "Alexandra," interview with Katherine Currin, Durham, N.C., 8 April 2003.

125. On "uplift" efforts by and among black Baptist and African American club women, see further Evelyn Brooks Higginbotham, *Righteous Discontent: The Women's Movement in the Black Baptist Church, 1880–1920* (Cambridge, Mass.: Harvard University Press, 1993), esp. 185–229, and Giddings, *When and Where I Enter*, 95–117. On the NOI's appropriation of rituals and symbols from the black fraternal orders, including the Shriners and Masons, see Ernest Allen Jr., "Identity and Destiny: The Formative Views of the Moorish Science Temple and the Nation of Islam," in *Muslims on the Americanization Path?*, ed. Yvonne Y. Haddad and John L. Esposito (New York: Oxford, 2000), 180–82.

126. A useful introduction to the dominance of public Protestantism can be found in Catherine L. Albanese, *America, Religions, and Religion*, 3rd ed. (Belmont, Calif.: Wadsworth, 1999), 396–431. See also Robert T. Handy, *A Christian America: Protestant Hopes and Historical Realities*, 2nd ed. (New York: Oxford University Press, 1984); Martin E. Marty, *Protestantism in the United States: Righteous Empire*, 2nd ed. (New York: Scribner's, 1986); and Ernest Lee Tuveson, *Redeemer Nation: The Idea of America's Millennial Role* (Chicago: University of Chicago Press, 1968).

127. See Sacvan Bercovitch, *The American Jeremiad* (Madison: University of Wisconsin Press, 1978).

128. Baer and Singer, *African-American Religion*, 143. Baer and Singer label the NOI a "messianic-nationalist sect," grouping the NOI with other "separatist," "militant," and "counter-hegemonic" movements that have offered a "fundamental critique of the place and treatment of people of African heritage in American society" (111–12).

129. E. Frances White, *Dark Continent of Our Bodies: Black Feminism and the Politics of Respectability* (Philadelphia: Temple University Press, 2001), 43.

130. See "Nation of Islam: Cult of the Black Muslims," May 1965, available through the FBI site: ‹http://foia.fbi.gov/nation_of_islam/nation_of_islam_part02.pdf›.

131. See Robin D. G. Kelley, *Race Rebels: Culture, Politics, and the Black Working Class* (New York: Free Press, 1994), 163–65.

132. Ibid., 169.

133. Ibid., 10.

134. For an intelligible introduction to literary structuralism, semiotics, and poststructuralism, see Terry Eagleton, *Literary Theory: An Introduction* (Minneapolis: University of Minnesota Press, 1983), esp. 91–150.

135. Amanda Porterfield, *The Transformation of American Religion: The Story of a Late-Twentieth-Century Awakening* (New York: Oxford University Press, 2001), 6.

136. Robert Wuthnow has identified the civil rights movement as a key context for the "restructuring" of American religion. See Robert Wuthnow, "Old Fissures and New Fractures in American Religious Life," in *Religion and American Culture: A Reader*, ed. David G. Hackett (New York: Routledge, 1995), 378, and see further Robert Wuthnow, *The Restructuring of American Religion: Society and Faith since World War II* (Princeton, N.J.: Princeton University Press, 1988).

137. Peggy Phelan, *Unmarked: The Politics of Performance* (New York: Routledge, 1993), 6.

138. See further Sean McCloud, *Making the American Religious Fringe: Exotics, Subversives, and Journalists, 1955–1993* (Chapel Hill: University of North Carolina Press, 2004), 55–94.


## Chapter 5

1. For many Muslims, a classical understanding of Islam's basic ritual requirements can be found in the five pillars of practice, which include prescribed prayers, alms, fasting during Ramadan, the pilgrimage to Mecca, and the witness that there is no god but God and that Muhammad is his Messenger. NOI members discussed the five pillars in various places. See, for example, Hubert X, "Marcus Garvey Said: 'A Messenger Will Follow Me,'" *MS*, 5 June 1964, 7; Minister Carl X Hayden, "Nothing Can Destroy the Messenger or His Program," *MS*, 25 September 1964, 12; Sister Ruqaiyah Muhammad, "A Look at the University of Islam from a Graduate," *MS*, 23 August 1968, 31.

2. Malcolm X and Alex Haley, *The Autobiography of Malcolm X* (New York: Ballantine, 1973), 333.

3. Abdul Basit Naeem, "U.S. Muslims' Good Deeds Are Prayers in Action," *MS*, 8 July 1966, 10, 27.

4. See Elijah Muhammad, *Muslim Daily Prayers* (Chicago: University of Islam, 1957).

5. Ibid., 8–9, and compare Frederick Mathewson Denny, *An Introduction to Islam* (New York: Macmillan, 1985), 105–11. The manual explained that the five prayers are the dawn prayer or *fajr*, the early afternoon prayer or *zuhr*, the late afternoon prayer or *'asr*, the sunset or evening prayer called *maghrib*, and the late evening or nightfall prayer called *'isha*.

6. Muhammad, *Muslim Daily Prayers*, 10–11. Believers were told that the ablutions included "washing hands to the wrists; rinsing the mouth three times; cleansing the inside of the nose with water three times; washing the face three times, washing the arms to the elbows three times (The right arm should be washed first); wiping over the head with wet hands; wiping the ears with wet fingers; wiping around the neck with wet hands; and washing the feet (the right one first) to the ankles." Believers were also instructed to ask their local ministers about a "complete bath" (Ar. *ghusl*).

7. Ibid., 12–13. The prayer-caller is directed to stand "erect on the prayer rug or sheet, facing the Holy City of Mecca (East), with your hands upright touching the ears, and [to] recite: Allah is the Greatest (Four times) / I bear witness that there is none wor-

shippable other than Allah (Twice) / I bear witness that Muhammad is Allah's Messenger (Twice) / Come to Prayer (Twice) / Come to Success (Twice) / There is non [*sic*] worshippable but Allah (Once)." Included is a reminder to add the line "prayer is better than sleep" in the call for the *fajr* prayer.

8. Ibid., 14–20. It also directs believers to recite their intention to perform the prayer, or the *niyya*, which is translated into English. The manual does not discuss what one does with one's hands during the prayer cycle nor does it outline which bodily positions accompany the various spoken parts of the prayers.

9. "A Believer in Prayer," *MS*, 13 September 1968, 4.

10. See *MS*, 7 July 1972, S5, and *MS*, 8 June 1973, S6.

11. Piri Thomas, *Down These Mean Streets* (New York: Alfred A. Knopf, 1967), 288–97. Thomas strikes me as a particularly credible source since he seems to have had no other official relationship to the movement.

12. See further Abdul Basit Naeem, "Explains Muslim Annual Observance of the Ramadan 30-day Fasting Period," *MS*, 22 December 1967, 10, and my discussion of diet in chapter 4.

13. Elijah Muhammad, "How to Eat to Live," *MS*, 3 January 1969, 17.

14. Elijah Muhammad, "Fasting," 18 December 1970, 15.

15. Elijah Muhammad, *How to Eat to Live, Book No. 2* (1972; repr., Newport News, Va.: National Newport News and Commentator, n.d.), 49, 51.

16. See Yusuf Shah, "Ramadan," *MS*, 15 December 1972, 18.

17. Sister Ivyln X, "Recalls Spiritual Devotion during Ramadan," *MS*, 19 January 1968, 25.

18. Brother Clifton 3X, "Once Christian Preacher Praises Ramadan Effects," *MS*, 1 February 1974, 3.

19. See, for example, "Pre-Ramadan Fete Delights Audience," *MS*, 1 November 1971, 18.

20. Charles D. X, "Muslims at Milan Released To Attend Ramadan Services," *MS*, 30 December 1966, 16.

21. Delbert X, "Ramadan in Marion, Illinois," *MS*, 8 January 1971, 18.

22. Catherine Bell, *Ritual Theory, Ritual Practice* (New York: Oxford University Press, 1992), 204–5. And compare Jonathon Z. Smith, *To Take Place: Toward Theory in Ritual* (Chicago: University of Chicago Press, 1987), 102–3, 108–10.

23. Bell, *Ritual Theory*, 197.

24. Ibid., 211.

25. References to the NOI as a cult appear in several places, including Robert Dannin, *Black Pilgrimage to Islam* (New York: Oxford University Press, 2002), 4; Louis A. DeCaro Jr., *On the Side of My People: A Religious Life of Malcolm X* (New York: New York University Press, 1996), 84, 88, 183, 193–95; and Michael Wolfe, ed., *One Thousand Roads to Mecca* (New York: Grove Press, 1997), 486.

26. Tom F. Driver, *Liberating Rites: Understanding the Transformative Power of Ritual* (Boulder, Colo.: Westview Press, 1998), xi–xv.

27. As quoted in E. U. Essien-Udom, *Black Nationalism: The Search for an Identity in America* (Chicago: University of Chicago Press, 1962), 149.

28. *MS*, 17 February 1967, 25.

29. Reproduced from a prospectus obtained by Essien-Udom in the late 1950s. See Essien-Udom, *Black Nationalism*, 155–56.

30. C. Eric Lincoln, *The Black Muslims in America*, 3rd ed. (Grand Rapids, Mich.: William B. Eerdmans, 1994), 201.

31. Essien-Udom, *Black Nationalism*, 208–9. This mechanism of control was widespread. See further Sonsyrea Tate, *Little X: Growing Up in the Nation of Islam* (New York: HarperSanFrancisco, 1997), 102–3.

32. *MS*, April 1962, 19.

33. *MS*, 9 September 1966, 5.

34. Beverly 3X, "The Messenger's Teachings Makes Men and Women," *MS*, 14 July 1972, 18.

35. For other featured articles on the success of FOI salesmen, see "Subscription Drive Picks Up Momentum," *MS*, 15 July 1962, 10; Sylvester Leaks, "Route of Ace Salesman," *MS*, 9 October 1964, 20; "Muhammad Speaks at the Golden Gate," *MS*, 13 August 1965, 27; *MS*, 20 May 1966, 25; "Muhammad Speaks Circulation Drive Spearheaded by 7 East Coast Mosques," *MS*, 17 November 1967, 4; Lonnie Shabazz, "Education Center Spur for Stepped-Up Sales Campaign," *MS*, 24 November 1967, 25; "Messenger's Teachings Build Top-Rated Salesmen in Nation's Mosques of Islam," *MS*, 3 May 1968, 25; *MS*, 21 February 1969, 27; *MS*, 21 February 1969, 28.

36. Abdul Shabazz, a carpenter, was born in 1948. I interviewed him on 27 February 1994 as part of a larger oral history project conducted among African American Muslims in St. Louis. See Edward Curtis, "Islam in Black St. Louis: Strategies for Liberation in Two Local Religious Communities," *Gateway Heritage* 17, no. 4 (Spring 1997), 30–43.

37. *MS*, 9 April 1965, 19.

38. Tate, *Little X*, 79.

39. *MS*, 4 July 1969, 32.

40. "To Our Readers," *MS*, 5 December 1969, 2. For a more comprehensive account of the printing process, see Allen 3X, "Messenger Directs Progress of Muhammad Speaks Pressmen," *MS*, 18 December 1970, 18.

41. "How New York Team Took Top Prize," *MS*, 19 June 1964, 15.

42. Sylvester Leaks, "Single Salesman Sells Thousands for Messenger," *MS*, 25 September 1964, 18.

43. "Baltimore News Vendor Stays Out and Sells Out," *MS*, 18 June 1965, 15.

44. Jeyone X, "Muslim's Appearance, Manner Noted by Black and White Alike," *MS*, 27 November 1970, 18. In 1972, Elijah Muhammad issued a ban on selling the newspaper to white persons. See "Warning: To Muhammad Speaks Salesmen," *MS*, 28 July 1972, 3. Abass Rassoull, national secretary, said that anyone who did so would be dismissed. Given the pressure to sell one's quota, it is no wonder that many men sold the paper to any person who would buy it.

45. Kevin X Burke, "Dope Pushers and Pimps Wish Muslims Would Stop Selling M.S.," *MS*, 24 April 1970, 15.

46. Gerald L. Early, *The Culture of Bruising: Essays on Prizefighting, Literature, and Modern American Culture* (Hopewell, N.J.: Ecco Press, 1994), 250.

47. Leon Forrest, *Relocations of the Spirit* (Wakefield, R.I.: Asphodel Press, 1994), 74.

48. See, for example, Sylvester Leaks, "Harlem Gets Word of the Messenger from Top Salesman," *MS*, 11 September 1964, 24.

49. See, for example, Sister Onetha X Berry, "Islam Rescued Her from a Bleak Life of Abject Fear, Inhuman Deprivation," *MS*, 29 October 1965, 25.

50. George 11X, "Work of Righteousness Turns Toil into Joy," *MS*, 10 September 1971, 15.

51. *MS*, 8 December 1972, 18.

52. Sylvester Leaks, "Brother Lopez Broke with Old Order, Joined Islam," *MS*, 19 February 1965, 23. See also Walter 3X Kemp, "Islam Made a Man of Me," *MS*, 18 December 1964, 15.

53. Abraham Pasha, "Here Stand Men," *MS*, 6 July 1973, S3.

54. George E. X Berry "Salute to the F.O.I," *MS*, 10 November 1967, 22. The final two lines of the poem are borrowed and adapted from "Lift Every Voice and Sing," the "Negro National Anthem" by James Weldon Johnson.

55. Various Muslim prisoners cited multiple changes in case law, including *Walker v. Blackwell*, 1969. See further Samuel 17X, "Prison News in Black," *MS*, 15 September 1972, 23.

56. Clarence R. X Mitchell and McKinley X Thomas, "Prison Officials Praise Followers of Muhammad," *MS*, 10 September 1971, 18.

57. "Muslim Prisoners File Charges under U.N. Genocide Petition," *MS*, 11 September 1970, 9–10.

58. Sandra 17X, "Muslim Wife Details Attica Horrors of Husband Inmate," *MS*, 29 October 1971, 20.

59. Charles 19X, "Assistant Minister Lauds Teaching Inmates," *MS*, 26 February 1971, 18.

60. Norman X Jones, "Florida Inmates Grateful for Literature," 8 October 1971, 20.

61. Clarence R. X Mitchell, "Lorton Reformatory," *MS*, 31 March 1972, 15.

62. Samuel 17X, "Prison News in Black," *MS*, 15 September 1972, 23.

63. Willis X Smith, "Brothers Celebrate in Missouri Prison," *MS*, 18 June 1971, 15.

64. Dilbert X, "Muslims Present Solution to Savagery Inside Prison," *MS*, 12 November 1971, 20.

65. For more evidence of the ritualized nature of NOI activities in prison, see also Chester A. X (Mapp), "Calls Purity of Islam Spiritual Mathematics," *MS*, 18 September 1970, 18.

66. Lincoln, *Black Muslims*, 24.

67. *MS*, 11 March 1967, 25.

68. Essien-Udom, *Black Nationalism*, 157–59.

69. Cynthia S'thembile West, "Nation Builders: Female Activism in the Nation of Islam, 1960–1970" (Ph.D. diss., Temple University, 1994), 101.

70. *MS*, 10 January 1969, 8.

71. *MS*, 21 February 1969, 31.

72. Tate, *Little X*, 89–90.

73. Ibid., 94–95.

74. Ibid., 71.

75. Ibid., 85.

76. Moreover, for many female members, the question of whether one *should* find employment outside the home was moot, due to their economic circumstances. They simply had to find work to survive.

77. Tate, *Little X*, 90–91.

78. "Nancy," interview with Katherine Currin, Durham, N.C., 8 April 2003.

79. "Amina," interview with Katherine Currin, Washington, D.C., 2 November 2003.

80. Ibid.

81. "Fatima," interview with Katherine Currin, Washington, D.C., 2 November 2003.

82. "Anna," interview with Katherine Currin, 29 October 2003.

83. Ibid.

84. West, "Nation Builders," 156.

85. Charles 67X, "Chicago Salutes Muslim Graduates," *MS*, 9 March 1973, 15, and Lincoln, *Black Muslims*, 120. According to Lincoln, the schools were located in Oakland, Los Angeles, Detroit, San Diego, Chicago, Cincinnati, New York, Youngstown, Washington, Newark, Philadelphia, Baltimore, and Miami.

86. Essien-Udom, *Black Nationalism*, 231, 234.

87. Ibid., 234–35.

88. Lincoln, *Black Muslims*, 121.

89. Tate, *Little X*, 29.

90. *MS*, 5 March 1965, 18; *MS*, 22 July 1966, 20; "Portrait of Top Educator Reveals Messenger's Inspiring Teachings," *MS*, 28 October 1966, 16; "Messenger's Educational Program Gets New Principal, Modernization Plan," *MS*, 13 January 1967, 20.

91. *MS*, 15 November 1962, 16.

92. "Muslim School Building Top Education Center," *MS*, 31 January 1968.

93. *MS*, 3 January 1964, 7.

94. Essien-Udom, *Black Nationalism*, 239.

95. Ibid., 241.

96. Tate, *Little X*, 29.

97. Sister Audrey 3X, "N.Y. Program Points Way to Youth Growth," *MS*, June 1962, 15.

98. See, for example, *MS*, 22 July 1966, 20.

99. *MS*, 24 April 1964, 18.

100. *MS*, 19 July 1968, 11.

101. "Winner in Muhammad's 1st Annual Science Fair," *MS*, 16 July 1965, 18.

102. *MS*, 1 October 1965, 12.

103. See further Darlene Clark Hine, *Black Women in White: Racial Conflict and Co-operation in the Nursing Profession, 1890–1950* (Bloomington: Indiana University Press, 1989).

104. *MS*, 6 November 1964, 14.

105. "Muslim School Grads Go on to Nation's Top Colleges," *MS*, 30 July 1965, 23.

106. See Tate, *Little X*, 7–9.

107. "We Need Our Textbooks," *MS*, April 1962, 7. Other writers emphasized the need for an all-black school as well. See Sister Velma X, "Education or Indoctrination," *MS*, 15 July 1962, 16.

108. Essien-Udom, *Black Nationalism*, 240. The school also used a world history

text, Carl L. Becker, *The Past That Lives Today* (New York: Silver Burdett Company, 1952).

109. "1st Muslim Grade School Text May Start New Trend," *MS*, 5 July 1963, 19.

110. Sister Agnita X, "The Fruits of Muhammad's Amazing Education Program," *MS*, 14 June 1968, 27.

111. Essien-Udom, *Black Nationalism*, 243.

112. Tate, *Little X*, 71.

113. Essien-Udom, *Black Nationalism*, 242.

114. *MS*, 15 April 1963, 17.

115. *MS*, 5 July 1963, 19.

116. Tate, *Little X*, 8.

117. "Islam U. Program Features Dramatic 'Speaking Choir,'" *MS*, 31 August 1962, 17.

118. *MS*, 4 May 1973, 16.

119. Tate, *Little X*, 30–31.

120. Essien-Udom, *Black Nationalism*, 202–3.

121. *Student Enrollment* and *Actual Facts* are reproduced in pt. 1, pp. 72–87, of an FBI report on the NOI available through the agency's web-based Electronic Reading Room; see ‹http://foia.fbi.gov/foiaindex/nation_of_islam.htm ›.

122. For general accounts of modern esotericism, see Antoine Faivre and Jacob Needleman, eds., *Modern Esoteric Spirituality* (New York: Crossroad, 1992), and Wouter J. Hanegraaff, *New Age Religion and Western Culture: Esotericism in the Mirror of Secular Thought* (Leiden: E. J. Brill, 1996).

123. "How Students Dig Into the Roots of Wisdom by Analyzing Philosophies," *MS*, 9 August 1968, 30.

124. "Where Education Is Life Itself," *MS*, 7 March 1969, 31, 34. And to compare a similar ceremony in Washington in 1970, see Carl 4X, "Student Speakers Star at D.C. Graduation," *MS*, 12 March 1970, 20.

125. See also "Sister Beverly Maurad Addresses All Islam Grads," *MS*, 19 March 1971, 15.

126. "Whoever Controls School, Controls Future," *MS*, April 1962, 11–12.

127. Essien-Udom, *Black Nationalism*, 211.

128. Ibid., 218–19.

129. His account was largely confirmed by C. Eric Lincoln, although Essien-Udom described temple meetings in much greater detail than Lincoln did. Cf. Lincoln, *Black Muslims*, 110–19. See also the FBI's descriptions of temple meetings in pt. 1, pp. 31–35 of an internal report on the movement available through the FBI's Electronic Reading Room at ‹http://foia.fbi.gov/foiaindex/nation_of_islam.htm›.

130. Essien-Udom, *Black Nationalism*, 213.

131. Ibid., 215.

132. Ibid., 216.

133. Tate, *Little X*, 49.

134. Ibid., 50.

135. Essien-Udom, *Black Nationalism*, 215–19. The same symbols existed in the Washington mosque in the early 1970s, according to Tate, *Little X*, 52–53.

136. *MS*, 26 February 1965, 23.

137. Essien-Udom, *Black Nationalism*, 160.

138. *MS*, 13 March 1964, 3. The image of the Messenger was also displayed in temples, homes, and businesses. Sister Pearl X Allen of Racine, Wisconsin, said that she first learned about the NOI by encountering a portrait of Elijah Muhammad in Henry's Barber Shop. "The picture on the wall seemed to be looking only at me and trying to tell me something," she said. "It was so clean, honest-looking, alive and sincere, I just couldn't pass without asking who the handsome man was." See "Born Near Messenger's Home in Georgia, Found Life and Path to Islam in Milwaukee," *MS*, 3 September 1965, 25.

139. Steven Barboza, *American Jihad: Islam after Malcolm X* (New York: Doubleday, 1994), 151.

140. "Candid Comments from Cross Section of 5,000 Attending," *MS*, 13 March 1964, 5.

141. Ibid, 5.

142. Leo P. X McCallum, "On the Meaning of Savior's Day to the Black Man," *MS*, 11 March 1966, 25.

143. Bayyinah Sharrieff, "How the Beauty of Unity Was Apparent in Chicago at the Muslim Convention," *MS*, 8 March 1968, 10.

144. *MS*, October/November 1961, 7.

145. "Thousands Hail Muhammad in Cobo Arena," *MS*, 20 August 1965, 5.

146. Lincoln, *Black Muslims*, 184.

147. Ibid., 184–85.

148. Malcolm X and Alex Haley, *The Autobiography of Malcolm X* (New York: Ballantine, 1965), 252.

149. Tate, *Little X*, 51.

150. *MS*, 2 June 1972, 4.

151. Lincoln, *Black Muslims*, 182.

152. Tate, *Little X*, 51–52.

153. Roosevelt 6X, "What Islam Has Done For Me," *MS*, 20 October 1972, 18.

154. See "Leadership," in "Nation of Islam: Cult of the Black Muslims," May 1965, pt. 3, pp. 15–16, available at ‹http://foia.fbi.gov/foiaindex/nation_of_islam.htm›.

155. Essien-Udom, *Black Nationalism*, 225–26.

156. Abdul Shabazz, interview with the author, St. Louis, 27 February 1994.

157. Abdul Shakir, interview with the author, St. Louis, 25 February 1994.

158. Tate, *Little X*, 60.

159. Ibid., 10.

160. Ibid., 21, 23.

161. Ibid., 52.

162. "'Nite with F.O.I.' Success in Buffalo, N.Y.," *MS*, 12 August 1966, 25.

163. "300 Enjoy Dinner, Drama Music at Muslim Social," *MS*, 23 December 1966, 12.

164. Louis E. Lomax et al., "The Hate That Hate Produced," on "Newsbeat," WNTA-TV, 23 July 1959, a transcript of which is available in a declassified FBI report.

See Office Memorandum to Director, FBI, from SAC, New York, 16 July 1959, ‹http://wonderwheel.net/work/foia/1959/071659hthp-transcript.pdf›.

165. *MS*, June 1962, 12.

166. "Buffalo Bazaar Highlights Messenger's Program," *MS*, 28 October 1966.

167. "Unity Bazaar a Success," *MS*, 14 November 1969, 19.

168. "Evening with F.O.I. Key Event Even in Washington," *MS*, 14 April 1967, 26.

169. Thomas Sharrieff, "Miami Mosque Entertains Top Black Professionals," *MS*, 16 December 1966, 16.

170. *MS*, 10 March 1967, 27.

171. *MS*, 2 September 1966, 25.

172. *MS*, 31 March 1967, 24; "Record Unity Bazaar Throng Treated to Outstanding Musical Entertainment," *MS*, 21 April 1967, 18.

173. Darryl Cowherd, "Muslim Musicians Reveal Trials of Black Artists," *MS*, 7 April 1967, 12, 19.

174. Abdul Basit Naeem, "Cites October 19th Benefit Concert as Example of New Outlook on Music," *MS*, 20 October 1967, 10.

175. *MS*, 4 November 1966, 16.

176. "Chicago Muslim Takes Black Jazz to Ethiopian Television," *MS*, 2 June 1967, 27.

177. "Special: Notice from the Messenger," *MS*, 12 May 1968, 3.

178. "Messenger's Task Is to Raise a Nation, Not Funds," *MS*, 10 October 1969, 12.

179. "12,000 Hear Min. Farrakhan Address Harlem Unity Rally," *MS*, 12 November 1971, 2.

180. "Muslim Unity Bazaar Like 'Marketplace in Mid-East,'" *MS*, 20 December 1968, 38.

181. *MS*, 3 January 1969, 37.

182. "20,000 New Yorkers Attend Giant Muslim Bazaar," *MS*, 25 May 1973, 18.

183. Sister Lt. Demetria X, "Messenger's Brother Enlivens Va. Affair," *MS*, 2 August 1974, 22, and Larry 14X, "Our Purpose Is to Reflect the Teachings of Messenger Muhammad," *MS*, 1 November 1974, 6.

## Conclusion

1. "Elijah Muhammad Dead: Black Muslim Leader, 77," *New York Times*, 26 February 1975, 1, 42. Two days later, the *Times* declared in an editorial that, while most Americans found his religious teachings to be abhorrent, Elijah Muhammad's "success in rehabilitating and inspiring thousands of once despairing men and women . . . suggests a need for deeper popular understanding." See "Black Muslim," *New York Times*, 28 February 1975, 32.

2. See Paul Delaney, "Son of Elijah Muhammad Succeeds to the Leadership," *New York Times*, 27 February 1975, 35, and *MS*, 14 March 1975, 1.

3. See "Nation of Islam Changes Name to Fight Black Separatist Image," *New York Times*, 19 October 1976.

4. See *Bilalian News*, 13 February 1976, 6.

5. See "First Official Interview with the Supreme Minister of the Nation of Islam," *Muhammad Speaks*, 21 March 1975, 3.

6. Aminah Beverly McCloud, *African American Islam* (New York: Routledge, 1995), 9–26.

7. See Robert Dannin, *Black Pilgrimage to Islam* (New York: Oxford University Press, 2002), esp. 141–87.

8. See Sonsyrea Tate, *Little X: Growing Up in the Nation of Islam* (New York: Harper-SanFrancisco, 1997), 105–12, 138.

9. "Alexandra," interview with Katherine Currin, Durham, N.C., 8 April 2003.

10. Devin DeWeese, *Islamization and Native Religion in the Golden Horde* (University Park: Pennsylvania State University Press, 1994), 55.

11. Carolyn Rouse, *Engaged Surrender: African American Women and Islam* (Berkeley: University of California Press, 2004), 87.

12. Ibid., 121.

13. Ibid., 114.

14. "Alexandra," interview with Katherine Currin, Durham, N.C., 8 April 2003.

15. *MS*, 7 November 1975, 1.

16. See Alex Haley, *Roots* (Garden City, N.Y.: Doubleday, 1976), but note that portions of the book were published in *Reader's Digest* in 1974, some time before Wallace Muhammad decided to explore the roots of his black Muslim ancestor, Bilal.

17. See Muhammad Abdul-Rauf, *Bilal ibn Rabah: A Leading Companion of the Prophet Muhammad* (Indianapolis: American Trust Publications, 1977); Z. I. Ansari, trans., *Bilal: The First Moezzin of Islam* (Chicago: Kazi Publications, 1976); and H. A. L. Craig, *Bilal* (New York: Quartet Books, 1977).

18. *Bilalian News*, 28 November 1975, 25.

19. Samuel Ansari, interview with the author, St. Louis, 29 March 1994.

20. Ahmed and Lorene Ghani, interview with the author, St. Louis, 1 March 1994.

21. Khadijah Mahdi, interview with the author, St. Louis, 18 February 1994.

22. See further W. Arafat, "Bilal b. Rabah," in the *Encyclopaedia of Islam*, WebCD ed. (Leiden: Brill, 2003), 1:1215a.

23. See Edward E. Curtis IV, "African American Islamization Reconsidered: Black History Narratives and Muslim Identity," *Journal of the American Academy of Religion* 73, no. 3 (September 2005): 665.

24. One example can be found in Malcolm X's interactions with Arab Muslims both in the United States and abroad.

25. Mahdi, interview with the author, 18 February 1994.

26. Abdul Shakir, interview with the author, St. Louis, 25 February 1994.

27. Abdul Shabazz, interview with the author, St. Louis, 27 February 1994.

28. These are the figures generally cited in press accounts and scholarly introductions to Islam in the United States, but there is no scholarly consensus on the number of Muslims in the United States. For various introductory treatments of American Islam and Muslims in the United States, see Karen Isaksen Leonard, *Muslims in the United States: The State of Research* (New York: Russell Sage Foundation, 2004); Jane I. Smith, *Islam in America* (New York: Columbia University Press, 1999); and Yvonne Yazbeck

Haddad and John L. Esposito, eds., *Muslims on the Americanization Path?* (New York: Oxford University Press, 2000).

29. For one approach to the racial divide in American religions, see Michael O. Emerson and Christian Smith, *Divided by Faith: Evangelical Religion and the Problem of Race in America* (New York: Oxford University Press, 2000).

30. See Leonard, *Muslims in the United States*, 3–15, 75–79.

31. See further Zachary Lockman, *Contending Visions of the Middle East: The History and Politics of Orientalism* (Cambridge: Cambridge University Press, 2004), esp. 215–72.

# Index

and adornment, 117; and ritualized activities, 136; and images of Elijah Muhammad, 138 (n. 224); and bazaars, 170

Byrd, James, 96

Campbell, C. W., 145
Caribbean voodoo, 89
Carmichael, Stokely, 90, 212 (n. 84)
Carr, Louis X, 27
Cartoons: and image of Qur'an, 51, 53, 54, 55; and history of slavery, 71–72; and myth of black origins, 76; and historical narratives of Nation of Islam, 79–81, 83, 87–88; and depictions of women, 84; and bodily care, 101–2, 118–20; and dress and adornment, 110; and birth control, 122–23
Chancey, Harrell, 140
Chancy, George X, 145
Charles 19X, 144
Charles 67X, 91–92, 99, 101, 153, 192 (n. 29)
Christianity: links with state, 9; as superstitious, 17, 22–23, 32, 33; Islam as religious alternative to, 17–24, 178, 197 (n. 3); other-worldly nature of, 19; slavery associated with, 19–20, 51, 90, 118, 134; as hypocritical, 20, 90; in religious culture of Nation of Islam, 56; apocryphal texts of, 64, 65, 207 (nn. 91–93); and historical narratives of Nation of Islam, 69, 80, 83, 210 (n. 55); and black Latinos, 85–86; and prejudices toward Islam, 90; and bodily protection, 119; and civil rights movement, 119; and birth control, 122. See also Protestantism
Christmas celebrations, 101–2, 134
Church of God in Christ, 97
Ciccone, P. J., 145
Civilizationism, 96, 97, 129, 161
Civil Rights Act of 1964, 54
Civil rights movement: and Malcolm X, 3; leaders' attitudes toward Nation of

Islam, 4; and conservative and liberal Christians, 9; and Islam's rejection of integration drive, 30–31; and extremism, 36; and black consciousness movement, 86; leaders of, as undignified black bodies, 118; and Christianity, 119; and restructuring of American religion, 218 (n. 136)
Clarence 6X, 142
Claudine X, 111
Clayton X, 140
Cleaves, Ezekiel X, 171
Clifford 8X, 144
Clifton 3X, 134
Cold War, 38, 130
Colonialism, 3
Commandment Keepers of the Living God, 97
Communal affiliations: and religious identity, 14; Islam as vehicle for, 23, 27, 33, 93; and ritualized activities, 136, 168, 174
Community bazaars, 170–71, 172, 173
Countercultural movement, 130
Cowherd, Darryl, 171
Cross, Lonnie, 60, 65
Crummell, Alexander, 96, 97
Cummings, Larthey X, 171
Curtis Amy Quintet, 173

Davis, Ralph X, 144
Dawud, Talib Ahmad, 5
Day, John, 5
Deanar, Tynnetta: and defense of Elijah Muhammad's Islamic legitimacy, 54–55, 60, 62–65, 207 (n. 92); and historical narratives of Nation of Islam, 72–73, 78, 85; writes "Black Beauty," 78, 79; and dress and adornment, 110–11
Debonairs, 173
Decolonization, 36–37, 86
Defense of Elijah Muhammad's Islamic legitimacy: and Nation of Islam intellectuals, 7, 37, 44, 56–59, 61–65; and

Qur'an, 8, 37, 39, 41, 48–51, 53–56,
60, 64, 65, 93; and foreign Muslim
leaders, 36, 37, 38–44, 61, 65; and
Arabic language study, 44–45; debates
about orthodoxy of, 60–65
Delphonics, 173
DeWeese, Devin, 178
Diab, Jamil, 44
Diggs, Eugene C. X, 145
Dilbert X, 145–46
Dogs, 99
Douglass, Frederick, 70, 157
Driver, Tom, 136
DuBois, W. E. B., 90
Durham, Richard, 72, 191–92 (n. 29)

Early, Gerald, 141
Eaton, Richard, 13
Economic self-sufficiency, 12, 19, 75
Edna Mae 2X, 71, 113–14
Edward 4X, 24–25
Egypt, 88, 89
Ehrman, Bart, 207 (n. 91)
Elvin X, 170
Employment, 26, 41, 148, 200 (n. 38),
222 (n. 76)
Equal Rights Amendment, 112, 148
Ernesto X, 170
Esotericism, 158
Essien-Udom, E. U.: and Akbar Mu-
hammad, 45; and Christianity's asso-
ciation with slavery, 118; and Muslim
Girls Training, 146–47; and Universi-
ties of Islam, 156, 157–58; and temple
meetings, 160–61, 162, 223 (n. 129);
and total ritualization, 167–68
Ethical code: and religious culture of Nation of Islam, 6, 33; and middle-class
values, 12, 127, 129, 130; and religious
identity, 14; as form of safety, 29; and
defense of Elijah Muhammad's Islamic
legitimacy, 41; and businesses, 101;
practice of, 107, 127, 141, 169, 173;
and Bilal, 181–82. *See also* Bodily care
Ethnic pride: and Elijah Muhammad, 2;

Islam as vehicle for, 23; and Universi-
ties of Islam, 155; and Wallace D.
Muhammad, 180
Eugenics, 121
Ewell, Ulysses A., 163

*Fall of America, The* (Elijah Muhammad), 29
Fard, W. D.: and Lost-Found Nation
of Islam, 2; Elijah Muhammad's belief in divinity of, 5, 10, 11, 18, 195
(n. 44), 204–5 (n. 40); and Savior's
Day, 162–63; Elijah Muhammad's
addresses on, 163; and Wallace D.
Muhammad, 176
Farms, 105
Farrakhan, Louis: on Qur'an, 50–51;
and defense of Elijah Muhammad's
Islamic legitimacy, 56, 58–59, 60, 65;
on Malcolm X, 58–59; and businesses,
102–3; and African dancers, 172; and
reconstituted version of Nation of
Islam, 185
Farrow, Thomas X, 144
Fasting, 99, 108, 133–34
Federal Bureau of Investigation (FBI):
attention to Nation of Islam, 4, 128;
and religious culture of Nation of
Islam, 9; and religious nature of Nation of Islam, 16, 193 (n. 29); and
Akbar Muhammad, 57; and temple
meetings, 158; and Muhammad's charisma, 167; and revolutionary potential
of Nation of Islam, 187; and membership of Nation of Islam, 190 (n. 12);
and content of *Muhammad Speaks*,
192 (n. 29)
Feminism, 112
Ferguson, James, 68
Financial success, Islam as source of, 26,
28
Fish businesses, 105–6
Five Percenters, 185
Foreign Muslim leaders: and endorsement of Elijah Muhammad, 36,

37, 38–44, 61, 65; and theological differences, 38, 39, 44

Forrest, Leon, 77, 141, 191 (n. 29), 192 (n. 29)

Fruit of Islam: and organizational infrastructure, 3; and selling of *Muhammad Speaks*, 136, 137, 139–43, 220 (n. 44); training of, 136, 137–38; and ritualized activities, 136–46; as hierarchical organization, 138; and discipline, 138–39; and recruitment in prisons, 144–46; and search at temple meetings, 161, 162; and Muslim conventions, 163; and religious rallies, 165; and place of musical performance, 169–71

Garvey, Marcus, 72, 90

Gender: and moral renewal of Islam, 28–29; and historical narratives of Nation of Islam, 83, 84; and dress and adornment, 109, 112–13, 118; and Fruit of Islam, 139; and Sunni Islam traditions, 185. *See also* Men; Women

George 11X, 142

Ghani, Ahmed, 181–82

Ghani, Lorene, 182

Ghetto sociological literature, 71

Grassal, Diogenes X, 85–86, 91

Great Migration, 20

Green, Gail, 31

Gregory, Dick, 170

Griffith, Delores, 164

Gross, Yusuf A. X, 110

Gupta, Akhil, 68

Guy X, 170

Hair care, 109–10, 114–15, 116

Haleem, M. A. S. Abdel, 48

Haley, Alex, 180

Hamiyd, Rafiyq Ahmad A., 45

Hannibal of Carthage, 70

Harold X, 170

Harrison, Tom, 77

Harvey X, 107

Harvey 3X, 101

Hassain, Margary, 103, 105, 192 (n. 29)

Hate, Nation of Islam associated with, 4–5, 193 (n. 29)

Hattie C. 3X, 26

Hazziez, Lydia, 107

Henderson, Helen, 163

Henry 15X, 31

Hilda X, 29

Hine, Darlene Clark, 9

Hinis, Elder L., 20

Hiram X, 19

Historical narratives of Nation of Islam: and complexity of Nation of Islam, 68; and African American Muslim identity, 68–69, 73–74, 82, 91, 92–93, 180, 184–85; and black origins, 69, 74, 75–76, 77, 82, 88, 90, 93; and Negro History Week, 70–77; and slavery, 71–72, 73, 208 (n. 12); supralocative perspective of, 74, 75, 77, 90–93, 184; translocative perspective of, 77, 79, 86, 90–91, 93; transtemporal perspective of, 77, 79, 86, 93; and Afro-Asian sitings of, 77–86; African siting of, 86–92; and shift in communal consciousness, 179–80

Homosexuality, 124

Howard, Thomas X, 145

Howe, Stephen, 89–90

*How to Eat to Live* (Elijah Muhammad), 99, 101, 134, 145

Hubbard, Richard, 164

Hubert X, 125

Hudson, George X, 171

Hughes, Langston, 157

Husain, Shukar Ilahi, 5

Identity politics, 8

Illegal drugs, 99, 101, 141, 172

Imagined community, and African American Muslim identity, 68, 85

Immigrant Muslims: and hatred of Nation of Islam, 4–5; and criticisms of Nation of Islam, 8, 36; and defense of

rallies, 165–66; and temple meetings, 223 (n. 129)

Liston, Sonny, 120

Lomax, Louis, 190 (n. 12)

Lopez, Frank 8X, 143

Lorton Reformatory (Virginia), 144, 145

*Lost Books of the Bible, The*, 64, 207 (nn. 92, 93)

Lost-Found Nation of Islam, 2

Louima, Abner, 96

L'Ouverture, Toussaint, 70

Lowe, Ermine X, 110

Maceo X, 45, 46

Maffly-Kipp, Laurie, 69

Mahdi, Khadijah, 182–83

Mainstream press, 4, 5, 41, 187, 193 (n. 29)

Majied, Eugene: "The Great Physician," 51; "As It Was in the Days of Daniel, So It Is Today," 51, 53; "As It Was With Pharaoh So It is Today," 54; "As It Was in the Days of" series, 55–56; McCallum compared to, 61; and history of slavery, 71–72; and myth of black origins, 76; and historical narratives of Nation of Islam, 79–81, 82, 83, 84, 87–88; and bodily care, 101–2, 118–19; and dress and adornment, 110; and birth control, 122–23

Makeup, 109, 110, 111, 113, 161

Malcolm X: leaves Nation of Islam, 3, 53, 60, 65; and Afrocentrism, 8; autobiography as conversion narrative, 24; and Afro-Asian Conference in Bandung, 38; rhetorical skill of, 54; as orthodox Islam spokesperson, 58; and Farrakhan, 58–59; role of Nation of Islam in assassination of, 59, 193 (n. 29), 206 (n. 78); and Negro History Week, 70; and bodily protection, 119; as zoot suiter, 129; and ritualized activities, 132; joins Nation of Islam, 146; on religious rallies, 166; and Sunni Islam tradition, 176

Marginal Muslims, 13

Marilyn A. X, 28

Martin, Louis, 53–54, 166

Masonic teaching, 18, 197 (n. 7)

Mathis, Marvin X, 144

Mayes, Margaret J. X, 28–29

McAlister, Melani, 69, 89

McCallum, Leo X, 17, 61–62, 75–76, 164–65

McCloud, Aminah, 176

McKay, C. M., 99

McKinley 2X, 163

Mecca, pilgrimage to, 3, 164–65, 176

Memory, construction of, 193 (n. 29)

Men: and moral renewal of Islam, 29; and historical narratives of Nation of Islam, 84; and dress and adornment, 109, 112–13, 118; and bodily protection, 118, 119–21; and sexuality, 125, 126; and Universities of Islam, 153, 154, 157. *See also* Fruit of Islam

Menelik (king of Ethiopia), 70

*Message to the Blackman in America* (Muhammad), 50

Middle East, 69, 85, 90

Millennialism, 29, 63, 64, 93, 146

Miscegenation, 78

Mitchell, Clarence X, 145

Moore, Johnny Percy X, 197 (n. 1)

Moorish Science Temple, 59, 185, 197 (n. 7)

Moses, Wilson Jeremiah, 96

Moton, Shirley, 113

Muhammad, Akbar, 45, 57–58, 60, 65, 176

Muhammad, Elijah: as prophet of Nation of Islam, 2, 7; Malcolm X as missionary of, 3; businesses owned by, 4, 12; condemnation of, 4–5; and divinity of Fard, 5, 10, 11, 195 (n. 44), 204–5 (n. 40); defense of Islamic legitimacy, 7, 8, 36; Qur'anic exegesis of, 7, 47–48, 50–51, 53, 65, 184, 205 (n. 53); death of, 8, 176, 185; ethical code of, 12; defense of status as religious leader, 16, 44; sees teachings of Bible as logical, 17–18; and Ahmadi translation of Qur'an, 46; as *mujaddid*, 47; lack of oratorical skills, 53–54, 166; and bodily care, 96, 97; and African dress and hair styles, 115–17; and prescribed prayers, 132–33, 218–19 (nn. 5–8); images of, 163, 224 (n. 138); and religious rallies, 165–67; charisma of, 167; and music, 172, 173; legacy of, 186; ownership of *Muhammad Speaks*, 191–92 (n. 29); success of, 225 (n. 1)

Muhammad, Elijah, Jr., 106

Muhammad, Emerson, 157

Muhammad, Harriett, 123–25, 163

Muhammad, Jamil, 47, 60–61, 62, 64, 65

Muhammad, Jamillah, 99

Muhammad, Murad, 163

Muhammad, Sonji, 120

Muhammad, Wallace D. (W. D.): and Arabic language study, 44; estrangement from Elijah Muhammad and Nation of Islam, 58, 60, 65, 206 (n. 71); as new leader, 176, 177, 178, 179, 184; and Bilal, 180, 181, 183, 184, 226 (n. 16)

Muhammad Ali, Mawlana, 46, 47, 49, 205 (nn. 43, 53)

*Muhammad Speaks*: and defense of Elijah Muhammad's Islamic legitimacy, 37, 38–39, 42, 48, 53, 62; disagreements aired in, 39–40, 163–64; and Arabic language study, 45; and Qur'an, 45, 53; and Ahmadi translation of Qur'an, 46; and Negro History Week, 70; and historical narratives of Nation of Islam, 72, 77, 81–82, 83, 88, 91, 92; and eating habits, 99, 101–3, 105–6; and businesses, 102–3, 105–6; and dress and adornment, 110–13; and bodily protection, 118, 119–20; and birth control, 121–23; and sexuality, 123–25; and ritualized activities, 136; and Fruit of Islam, 136, 137, 139–41, 220 (n. 44); and prison abuse, 144;

in prisons, 145; and Universities of Islam, 153–55, 157, 159; and Muslim conventions, 163–65; and musical performance, 172–73; name change of, 180; circulation of, 191 (n. 29); content of, 191–93 (n. 29). See also *Bilalian News*

—testimonials: as descriptions of being Muslim, 7; and religious conversion narratives, 16, 21, 24, 31–34; characterize Christianity as superstitious and spooky, 17, 22–23, 32, 33; and Islam as religious alternative to Christianity, 17–24, 178, 197 (n. 3); characterize Islam as logical and scientific, 18–19, 23; and Islam as religion of resistance and action, 19; associate Christianity with slavery, 19–20; and abandonment of religious community, 21; and positive characteristics of Islam, 22–23; and practical benefits of Islam, 23–24; and forgiveness, 24–25, 33; and financial success, 26; and self-improvement, 26, 33; and employment, 26, 200 (n. 38); and moral renewal of Islam, 28–29; and protection of Islam, 29–31; and Islam as total way of life, 31–34; and historical narratives of Nation of Islam, 82, 90; and bodily care, 97

*Mujaddid*, Elijah Muhammad as, 47, 60

*Mumbo Jumbo* (Ishmael Reed), 89

Murwar, Yessef al, 42–43

Muslim conventions, and ritualized activities, 136, 162–65

Muslim Girls Training and General Civilization Class: and organizational infrastructure, 3; requirement to attend, 84; and ritualized activities, 136, 146–53; and drill team, 148; criticism of, 148–49; and discipline, 149–53; and search at temple meetings, 161, 162; and Muslim conventions, 163

Muslim Mosque, Inc., 53, 54

Muslim naming, 182

83; and school ceremonies, 133; enrollment of, 153; and ritualized activity,
153–60; curriculum of, 154, 157; and
pride in being black, 155; and discipline, 156; dress codes of, 156; and
prescribed prayers, 157; and student
performances, 157; and esotericism,
158–59; and graduation ceremonies,
159

Van Ess, Dorothy, 85
Vesey, Denmark, 72
Vietnam War, 9
Violence: and police, 142; in prisons, 144,
145–46

Wahhabi Islam, 185
Wallace, Mike, 4, 170, 190 (n. 12)
Warren, Gwendolyn X, 28
Washburn, Harold, 145
Washburn, Mrs. Harold, 145
Washington, Booker T., 70
Watford, Clint, 27
Watkins, Frances Ellen, 96, 97
Watts riot, 86
Weber, Max, 202 (n. 3)
Webster Young Quintet, 170
Wedad, Dorothy, 112–13
Wells, Ida B., 96
West, Betty X, 88
West, Cynthia S'thembile, 25, 121, 152–
53
West, Leroy X, 88
Whitcomb, Charlene M., 19–20
White, E. Frances, 128
White devil: role in God's divine plan,
18; foreign Muslim leaders' reaction
to, 38, 40; and defense of Elijah Mu-
hammad's Islamic legitimacy, 49–50;
and birth control, 121–22; and prison,
145, 146; and Wallace D. Muhammad,
176

White racism: Christianity associated
with, 17, 20; and slavery, 19; Islam
as protection against, 29–31; and
black body, 97; and birth control, 122;
within Islam, 186
Whites: and Elijah Muhammad's apocalyptic views, 12; and dress and adornment, 110–11, 113, 117; and seduc-
tion of blacks by, 118–19
White supremacist scientists, 77
Wilkins, Roy, 4, 80
William E. X, "Black Man," 78–79
Williams, Chancellor, 89–90
Wilson, Jerry, 21
Witherspoon, Jimmy, 171
Women: and moral renewal of Islam,
28–29, 32; and protection of Islam,
31; and historical narratives of Nation of Islam, 70–71, 78, 83–85, 208
(n. 12); and separate spheres, 84–85;
and bodily care, 96, 97; and dress
and adornment, 109–18, 185; and
bodily protection, 119, 121, 137; and
sexuality, 123–25; and *Muhammad
Speaks*, 142; and employment outside
home, 148, 222 (n. 76); and Universi-
ties of Islam, 153, 154, 157; as nurses,
154–55. *See also* Muslim Girls Training and General Civilization Class
Women's Club movement, 127
Woodford, John, 192 (n. 29)
Woodson, Carter G., 70
Working class, 129
Workplace discrimination, 29
World Community of al-Islam in the
West, 176

Yoruba language, 91
Young, Margaret B., 72

Zubayda, 85